Chelsea's Century

THEY'VE WON THE PREMIERSHIP. THEY'VE WON THE CARLING CUP. HERE ARE THE GREATEST MOMENTS FROM 100 YEARS OF THEIR HISTORY.

CHELSEA'S CENTURY

HARRY HARRIS

JB
JOHN BLAKE

Published by John Blake Publishing Ltd,
3, Bramber Court, 2 Bramber Road,
London W14 9PB, England

www.blake.co.uk

First published in hardback in 2005

ISBN 1 84454 110 X

British Library Cataloguing-in-Publication Data:

A catalogue record for this book is available from the British Library.

Design by www.envydesign.co.uk

Printed in Great Britain by Creative Print and Design

1 3 5 7 9 10 8 6 4 2

Papers used by John Blake Publishing are natural, recyclable products made from wood grown in sustainable forests. The manufacturing processes conform to the environmental regulations of the country of origin.

To my Father-in-Law, Ken, who was there in '55 and has
never stopped dreaming of the day The Blues would do it again.
Enjoy your dream come true!

Foreword by Peter Osgood

The centenary season has become a fantastic time to be a Chelsea fan or a Chelsea player: in general, it is a great time to have any connection with the club and I consider myself fortunate to be in that position, as I work at the Bridge on match days in the hospitality suites.

Yes, hospitality probably suits my image and, yes, what was said about what we got up to in the 1970s was true: we certainly lived up to the reputation of the King's Road set. I shall be telling you a few of the secrets of that era in this book.

But it is the present, the centenary year itself, and the future which fascinate us all, and, as long as someone like Roman Abramovich owns the club and someone with the calibre of Jose Mourinho manages the team, it won't only be true-blue Chelsea fans who are fascinated by events at the Bridge.

As long as Abramovich is there, the future is just fantastic, mind boggling. Chelsea have a fabulous team already and, with Abramovich, they can go out and buy even more great players: they will be a force to be reckoned with for years to come.

What a time to be enjoying a centenary year, particularly as the last championship win came fifty years ago.

What Mourinho has achieved in such a short space of time is equally unbelievable. Mourinho is cocky, arrogant and confident – but all in a nice, positive way. The players think the world of him and there is a remarkable camaraderie among them: with that kind of atmosphere and with the quality of the players, Chelsea have become a major force.

I've met Jose a couple of times and introduced my son Darren to him. He came across as one of the game's absolute gentlemen. He told me I was welcome at Stamford Bridge any time, which is more than I used to get when Ken Bates was in control of the club!

But the supporters are only really interested in the players, the results and the performances and, under Mourinho, Chelsea have become an awesome team; a team that can only get better and better and one which is guaranteed to fill the stadium all the time.

Introduction

To mark the club's centenary, the A–Z of Chelsea's history includes exclusive interviews with names synonymous with Chelsea's traditions for flamboyant football and success at crucial stages of the club's development.

From Jimmy Greaves and Kerry Dixon to Peter Osgood and Ron Harris, from Ray Wilkins and Glenn Hoddle to Ruud Gullit, this book contains insights, recollections and reminiscences of Chelsea's past, comments about their present and a glance ahead to the club's future.

I would like to express my gratitude to all those who gave their time and energy in recalling their part in Chelsea's history.

The club nominated the 2005–06 season as its centenary year rather than choosing the calendar year of 2005. The birth of Chelsea FC can be traced to three alternative dates in 1905:

1. On 14 March 1905, Chelsea FC was founded at The Rising Sun pub (now The Greene Room) opposite the main entrance to the ground on the Fulham Road.
2. On 29 May 1905, Chelsea were elected into the Second Division at the Football League AGM.
3. On 2 September 1905, the first match took place, away at Stockport County. The reason the club opted to make the centenary year the 2005–06 season is that it is the closest date to Chelsea's first match and 100 years since the club's first full season.

However, the club also recognised the importance of their foundation in March and their election to the Football League in May. Football was the centrepiece of the club's plans for its centenary, but their name Chelsea goes beyond football. It is synonymous with fashion, music and art and is part of the social history of not just our immediate home in Hammersmith and Fulham, but of London as a whole. The celebrations will reflect this, so there should be something for all ages and tastes to participate in.

A centenary committee was formed to oversee the project, packed full of personalities from the worlds of football, politics and business, all of whom have an intimate knowledge of Chelsea, as well as executives from the club.

The members of the committee are Chelsea's life vice-president Lord Attenborough CBE; Tony Banks, Labour MP and fanatical Chelsea fan; Charles Trellogan, the Mayor of Fulham; Terry Venables, one of the club's most famous former players; Charles Dunstone, chief executive officer of Carphone Warehouse; and Richard King, chairman of Chelsea Pitch Owners.

The club are represented by Bruce Buck, chairman; Peter Kenyon, chief executive; Paul Smith, business affairs director; Alan Shaw, company secretary; and Simon Greenberg, director of communications.

The committee met for the first time before the match against FC Porto in the Champions League, and endorsed the concept that the centenary year should be celebrated during the 2005–06 season. A number of sub-committees, or task forces, covering various areas of the centenary will also be set up to execute the wishes of the committee.

Harry Harris

Contents

A

Roman Abramovich and Lord Richard Attenborough

Roman Abramovich plans to make the club a central part of his family dynasty with Jose Mourinho leading Chelsea through a ten-year campaign to dominate the world game. That is the vision of the Russian billionaire who has fallen in love with the club and who has hinted that he will never walk out on them. In fact, he has even promised that one day Chelsea will be in the hands of his son Arkady: he is only eleven years old!

Business manager Paul Smith said, 'Roman is such a huge fan of Chelsea, and of football in general. Not only does he fly into the country just to watch every Chelsea match, he wants to watch other games in the Premier League as well, because he likes it so much. He spent his birthday watching the Manchester United–Arsenal game. There is no doubting how passionate he is about football and Chelsea. And he has indicated to us that, when the time comes for him to leave, he will be passing the club on to his son, Arkady.'

Much of the excitement at Stamford Bridge since the Russian's arrival has been tempered by the fear of what would happen should he suddenly decide to end his interest in the club. But Abramovich intends to oversee his dream of overtaking Manchester United and Real Madrid and making Chelsea the biggest global name in football.

Abramovich has pledged his commitment to Chelsea for maybe twenty-five or fifty years. 'I said from day one that I wanted to enjoy myself and that's what I've been doing. I like the English lifestyle. The English are used to mixing with people of different nationalities. Anyone could feel comfortable in England.'

His Moscow-based Public Relations chief, John Mann has said, 'He hopes that by increasing the fan base and merchandising and building the popularity of the club, it can become self-sustaining. He's put some money in there to set the ball rolling and the club is winning at the moment. Let's hope that continues, but we'll go through the hard times, too. Obviously there are bad days when you lose 2–1 at Bolton and the criticism starts, but he's definitely in it for the long term.'

Suspicions of his enormous wealth have abounded in England, while politicians in Russia have called for an investigation into the oil deals that made him such a colossal fortune. It was reported that ex-spy chief Sergei Stepashin accused him of illegally acquiring Chelsea, but Abramovich implies Chelsea were bought with Russian President Putin's blessing. 'The President knew I was going to buy Chelsea, and I can't say he put me off doing so.'

He plans to stand down as governor of the eastern Siberian region in two years. 'My time in Chukotka has been very expensive for me. It's not like a real job, and I don't get the satisfaction from it I once did. I'm not a hereditary oil industry worker. Nor am I a gas industry worker or a pig-breeder. Every part of my business may be sold. It's just a question of time and price.'

Mann adds, 'Roman has become a kind of ambassador for Russia in England. He feels at home in England because it has had a colonial past and can deal with people from all over the world. He wants to make a business of it, but he doesn't want another Leeds. He wants to win trophies. You can see the excitement on his face at all the games. He's caught the Chelsea bug. The moment he set foot in Stamford Bridge that was it. It's such a great ground and the people are wonderful. He is seen as a god and it obviously makes him feel great. The only thing is, he's been a shy, private person for as long as I've known him. The interest in England in his personal life is unprecedented for any Russian businessman. The UK press is much more aggressive.'

Oleg Tarovinksi, who started a Chelsea Supporters' Club in Moscow, thinks that Abramovich will improve Russia's image in Britain. 'It is good that he bought a foreign club. It's very good PR for Russia. And very good for the Russian people. English people see Russia as just a big, cold country with bears. Mr Abramovich is changing all that.' Abramovich has an estimated fortune of £7.5 billion and heads the *Sunday Times* Rich List of the 1,000 wealthiest people in Britain, knocking the Duke of Westminster off top position.

Abramovich is the sixth-richest person in Europe and the twenty-second-richest in the world. He is the richest man in the world under the age of forty. he has all the trappings of enormous wealth: a £72 million 378ft yacht, *Pelorus*, so luxurious that it even has its own submarine and, of course, all the extras that any security-conscious oil baron could wish for – bulletproof glass, a missile-detection system and quarters for the security guards. The five-level vessel has a crew of forty, boasts a restaurant, casino, dance floor, luxury bedrooms, bars, a state-of-the-art gym and sauna and on the deck there is a helicopter landing pad as well as a massive sun deck with whirlpool. Works of art and crystal chandeliers decorate the rooms. This, the world's sixth-largest yacht, was purchased from German shipping giant Lurssen. Abramovich already owns one giant yacht, *Le Grand Bleu*, which has a huge aquarium and a glass bottom to observe the sea bed.

Abramovich likened himself to Moses: 'Do you remember Moses? He spent forty years in the desert with his people to make them forget slavery.' He pledged, 'I haven't thought about how much money I am prepared to spend. I suppose that depends on how well we play and how determined we are to win. If I feel we need to buy any particular player to get the results we want, I'll just spend more money. British football is a business venture and a very competitive one; the quality of the teams is pretty similar – there is not one big name overshadowing the other. That is why I liked British football.

'I guessed the papers would write stories, but I didn't expect them to write so many or for so long. Football is almost a religion in Britain, so I knew that such an event would produce a big bang.'

Chelsea fans adore him and they couldn't care less where his money comes from. Abramovich responds to his critics in Moscow. 'In Russia we have lived in a free country for a relatively short time. People are not used to the idea that someone can spend his own money the way he wants. Every little politician readily gives away advice on how to live.'

The foundation stone of Roman Arkadyevich Abramovich's fortune lies in oil. He does not sit and count it, though. 'It is very difficult for me. I do not sit with a calculator and work out how much I am worth.' His share of the aluminium industry in Russia adds to his vast wealth. There were no pictures published of this intensely private 'oligarch' until 1999, he rarely gives interviews and there is scarcely any television footage.

He is quietly spoken, has an unassuming appearance and seems perfectly comfortable conducting business in trademark jeans, a T-shirt and designer stubble. His appearance is hardly that of one of the world's wealthiest individuals.

His business empire ranges from aluminium, trucks and hydro-electricity to meat processing and pharmaceuticals; he owned 26 per cent of Aeroflot, Russia's national airline, but sold his stake to the National Reserve Bank.

From the outset, Abramovich made no demands that Chelsea excel in his first season. 'I would love to think we will, but we have made many acquisitions and so it is hard to say if it will be the most successful season in the history of the team. Even the best players don't immediately make a team. The internal structure of the team has been destroyed and the players need time to play together; only then can you hope for a result.'

However, having come so close to real glory, Abramovich sacked Claudio Ranieri and hired Jose Mourinho, whose unfancied Porto side won the Champions League. Trevor Birch was the chief executive at the time of the first and biggest wave of spending. He admitted, 'Prior to the company being sold, we were pursuing one plan, but the arrival of Mr Abramovich allowed us to pursue another. And long may it continue; it's been a terribly exciting time.' Birch was replaced by former Manchester United chief executive Peter Kenyon, as Abramovich started to put in place the infrastructure that he hoped would take the club on to a different level.

The remarkable story of how Abramovich came to buy Chelsea has its roots in the Russian's introduction to football agent Pini Zahavi in March 2002 by German Vladimirovich Tkachenko, the owner of Russian club Sovietov Krylya, in Samara. Tkachenko is an influential member of the council of the Russian Federation and is the equivalent of an MP.

Abramovich's passion for football was activated when he went to watch the World Cup finals in Japan and Korea. He finally set his heart on owning a club when he sampled the atmosphere of Old Trafford in a Champions League tie with Real Madrid and seriously thought about buying Manchester United. Zahavi, through his multitude of contacts at Old Trafford, arranged tickets for the Russian in the directors' box, but no one knew the unfamiliar face watching the Champions League quarter-final game.

Abramovich says, 'That's when I decided I really wanted to be involved in football. The whole atmosphere got to me and that is when I knew I had to be involved. On the way back to Moscow, I couldn't stop thinking about it.

So I said to my people, "Find me a football club."'

England captain David Beckham had been controversially left on the bench for that game, but he came on and scored twice in United's 4–3 victory, although the Spanish club progressed 6–5 on aggregate.

Abramovich added, 'It was a very beautiful game and I realised I couldn't pass it by. I decided less than a year ago to get involved, and looked at ten clubs in England, of which four were "possibles"'

On Wednesday, 23 April 2003, a meeting took place between football agent Jonathan Barnett – who, among others, represents Ashley Cole – Zahavi and Birch at Les Ambassadeurs Club in Hamilton Place, Park Lane. They enjoyed a convivial lunch paid for by Zahavi.

Chelsea had debts of £90 million plus; it was imperative for the club to unload surplus playing staff as discreetly as possible. As the lunch progressed, it was clear that the financial problems were worsening and that, while the aperitif may have been about the players, the main course was whether Zahavi could find a suitable buyer for Chelsea.

The ultra-well-connected Israeli knew Spurs fan Phillip Green, who might be persuaded to invest in a club but, through his connections in Russia, he also knew that Abramovich would be keen.

Zahavi travelled to Moscow for a working holiday. It was there that he had the opportunity to discuss the possibility of involving Abramovich in a takeover deal with Tkachenko. A shortlist of clubs was drawn up which comprised Lazio, Manchester United, Arsenal, Tottenham ... and Chelsea.

Abramovich first met with Spurs chairman Daniel Levy to discuss 'general issues', and the question of whether Levy would be interested in selling his shares did crop up. Levy confesses, 'Yes, we did have a meeting at his request, because he wanted ENIC's perspective on the European football market. It is important to note, however, that at no time did we discuss, either then or subsequently, his desire to acquire a Premiership club.'

Levy later received a telephone call from Zahavi, who made a more formal declaration of intent, asking whether he would be keen to sell and at what price. Levy asked far too high a price for the shares – £50 million for 29.9 per cent. At the time, the share price was 18 pence, which valued the club at just £20 million. Ironically, a further appointment had been made for the day after the announcement of the Chelsea takeover. Naturally, there was no need for that second meeting!

Bates was running out of time and examined several options before finally selling to Abramovich. Bates was confident of a deal with one of the interested parties, so he declined to sell Jimmy-Floyd Hasselbaink to Barcelona whose £6 million offer he described as 'derisory'. Eidur Gudjonsson's agent was aiming for a pay rise, while William Gallas had an escape clause in his contract that, with Arsenal sniffing around, needed to be addressed.

On Monday, 23 June 2003, an 8am meeting was arranged with Birch at Zahavi's Marble Arch flat. The value of the Chelsea Village shares at the time was languishing below 20 pence and Zahavi wanted to know the price required to buy the club. Birch demanded 40 pence a share, but conceded that, if Zahavi's man was serious, the price would be negotiable. Zahavi passed on the information to Abramovich in Moscow via a call to his friend German. The call came back to arrange a meeting to conclude a deal. Just three days later, Birch met the Russian delegation of Abramovich, German Tkachenko and Eugene Tenenbaum at Stamford Bridge. Birch was on the line virtually every minute to Zahavi to keep him fully updated about the talks. No one had any doubts about Zahavi's pivotal role in the deal.

The deal was done in about twenty minutes. They broke up at 11.30am and decided to go out to lunch to celebrate. Later that day, Zahavi received a call from Birch. Could Roman meet Bates? Through German, Zahavi persuaded Abramovich to delay his flight back to Moscow. The meeting was arranged at the Dorchester Hotel. Zahavi didn't need to attend that meeting between Abramovich and Bates as the deal had already been done.

At 7.10pm, Bates marched along the narrow corridor, past the check-in for the coats and on to the plush Dorchester bar, to greet Abramovich and his entourage. Bates and Abramovich drank Evian water. Forty-five minutes later, they shook hands on the deal. Bates had a dinner date later that evening: he celebrated it with champagne.

On Friday, 27 June, Richard Creitzman, Tenenbaum and Abramovich met with Chelsea's financial advisers and stockbrokers Seymour Pierce at a hastily arranged meeting at Chelsea Village. Seymour Pierce's chairman Keith Harris said, 'It was break-neck speed; I have never experienced anything as quick as this. I thought the deal to buy the *Express* by Richard Desmond was quick, but we had to raise the money. We arrived on Friday afternoon, around 4pm, and were told of the meetings the previous day. It was all relatively straightforward: the finances were in place and verified by Citibank, who knew Abramovich from deals in Russia, so I had no problem with them.'

Estimates as to his fee for his advice on the Chelsea deal totalled a cool £1 million for his firm, of which he owns a 20 per cent stake. Harris remarked, 'This deal has lifted the shadow over the entire football industry. Everyone was down, forecasting gloom and doom and suddenly it all looks a bit brighter. Whether or not more Russians will end up owning football clubs over here is an interesting point, but Abramovich has shown he is deadly serious with the welter of player purchases and that can only encourage others to follow suit. All the accusations that it is a toy, well, anyone who commits to something like half a billion dollars is hardly playing at it. That shows commitment in my book.'

Harris suggested that Abramovich snubbed Manchester United because it would have cost £700 million to take over. He said, 'There was a great deal of research done by him and his advisers before going for Chelsea. He looked at a number of Premiership clubs. They were Manchester United, Arsenal, Spurs and Chelsea. Why not Manchester United? If you think of the sums of money involved, United are the most successful financially. They would have cost £650–700 million. That's a huge chunk of change. He paid £60 million for the shares outstanding at Chelsea, but buying the company meant assuming responsibility for the debts: another £80 million. So he got Chelsea for £140 million.'

Although the debts were £90 million, there were reserves of £10 million, so Harris is right to put the real debt figure at £80 million.

'As for United, what can you do with them? How can you improve them? At Arsenal, you would have to spend to build a stadium. Spurs have spent money on the ground, but is it big enough and is it in the right place? And how much would you have to spend on the team? You look at Chelsea ... the assets are in place and they have spent a lot of money developing the ground into one of the best in the Premiership. The infrastructure of the team is good. Sure there is money to be spent, but the backbone is strong. Only time will tell whether it was money well spent. One suspects that this is a good investment.'

Bates said, 'He went to United to watch a game, but he didn't like the atmosphere. He decided he wanted a club in London and opted for Chelsea as they had more going for them than other teams. We have no problems with stadium redevelopment.'

Roman Abramovich was born on 24 October 1966 in Saratov, a city on the Volga. His parents were of Jewish-Ukrainian extraction from southern Russia. Roman's mother Irina, known affectionately as 'Irochka', was a piano teacher. She died tragically at the age of twenty-eight as the result of a termination: the only reason she had the operation was because she could not afford another child. Her only son, Roman, was a day short of his first birthday when she died from blood poisoning in Komi, one of Russia's most remote regions. Irina's decision was hardly uncommon; many women chose to have abortions rather than to give birth to more than one child during a time of severe housing shortages and poor financial prospects. Eighteen months later, Abramovich's dad Arkady, known by the family as 'Arkasha', was killed after a crane collapsed on him. He was thirty-two. Arkady discovered a broken jib on the crane during a site visit and, on an already delayed project, tried to fix it himself. But the jib fell, crushing his legs and leaving him trapped. He died in hospital of post-traumatic shock ten days later.

After his father's death, Abramovich's close-knit Jewish family never considered sending him to a state orphanage. Arkady was the youngest of three brothers and, as Abramovich grew into a young man, he learned from his devoted uncles, Leib and Abram. As Arkady was the only brother to have had a son, Roman's future was especially important to the Abramovich name. He was raised by Leib and his wife Ludmilla. The couple also have two daughters, Natalya and Ida.

Roman was enrolled in Ukhta City Municipal School Number 2 at the age of six, in September 1973. He was sent to Moscow at the age of fourteen, where he shared a cramped, one-room flat with his grandmother, Tatyana, and enrolled at School Number 232. At the age of seventeen, he failed to get into Moscow's prestigious Gubkin Oil and Gas Institute. Without a place, which would have allowed him to postpone his compulsory two-year national service, he was forced to join the Army: as a truck driver in the artillery detachment. Aged twenty, Abramovich returned to Ukhta and enrolled at the town's Industrial Institute. He studied for two years there, before successfully applying for a transfer to the Moscow Auto Transport Institute – a prestigious engineering school – where he studied for a year.

It was around this time that he met Eugene Shvidler, who was studying at the Gubkin Oil and Gas Institute. He has remained a close friend and confidant ever since. Abramovich started his first company, Ooyut-Comfort, in 1987, while still a student: the company made plastic toys, dolls and ducks and sold them at the markets that were springing up around Moscow. The company also dabbled in retreaded tyres. He became extremely rich, extremely fast, by exploiting the hybrid law of the Gorbachev–Yeltsin transition which allowed companies to trade on the huge difference between Soviet and Western prices for raw materials.

In 1999, he was elected to the lower house of the Russian parliament, the State Duma, from the Russian Far East region of Chukotka, where he was invited to run by the local governor. He also founded the charity Pole of Hope and sponsors a Russian ice-hockey team, Omsk Avangard, which came second in the Russian premier hockey league in 2003.

He met his attractive second wife, Irina Malandina, a glamorous former Aeroflot air stewardess, on a plane. He was married at the time to Olga, a women three years his senior. Irina would return from some exotic locations with examples of Western goods and Roman copied them in Russia. He was living in a single-room Moscow flat with Olga and stepdaughter Anastasia at the time.

Now Roman and Irina and their five children – Anna, Arkady (who is named after Roman's father), Sonya, Arina and Ilya – have several luxury homes. Irina studied for a law degree as she started her family and, more recently, she enrolled for a doctorate in Fine Arts in Moscow – an affirmation of their growing mutual interest in collecting paintings. He lives in a 99-acre walled estate outside Moscow: the couple have entertained Vladimir Putin there on numerous occasions. They also own a castle in Bavaria, with nearby skiing, one of Roman and Irina's hobbies. Then there is a £10 million villa in Nice in the south of France.

One of the Russian's newest luxury homes is the 424-acre estate Fyning Hill. It consists of secluded woodland in Rogate on the South Downs near Midhurst in West Sussex, and was once the British bolthole for King Hussein of Jordan. The seven-bedroom house, built in the 1920s, has stabling for 100 horses, two polo pitches, a swimming pool, a tennis court, a clay-pigeon shoot, a rifle range, a trout lake, an equestrian centre and a go-kart track. There is a separate house, six cottages, a staff flat and four guest apartments. He has been spotted driving through the village in a red Bentley and arrives on the estate by helicopter. Putin is reputed to have flown in for lunch! The stables are being converted into a massive £2.5 million complex, comprising a bowling alley, a gym and an indoor swimming pool.

Abramovich also owns a plush, multi-million-pound apartment in Lowndes Square, Knightsbridge, and, although he plans a more permanent residence in this country, he has said publicly that he does not plan to leave Russia permanently.

'I'm most comfortable in Moscow. I spent most of my life there. But I like the seasons. I like the lifestyle in England. It's multi-national and multi-cultural. There are signs that remain from the Empire ... I like that. People are used to dealing with different people. Everyone can feel comfortable here. The same applies with the United States.'

His business life took off when he first traded in oil products using the Swiss-based 'vehicle' company Runicom, now absorbed into Sibneft. 'I used my own money,' he insists. 'I didn't use State money through bank loans. I completed my most important deals when I was unknown. Now you have to be a known name to be a success.'

In the early nineties, Abramovich consolidated the oil business in the Omsk region so successfully that, when the most powerful oligarch of that time, Boris Berezovsky, conceived the idea to create Sibneft, an amalgamation within the oil industry, Abramovich was his first choice for the Board and was then made head of the Moscow office. Due to Abramovich's loyalty to President Vladimir Putin, Berezovsky's sworn enemy, the pair are no longer on speaking terms. Berezovsky is now in exile in London.

The web of companies owned by Abramovich is largely controlled by a British-registered holding company, Millhouse Capital, based in Weybridge, Surrey. This, in turn, is controlled by a Cyprus-based organisation called Electus Investments.

In 1992, after the collapse of the Soviet Union, fifty-five railway wagons of diesel fuel – all of which were part of a deal in which he was involved – 'disappeared' between Siberia and Moscow and ended up several hundred miles to the west in newly independent Latvia. Abramovich was investigated, but no charges were ever brought. Despite all the suspicions as to how someone so young could have amassed so much money, there was nothing else on his 'file'. During the investigation, Abramovich shared a grim prison cell with ten crooks.

Police investigator Yuri Lyutoyev, the man who grilled Abramovich, said, 'He was really scared after spending time in the cell with ten criminals. It was interesting to observe how his behaviour changed from cheeky to polite and then to timid.' Abramovich's arrest warrant is dated 19 June 1992. The case

– No. 79067 – was brought in the name of Roman A. Abramovich. Before his jail experience was widely known, he was asked to give advice to young Russian entrepreneurs. He told them, 'Never think you will never go to prison!' The file on the train affair ran to four 600-page volumes.

As an eighteen-year-old he was conscripted into the Soviet Union's feared Red Army. He was called up in November 1984, four months before reforming president Mikhail Gorbachev came to power. His undistinguished Army service lasted two years, during which he failed to be promoted to the rank of sergeant, as high-flying conscripts could expect. His first wife Olga said, 'Roman hated his time in the Army – no one enjoys it. It is a duty. He served his conscription near Moscow, close to his uncle's house.'

Olga married Abramovich in 1988 and he began his wheeler-dealing in the grim Moscow tower block. Olga said, 'For our wedding my father gave us a present of 2,000 roubles [then worth around £1,000]. Roman used it to buy black-market goods like perfume, deodorants, tights and toothpaste. He then sold them at double or triple the price.' If caught, the future oil baron could have been locked up in a Siberian gulag for five years. Brunette Olga, who has since remarried, added, 'Roman invested the profits in more goods to sell on. It lasted for around six months until he went into business. It provided us with a nice lifestyle. It helped us buy fashionable Western clothes and let us eat out at good restaurants.'

Olga has heard rumours of questionable business methods used by some of Russia's new rich, but she said, 'Roman certainly didn't mix with criminals or gangsters.'

So how did he become so wealthy, so quickly? He says, 'I bought a company that was not the largest back then' – referring to the rapid privatisations of the 1990s that made billionaires of a few supporters of the former President Boris Yeltsin in return for their support in the 1996 elections – 'and it is important to remember that the people who took part then were willing to take a risk ... and there were all kinds of risks. I was not part of a system that would take care of me, I had to survive. In 1995 [when Sibneft was privatised], $250 million was a sum of money that people in Russia couldn't fathom. An apartment then cost $5,000.'

Most of these companies were bankrupt, extremely inefficient and poorly run: they were not competitive in a market economy and it was extremely important to save them quickly because thousands of jobs were at stake. The people who made the money were the ones who didn't sit back and skim money off the enterprises they bought, but who brought in good management and Western techniques and invested in new technology. In the process, they created shareholder value for both themselves and minority shareholders. There are plenty of enterprises out there that were privatised by non-famous (because they aren't as rich) people that are currently languishing.

He also runs the governorship of Chukotka, 4,000 miles away in Siberia. He has invested millions there, building homes, improving schools and public buildings for the area's 73,000 population, most of whom are reindeer herders and fishermen. He provided the region's first international-standard hotels, supermarket, cinema, a restaurant/billiards hall that brews its own beer, a college, a museum and a house of culture, an international-standard medical facility and a fish-processing plant. The list goes on: he is treated like a god there. He is also known to contribute to many charitable local causes.

Abramovich is now responsible for the biggest shake-up in the British football industry since the creation of the Premier League in 1992. Manchester United and Arsenal no longer have a monopoly on either cash or trophies.

Not everyone was sure from the outset. David Mellor said at the time, 'I cannot blame the Chelsea Board, or Ken, for taking that deal, because you only have to look at the finances involved to see why they did it, rather than go in our direction which would have, in all honestly, been applying the sticking plaster to the problem. I don't think it is good in the long run for a football club of Chelsea's standing to be owned by a foreign billionaire, even if he turns out to be an eminent one. There are consequences for football in the broader sense, and ramifications for the Premiership as an international brand. Naturally, I was furious when the Russian tied up a deal, because I had been trying to help sort something out for the past eighteen months: (a) because I am a friend of Ken's; (b) because I am a Chelsea fan; and (c) because when Ken decided to go, I would have preferred somebody to replace him that I got along with and believed in. Paul Taylor was that man. He had the potential to become Ken's favourite son, so that by the time that Ken felt it was right to retire he would have had somebody there to offer the whole of the club. I am just so very upset that it didn't happen. But, as it turned out, Ken met the Russian on the Thursday and the whole damn thing was done by the following Tuesday, and nobody outside of those involved knew.'

A leading City source laughed at Tony Banks's suggestion that there should be an inquiry into whether Abramovich has the right credentials. 'If we wanted a test to decide who is fit and proper to run a football club, we would have a very big orphanage!'

He added, 'Roman Abramovich, like Mr Banks, shares a passion for football. He is committed to Chelsea and, like Tony, wants the very best for the club. We have written to Mr Banks in order to introduce Mr Abramovich to him, and have offered further dialogue to assuage his concerns.'

Banks has been following Chelsea since he was a ten-year-old on the terraces, and has held a season ticket for thirty years. At the time of the takeover the MP said, 'I was one of those lucky people who managed to see all of Chelsea's home matches in 1954–55 – I've still got all the programmes – and that was the last time, in fact the only time, we won the championship. Hopefully, I shall see them do it again before I die.' Thanks, perhaps, to their new Russian godfather, about whom Banks has so far been so sceptical!

Chelsea Village shares shot up 40 per cent on their AIM listing, and jumped a further 7 pence twenty-four hours before the announcement to close at 35 pence, after Abramovich agreed to buy 84.9 million shares from Bates.

At the time of the takeover Abramovich observed, 'It is the right price. I don't feel like I saved the club.'

Abramovich insisted that his motives were simply 'to have fun', but fun for such men tends to involve winning. 'Buying Chelsea is a way to realise my ambitions,' he said. 'Chelsea is near the top of its league. It is one of the best teams, and England is a very competitive league. For me, that was a very important criterion. My message to the fans is, I will do everything possible to ensure they enjoy the game as much as me.'

Supporters were reassured by his record with the ice-hockey team Omsk Avangard, which he transformed from provincial also-rans into a leading power in Russia's superleague: they now have an annual wage bill of $15 million, a sum that approaches pay levels in North America's NHL. Omsk is a city out on the west Siberian plain, but Abramovich's money attracted top players. A spokesman for the new owner, is also keen to reassure fans. 'Chelsea fans should not worry. He is a very serious guy and has good intentions.'

Club spokesman Arkadi Alekseev said, 'We are so grateful that Abramovich decided out of the blue to help us. Since he bailed us out five years ago, the team has changed beyond recognition. Now we can go out and get the best players. This year, the coach of the Russian ice-hockey team, Sergei Gersonsky, started work with Avangard. It's the equivalent of Sven-Goran Eriksson taking over as manager of Chelsea. We have made great progress since Roman appeared in our life, climbing high in the league. I think this is a great chance for Chelsea. The players and fans should be very happy that Abramovich chose them. It means only the best in the future and lots of victories.'

The takeover caused shockwaves in Russia with some ice-hockey fans in Omsk expressing fears that he will neglect their little club now he has Chelsea as his new toy. Deputy local governor Sergey Shelpakov said, 'We hope very much that Roman Abramovich will not abandon this team.'

Russian Football Federation President Vyachelsav Koloskov was furious that Abramovich shovelled his cash into Chelsea, 'Russian money should be put into Russian sport for the Russian fans.'

The Mayor of Moscow, Yuri Luzkhov, one of Russia's most prominent politicians, who had previously not always seen eye to eye with Abramovich on other matters. Luzhkov, an avid amateur soccer player, told a gathering of the city government, 'In buying Chelsea for such a huge amount of money, they abandoned our Russian teams, which needed support.'

Former Prime Minister Sergei Stepashin, now head of Russia's auditing chamber, criticised the purchase as 'unpatriotic'. But John Mann said that the tycoon had carefully considered Russian teams before investing abroad. 'He looked at several Russian teams over the last couple of years, but there were no deals available that met his requirements.'

Abramovich countered objections with a pledge to build new stadiums in Russia, including a £65 million state-of-the-art football stadium in Moscow. Creitzman said, 'The fact that Roman loved central London helped, but we also took into account the fact that we would only have to deal directly with one person rather than go through the process of talking to numerous shareholders. The others were seriously considered but, once we did our homework, the appeal of purchasing Chelsea became even greater.

'It wasn't just the shares. He likes London, so that was a plus for Chelsea. Financially, it depends how you look at it, but if you are coming in to buy, and someone is in a weaker position, then it is better for you as a buyer.

'They are in the Champions League, as are Manchester. They have a good squad, as do Manchester, Arsenal and Newcastle, the teams that finished above Chelsea last year. They have a very strong team here and Ranieri is one of the top managers. The people we have bought are also very strong and the key thing now is to get them all to gel together.

'We prepared information for him about various clubs; he took out the ones he wasn't interested in and there were a few left, most of them English. We got a bank on board to show the turnover, debt, players, league positions, stadium information, non-football business and so on of the clubs. Then, one Wednesday night in Moscow, we sat down and he said, "Right, we are flying over to England tomorrow." We weren't coming to buy a particular football club, but we had focused in on two, one of which was Chelsea. We met Ken Bates on Thursday evening; on Friday, lawyers got involved and, by Tuesday, bang, that was it.'

As the Russian's private helicopter took him across London after his meeting with Spurs chairman Levy, he spotted a football pitch, stadium and complex. 'That looks a damn sight better than the ground I've just visited,' Abramovich apparently observed.

Abramovich said, 'I looked at a lot of clubs in England and one in Europe but, after studying everything and talking to my advisers, Chelsea was the one I wanted to buy. It was the obvious choice for us once we'd studied all the facts surrounding it ... now we have to build something special here.'

Bates said, 'This guy looked at four clubs, two of them in London, and felt there were too many problems.'

Abramovich adds, 'Being in the Champions League was also important. It helped, but it was not decisive. There were four or five other factors that helped me make up my mind. I love London and Chelsea is in the centre of London ... that was important to me. The English word "fun" sums it up for me. It is not about business. I want to be at every match.' Unable to ignore the value-for-money element of his investment, however, he adds, 'The price and quality of Chelsea made it the optimum choice.'

And he is also willing to commit to years of ownership. 'I see it as a very long-term commitment,' he says, although he refused to disclose the limit on funds he was willing to pour into the club, explaining that by doing so he would push up the price of future contracts.

Abramovich came close to buying Manchester United, but was told that the Irish connection, John Magnier and J.P. McManus, would prove an obstacle as they held a significant slice of the shares, and that he would also encounter problems with Sir Alex Ferguson. Abramovich explains, 'I am realising my dreams of owning a top football club. Some will doubt my motives, some will think I am crazy.'

It looked as though he was on a mission to expand his empire when he moved into football, but Abramovich insisted he is not driven to rule the world. He explains: 'I have no Napoleonic dream. I'm just hard working and pragmatic.'

From the outset he planned to spend money on players. 'I want a team that wins the league and Europe. The goal is to win. It's not about making money. I have many much less risky ways of making money than this. I do not want to throw my money away, but it's really about having fun and that means success and trophies.' He chose an English club 'because I can afford to fly in and out and back to my job in Russia. I enjoy England and I'd like to see every Chelsea game, but that may not be possible. I will do everything to ensure that you enjoy the game as much as I do. It should be an international team. The best players need to play. What they have now is nearly a top European team. I am prepared to invest in the club and see the club be successful. And, of course, I will be looking to buy players.'

Asked which players he likes most, Abramovich was quick to mention Thierry Henry. After some discussions with his advisers, he says, 'I also like Sol Campbell.' He went on, 'I'm not going to tell you other players because their price will just go up.'

Incredible headline-grabbing news followed the first few days and weeks of Abramovich's reign. First, an audacious attempt to sign back Gianfranco Zola, but the real blockbuster was the courting of the England coach. Zahavi accompanied Sven-Goran Eriksson to Abramovich's palatial apartment at 39 Lowndes Square. Zahavi told me later, 'Sven was never offered the job, and I should know. I introduced Sven to Abramovich a year earlier and they had met five times before this meeting.' If Eriksson couldn't become manager straight away, there can be no doubt that he indicated that he might become available after the 2004 European Championships, and the chit-chat also included his liking for a certain kind of English player, such as Glen Johnson, and a foreigner he would always select, Seba Veron. Both ended up signing for Chelsea!

Abramovich added to the uncertainty surrounding Claudio Ranieri by admitting that he was 'not sure' about him. Asked about his thoughts on Ranieri's position, Abramovich shrugged his shoulders and said, 'I am not sure, I just don't know. I am going to sit down with him in the very near future.'

Ranieri expressed fears, saying, 'I don't know anything about these rumours about another manager. But I know the rules of the game and that is that, when control of a club passes from one man to another, anything can happen. It's the right of the new man to decide who he wants in charge of the team. I don't know Mr Abramovich and I would like to speak to him.'

Ranieri, who had been in the Stamford Bridge hotseat since 2000, had steered the club to the coveted fourth place in the Premier League, and the promise of the lucrative Champions League that came with it. He naturally felt that such an achievement merited a chance under the new owner. Speculation, though, centred on Eriksson and Roma's manager Fabio Capello, who had made contact with intermediaries expressing his interest. Sir Alex Ferguson was also linked to the post.

Eriksson elaborated: 'It was not the first time I've seen him ... I've seen him many times. It didn't embarrass me. I could have spoken to him on the phone, I guess, but the big difference is that he invited me to take a cup of tea in the house of a so-called friend. I saw him many times and I was presented to him by Mr Zahavi, who I have known since I was manager of Benfica and he was involved in business with two Russian players I had. As Pini lives in London, when I came to England we have eaten together now and then, and on one occasion we dined with Mr Abramovich. Of course, we talked about football, but if I meet Arsène or Ferguson, we talk about players. That is normal. What do you expect me to talk to Abramovich about? The weather? Or cards? I have been to David Dein's house many times, but I don't think I will be the manager of Arsenal. It shouldn't be difficult to have friends in football without people assuming things. That he [Abramovich] bought Chelsea was a big surprise. All I knew was that he was going into football or maybe Formula One, which he told me a while ago. We were not going to discuss a contract. We [England] are trying to qualify for Euro 2004 and then to have a good championship. I can see myself being England manager until 2006. I stopped trying to convince you years ago that I am staying. I don't worry about it because then you have even more grey hairs.'

Had he spoken to Ranieri about the speculation? 'I talked to Ranieri.' Had he apologised to the Italian? 'I didn't say anything because there's nothing to say.' Had Abramovich asked him to be the manager in the future? 'No, no. You are invited to take a cup of tea in the house of a friend, and you are not going there to discuss making a contract with the club.'

Asked later if he thought that the meeting had been a mistake he said 'no', but then modified his response to 'maybe'.

Abramovich surrounds himself with bodyguards, including former KGB men, and travels in bullet-proof vehicles. Less than five years ago, his Aston Martin was found riddled with bullet holes in France. At his Moscow base, he travels in an armour-plated Mercedes. Abramovich feels that both he and his family will receive even greater protection in England.

One of Abramovich's key aides must hold the record for the shortest term of office as a Chelsea director. Eugene Shvidler, the thirty-nine-year-old graduate of the Gubkin Oil and Gas Institute, where he was studying when he first met Abramovich, who has an MBA in financial accountancy and who is also the chairman of the Investment Board of Millhouse Capital, resigned after only three-and-a-half weeks in the job because of his heavy workload. He was to be replaced on the Board by Bruce Buck, a partner at the law firm Skadden, Arps, Slate, Meagher & Flom, who acted for Abramovich during the takeover.

Abramovich discusses transactions from his offices in Chukotka, Moscow, his Knightsbridge home or on his private yacht. He says, 'I have videos sent to me of the players we want to buy before I agree to go ahead with it. Of course, there is no point having money if you can't spend it, but I don't throw my money away either.'

Abramovich spelled out his philosophy. 'This is not a business venture. I am focused on the game, the beauty of the game. This is simply for my love of football. Buying Chelsea is a way to realise my own ambitions. Through a great team you can realise your ambitions through a great game. Chelsea should be an international team. The best players need to play.'

Abramovich made it plain that money was no object in securing the players of his choice, although Zahavi told me, 'I won't allow him to be ripped off.'

Asked whether he would get involved in team matters, Abramovich said, 'This is what the pleasure is all about, to participate in the game and the selection process.' He was referring not to team selection, but to the selection process of the acquisition of new players. He explained, 'The coach will determine which areas are in need of new players. I will participate in that process, discussion and analysis.' Note 'the coach' as opposed to 'Claudio Ranieri'.

Abramovich took a wide range of soundings on football issues, not just from Ranieri and Zahavi, or even Eriksson, but also from Russian sports journalists and supporters. 'Their opinion is very important to me. They understand more than the press.' Abramovich received a letter from a ten-year-old fan. 'He described the situation in the team perfectly and we were already thinking about three of his five suggestions for new players,' he said. Abramovich was impressed. 'I couldn't even write at that age.'

A new £20 million training complex complete with enhanced youth facilities was now affordable. 'I don't believe the model of Real Madrid would fit in the English structure. I see Chelsea being in between Manchester United and Real Madrid,' the Russian said. 'At Manchester United, they have an academy to prepare future players. But when you have to make a purchase, you do.'

Abramovich's Moscow-based Sibneft paid CSKA Moscow £30 million over three years for exclusive rights to the club's name, trademark and image both in Russia and abroad. The deal was intended to placate those Russians who were angered by his takeover of Chelsea, but it caused an uproar when Chelsea were drawn against the Russian club in the opening group stage of the Champions League in the new owner's second season in control.

Abramovich paid for a group of fifty children from Chukotka to come and watch his team as the highlight of a five-day trip to London for a party of elite athletes and students aged eight to seventeen. They had been handpicked by Abramovich's advisers to demonstrate his continuing commitment to his homeland.

Interest in Chelsea is spiralling throughout Russia and has even reached outer Siberia. A Chelsea fan club was established in Chukotka and many Russians are adopting the Blues as their second team.

But it was English football that was feeling the shockwaves of the Abramovich era. It hadn't taken long before the whinging could be heard, from Highbury to Old Trafford. In the embryonic stage of the Abramovich spending spree, Wenger branded the Russian's rejuvenation of the stagnating transfer market as 'dangerous' for the game.

'Chelsea's transfer dealings are inflating an otherwise deflated transfer market. That could be a dangerous thing for football. Chelsea have won the lottery. They have always spent in the transfer market – usually as much as Arsenal – but now they are in Manchester United's bracket. Chelsea will be even more competitive next season because they will buy and have the potential to buy, but it doesn't always guarantee success. In recent years, the competition has come from United, but now I think we can add Chelsea as well.

'Chelsea buy a player a day – we do not buy any players in a month. To write us off just because we haven't spent £100 million is too easy ... I think we have got enough to compete at the top again. At the moment, the newspapers have already removed us from being favourites for the title, but I don't mind that. What's important is what's happening on the pitch and I know this team has great potential.'

Wenger remained unperturbed, even though Henry and Vieira had been top of the Chelsea wish list. The Frenchman was adamant. 'They are not for sale at any price. It is that simple. Patrick has not signed his new contract yet, but we are close. When he returns to pre-season training, we expect him to sign.'

Wenger added, 'It came as a huge surprise to me that the change was made so quickly at Chelsea, because it looked as though Ken Bates could manage the financial situation down there. What will the new resources do to Chelsea? I don't think it is a concern of ours, because we do not want to sell our good players to anyone. We want to maintain the stability here that we have developed in recent years. To build a great team is not all about money. First, you have to create the spirit and togetherness within a squad and that is not easy. Of course, it's not all down to money. But, if you want to be successful, it's better that you have it.'

Kenny Dalglish steered Blackburn to the title in 1995 when the late Jack Walker bankrolled their bid, pouring £60 million into his beloved club to achieve championship glory. Dalglish did not accept any similarities and made his point right from the outset of the Abramovich takeover, when he observed, 'Chelsea are in a much stronger starting position than we were at Blackburn. They have a Champions League place and finished fourth last season. What is happening now can only make the next title race even more exciting. Apart from United, Arsenal and Chelsea, Liverpool and Newcastle will also look to make a push.'

Dalglish added, 'Money alone won't win you the title – it's the players who will do that. I am sure Ranieri is comfortable with the situation. He has worked in Spain and Italy where the president buys the players and now someone else is providing the money to bring in the new faces. From his point of view, that is a great position to be in. He has already demonstrated that he is one of the best-equipped coaches in the game. He is shrewd and knowledgeable and, when you look at who they have signed so far, you have to say they are all good investments. Now it's a question of everyone gelling and, until we see the outcome of that, you cannot predict just how quickly Chelsea will rise to the top. They were a good side last season and will certainly be an even better one this time. By having so much cash at his disposal, it is inevitable that standards will rise and that is good for the game as a whole. That is why I am looking forward so much to the new season. These are exciting times for the Premier League and not just for Chelsea fans.'

Dalglish is the only other boss apart from Ferguson and Wenger to have won the Premiership title, 'I thought Chelsea were in with a shout of winning it even before they started signing new players. In recent years, United and Arsenal have set tremendously high standards, but now Chelsea are just as powerful as those two.

'How can it be a problem for the game if someone is investing in the Premier League? Don't forget, £30 million of the £37 million Chelsea have spent so far is invested in our league. Only the money for Geremi has gone out of this country. You have to take your hat off to Chelsea, because they are creating so much excitement, not only for their own fans but also because they are increasing the competition and standards for the rest of the country.'

Former Blackburn stars Tim Flowers and Tony Gale insisted that money can, indeed, buy you glory. Ex-England 'keeper Flowers, now coaching at Leicester, said, 'You only have to look at Real Madrid to see that you can buy success. They have spent more than anyone else on players like David Beckham, Zinedine Zidane, Ronaldo and Luis Figo and what have they got to show for it? Two European Cups in the last four years. Of course Chelsea can do it. The money is available and they are already a very good side. If Chelsea get the sort of players they are being linked to, then – Bang! – they are in business.'

Abramovich remained a mystery to outsiders, but the Chelsea players have seen quite a bit of him. Frank Lampard says, 'If we've won, he shakes your hand and, if you've lost he is the same. He's always there and he has never shouted, bawled or complained that he has spent all of this money. He comes to the training ground and sits in on meetings with a translator. It's great for the lads to see that he is not just a figurehead who doesn't care about the players or the results. He speaks to you. For instance, if you have an injury, he will come right up and see if you're OK and other times he will say "s**t result" and maybe we should have done that a bit better. His English is very broken, but he can say a few words.'

John Terry said, 'Roman is in the dressing room every week, win, lose or draw. He goes around and talks to the lads individually and asks how everyone is. He speaks through his translator and wants to know how everyone is feeling and whether they've got any problems ... Roman is a very open person and it's great to see him in the dressing room. It's a great boost to see how much he has put into the club and we just want to repay him.' Abramovich had been making visits to morning training sessions and to the players' lounge in an attempt to get to know his squad personally. Seba Veron observed, 'He's an everyday kind of guy. He doesn't turn up with twenty-five bodyguards. He's just got an ordinary manner, and dresses in an ordinary way, sometimes in jeans and trainers, and never a tie.'

Former Chelsea star Didier Deschamps, who played just one season at the Bridge, now manages Monaco. He often talks to his close friend Marcel Desailly who, up until last season, was a star of the Chelsea defence, and he observed, 'If football could find more Abramovichs, it would be very good thing for the game. He's brought significant resources into the club. He's bought a lot of players and, for the economy of English football, he's been beneficial, because some of the money has gone around the game there.' Will it work for Chelsea? 'Hard to know. He's bought in very good players, but making them work as a unit? There are a lot of players there now, maybe too many. That's not easy. Remember there was a team already there which was a good, competitive side.'

The knock-on effect of Abramovich's spending on players soon became apparent. Southampton chairman Rupert Lowe pointed out that the sale of Wayne Bridge had had a 'beneficial impact on the half-year figures'. Lowe noted, 'Bridge was a homegrown player and, therefore, had a nil book value. The proceeds were used to strengthen the squad further, with seven players added at a cost of £6.8 million.'

West Ham may have sold Jermaine Defoe to Tottenham for £9 million, but debts of £44 million could have crippled the club if Abramovich had not bankrolled summer raids for Glen Johnson and Joe Cole. Hammers' manager Alan Pardew said, 'In all honesty, if Abramovich hadn't gone into Chelsea, you would seriously have had to worry about the future of West Ham, because a lot of those deals kept us from a Leeds United situation.

You could say it's sliding down the scale. One of the big, big problems of the last six years was that money on players went abroad to other clubs and was never seen again. But the Abramovich money has come to us. It's been fantastic. We then spent it in the British market and so the money filters down.'

⚽ ⚽ ⚽

Lord Attenborough CBE has been a Chelsea fan for six decades and is still the club's life vice-president. Dickie Attenborough, eighty-one, heads a list of some exotic and famous personalities who are among Chelsea's celebrity set.

When Lord Attenborough first filmed the classic movie *Brighton Rock* in 1947, he trained for the part of Pinkie Brown – a small-town hoodlum whose gang ran a protection racket based at Brighton racecourse – by spending time with Tommy Lawton and John Harris.

He was a director of Chelsea FC when the club won the FA Cup in 1970 – he held a directorship between 1969 and 1982 – presided over the launch of Chelsea's new badge and made a keynote speech as part of one of the initial processes of the club's centenary.

Of the badge, he said, 'It is an emblem that personifies not only our past but also our excitement, dedication, ambition and aspirations for the future. I think it is terrific. It is beautifully designed and we could not ask for more artistically, because it says something.'

B

Roy Bentley and Ken Bates

Roy Bentley was the centre-forward and captain of Chelsea's league championship-winning team of 1955; he was the first Chelsea captain to lift a major trophy, and the first player to score 150 goals for the club. With the club's new manager Ted Drake – the former Arsenal and England centre-forward – Bentley initiated an era of tactical organisation and coaching at Stamford Bridge.

'When I look at Jose Mourinho's team,' reflects Bentley, who is now living in retirement in Reading, where he was manager for six years and secretary for another seven, 'I can see the fulfilment of Ted's original ambition, the maximum utilisation by each player of his particular talents.'

Before Drake's arrival, Bentley had never experienced any coaching, neither with Bristol Rovers, where he began as a fourteen-year-old, nor with Bristol City, where he moved as a groundstaff boy to increase his £2.50 wage by 10 shillings (50p), or even with Newcastle (transfer fee £8,000). 'We never saw a ball except in matches,' he says. 'All we did was fitness. Nobody talked about tactics, not even Walter Winterbottom with England. Ted was manager at Reading, though they knew he was angling to join Chelsea. But, before he would sign a contract at the Bridge, he spent hours on the golf course with me and our defender Johnny Harris, and all he talked about was football and Chelsea's players: about how he wanted our wingers, Eric Parsons and Frank Blunstone, to come back deep when the opposition had the ball; about attacking variations; about how he wanted them not always to cross the ball to the far post, but to hit sharp, low centres across the face of the six-yard box, because it was much more dangerous and you'll get more own goals as defences panic. The secret, he insisted, was repetition of moves, even when things were going badly.

'I'd talk for hours with Ted on the phone after each game, calculating how the team was developing. In the middle of the 1953–54 season, we lost a fine match against the powerful West Brom side 5–2, and Ted confidently said, "It's coming!" By Christmas the next season we were lying tenth, but with a sustained unbeaten run, it always looked like we could do it.'

Also vying for the England centre-forward position at that time, along with Bentley, was Tommy Lawton (Chelsea), Jackie Milburn (Newcastle), Nat Lofthouse (Bolton) and Ronnie Allen (West Bromwich). Because of the range of skilful players, Bentley reasons, it was harder to get into the England side and much harder then to win the league, as there were at least a dozen potential challengers in any year. 'Nobody could hope to go unbeaten like Arsenal last season,' he says.

Bentley served on destroyers and minesweepers in the Second World War, escorting the merchant fleets on the supply route to Murmansk during Russian winters: he also won Navy boxing titles.

He may only have earned a pittance from winning the championship with Chelsea, but he remains a legend at the club and occasionally hosts elderly tourist visitors to the Bridge. Brought up in freezing Geordie land, he suffered so much from the cold that it affected his breathing, but he was a demon in front of goal and in the championship season he scored a hat-trick against Newcastle at the Bridge, and also scored twice against Wolves in a thrilling 4–3 win that ultiamtely left the Midlanders as runners-up.

Roy followed his manager Ted Drake and chairman Joe Mears in addressing the wildly emotional fans who were gathered around the directors' box on the day that, barring a mathematical miracle, the championship was won. He said, 'On behalf of the boys, thank you all. There is no need for me to say how pleased we are to have won the championship, but we are pleased, too, for your sakes, because you have been behind us in other years when we needed your support. From the bottom of our hearts, thank you very much.'

When Bentley recalls the day they clinched the championship with a 3–0 win against Sheffield Wednesday, he has mixed emotions. There is humility.

'We defeated Wednesday without being particularly proud of it. Their goalkeeper was carried off and they were unlucky to have a penalty goal scored against them for a somewhat unlucky handball.'

But he also could not hide his jubiliation at winning the championship, which hinged on Portsmouth failing to win on the final day. 'The final whistle was music to my ears ... I could have wept. That wonderful crowd. They had been taking it on the chin for fifty years and always came up smiling.

'We clasped hands with the boss – each of us; with John Harris and Les Stubbs, too. They hadn't been in the actual league-winning line-up that day, but they had a very definite place with us in our hour of victory. We hurried back and changed into our suits to enter the boardroom for a jolly little celebration party that the directors had arranged.

'Telegrams of congratulations were read out; one of them, from Portsmouth, was despatched five minutes after the final whistle had sounded at Ninian Park.

'No longer could they call us the Clown of Clubs. Now we were the Champions Club.'

Ironically, Bentley joined Chelsea from Newcastle after the Second World War as an inside-right, just after the surprising departure of Tommy Lawton. He struggled at first, but manager Billy Birrell switched him to an unorthodox centre-forward, who could raid down the flanks as well as through the middle. He might only have been 5ft 10in, but he was dynamic in the air. He scored nine times in twelve games for England, including the goal that clinched qualification for the 1950 World Cup.

A year after the championship, when he finished as top scorer for the eighth successive season, he was sold to Fulham, helping them to promotion to the First Division, and he finished his career with QPR.

Ken Bates was Chelsea chairman for twenty-two years and, although the title always eluded him, he was credited for saving the club.

However, when he sold out to Roman Abramovich, the club had debts of £90 million plus. He stayed on with a two-year contract to remain as a figurehead chairman, but stormed out and sued, claiming that his contract had been breached.

He resurfaced just ten months later. Having failed to buy Sheffield

Wednesday, he took a 51 per cent stake in Leeds United, Chelsea's one-time dreaded foe.

Peter Lorimer remained on the Leeds Board when Bates arrived and observed, 'The rivalry with Chelsea dates back nearly thirty-five years to an FA Cup final when they beat us. It's no good saying that Chelsea and Leeds are enemies. We've gone a long way down the road since that Cup final. After talking to Ken Bates, I know how sincere he is in wanting to take Leeds back to the top. He sees it as his last challenge in football.'

Bates failed to fulfil fully his dream of making Chelsea the Manchester United of the south and he finally called an end to his reign when it was announced, at 8pm on 1 July 2003, that Roman Abramovich had bought the club. Bates told me on the very day of the Abramovich takeover, 'Because of what has happened at Leeds, football has become a dead duck as far as clubs getting bank loans and investors interested.' Little did Bates know that it wouldn't be long before he was trying to rescue the 'dead duck' at Elland Road!

Abramovich aquired Bates's shares and those of the five offshore trusts for £17.5 million to give him control from day one with 57 per cent. The next stage was to bid for the entire company, to de-list the club from the AIM Stock Exchange and to make it private.

Chelsea Ltd, a special-purpose vehicle, registered in England, was formed to buy Chelsea Village, but it is just an intermediate entity. Chelsea Ltd is wholly owned by Isherwood Investments Ltd, a company incorporated in Cyprus, which in turn is wholly owned by Taverham Holdings Limited, a company incorporated in the British Virgin Islands. Abramovich is the sole beneficial owner of Taverham. Taverham will be ultimately owned by Millhouse Capital, a holding vehicle for all of Abramovich's assets, which is registered in the UK and has its office in Weybridge, Surrey. Millhouse shares are all owned by an entity in Cyprus. Russia and Cyprus have a tax treaty which makes the Mediterranean island an attractive place for wealthy Russians to keep their money.

Claudio Ranieri was driving through France when he got the news from the then chief executive, Trevor Birch, that the club had been sold. Eidur Gudjohnsen was out with his two boys in Reyjkavik when he took a never-to-be-forgotten call on his mobile phone. It was from his father, Arnor, telling him that Chelsea had been bought by a Russian billionaire. He laughed and got on with his shopping! Curiosity got the better of him, though, and he rang John Terry, who told him that it was true.

Bates encapsulates what the twenty-one years as overlord of the Bridge meant to him when he told me, again on the very day that the takeover went through, 'Fantastic experience, wouldn't have missed it for the world. I have loved every minute of it.'

Bates bought the club for £1 back in 1982. The club had debts of £1 million and those, along with the valuable piece of real estate, the Bridge, were transferred into another company which was owned by the existing regime. Bates recalled, 'I took over when the club was bankrupt and at the bottom of the Second Division with a crumbling stadium. It is a great recognition of my achievements that when this guy wanted a football club he looked at Manchester United, Arsenal and Spurs, but he chose Chelsea because we had the most potential; we have a great ground, not necessarily the biggest but the best, and we have a good team.

'I won't go on forever and, at some stage, I'll want to sit back and retire. I'll enjoy the fruits of my past labours and Roman's future labours.'

Bates's vision of lavish hotels and a banqueting complex in one of London's trendiest areas also came to an end. Bates said, 'Roman is putting £200 million into the club in total. Do you think he'd spend that just to pour it into the Thames? That demonstrates that this guy means business and we have got a great future now. We'd been looking for an investment partner for almost a year. That's why, at our AGM, we got our shareholders to agree to issue 30,000 more shares. We were talking to four suitors and, of them, three actually approached us out of the blue. Roman wanted to get involved in Premiership football and looked at four clubs – but thought we were head and shoulders above the others. We're a good team and in the Champions League, which must have influenced him.

'When Trevor Birch first met them [the Russians], he was amazed they knew as much about Chelsea as he did. We arranged to meet and did the deal in forty-five minutes. He [Abramovich] is a young man and his wealth is quite phenomenal. He is the right man to take this club on to the next stage of its development. He feels that Chelsea is the only club in this country with real potential and, once we got talking, it didn't take us long to thrash out a deal. We have been working on it non-stop for the past few days and I am exhausted.'

Bates was not perturbed, at the time, about the jibes that selling out to a

Russian would start a trend of overseas 'sugar daddies'. He argued, 'There are several clubs already owned by Scandinavians, while an Egyptian owns Fulham. If there is a trend, and I don't think there is one, it won't have started with this transaction.'

He went on, 'This is a marriage made in heaven. Let's be honest about it, I have always had to run Chelsea on a shoestring. We could have continued to pootle along or we could go into the big league. I feel I have taken Chelsea into that big league, into the elite in this country, but, if we want to compete with the likes of Real Madrid and Barcelona, then we need more money ... much more money. Now along comes this man with plenty of money who wants to invest in Chelsea. With his financial muscle behind us, we can compete on the world stage and you know that has always been my main ambition – it has been the reason for all my hard work at this club.

'This is a great deal for the Chelsea fans. They are not too bothered who owns the club, they are mostly interested in how much money we can spend on new players. We are now entering a new era. Despite all our handicaps over the years, I have made Chelsea into one of the top four or five clubs in this country. With this guy's help and financial muscle, we can be one of the top four or five clubs in Europe. You have got to look at the wider spectrum, and he will sit back and have the pleasure of being associated with a club that can hit the heights – and know that he has made it possible.'

Despite buying the club, Abramovich could not be on the Chelsea Board. As Bates explained, 'He can't come on the Board because he is a governor of one of the Soviet provinces and that precludes him becoming a director.'

Bates refuted claims that he sold as the club was running out of money. 'I never comment on those reports because most of them are rubbish anyway, but our problems were behind us, apart from short-term cashflow which had actually been arranged to be covered anyway.' Two loans were proving difficult to service – a £5 million facility with the Royal Bank of Canada and an £18 million syndicated loan led by Barclays. Bates later told me that it was the refusal of the Harding Estate to continue with their £5 million facility that proved to be the difficult issue.

Abramovich was unperturbed about the level of debt. As Bates said at the time, 'When I told him he should clear the debts, he asked how much we were paying. I told him 7 per cent. He told me not to worry – in Russia they pay a lot more!'

Bates was in the departure lounge at Heathrow when he spotted his old mates from Anfield, Gerard Houllier, chairman David Moores and chief executive Rick Parry. The Chelsea squad were heading for Kuala Lumpur for the inaugural Premiership Asia Cup, while the Liverpool party were on their way to their own Far East tour. Bates couldn't resist the opportunity to show off his unique brand of humour as he shouted across the lounge, 'Hello, boys, anyone want to come and play for Chelsea? We'll double your money!'

Gerrard and Owen were on their list of potential signings! That is typical Bates. He has never been afraid to speak his mind, irrespective of who might be embarrassed as a result.

Bates also made some disparaging comments about Sven-Goran Eriksson that made huge headlines and caused a degree of disquiet within the Abramovich camp and, although it had been agreed that he'd stay on until 2005, mutterings began over whether his term of office might be shortened as a consequence.

Bates insisted that Abramovich is in it for the long haul and that no one is going to rip him off. 'How has Mr Abramovich made his fortune? He's a shrewd businessman. People seem to forget all of that. It would cost him £200 million to walk away. Even if he's worth so much money, then we are still talking about a significant amount of money. It would cost him 5 per cent of his wealth. Why would he have started something if he didn't want to see it through? He has his advisers. They know what a good buy Chelsea Football Club is and they know the potential here. The balance of power could be shifting; there is certainly a more level playing field now.

'I was very interested in what Graeme Souness said about us the other week. He said that teams would not roll over and give us points. We know we are going to have a fight on our hands and people will raise their game against us. We know that every game is going to be like a Cup final. Even if we are playing a workmanlike, journeyman team, they are going to be fighting us for everything. It has helped us to disturb the established order. Instead of viewing it as Manchester United, Arsenal and eighteen others, it is now Manchester United, Arsenal, Chelsea and seventeen others. I'm very happy, very happy indeed, about what has happened to Chelsea. Chelsea is a success story, it was a success story before Mr Abramovich arrived, a great success story, and now he has fast-tracked it far further and it's just great.

'Look back to season 1984–85 when Chelsea went head to head with one of the teams of the day, Sheffield Wednesday. What has happened to Sheffield Wednesday? They're in the Second Division, while Chelsea qualified again for the Champions League. Remember the Big Five of two decades ago – Manchester United, Arsenal, Spurs, Everton and Liverpool? What has happened to two of them? Spurs and Everton are now Premiership strugglers.

'When I look back over the twenty-one years, I feel as though we have done a pretty good job, and that is why it was the most exciting club for Mr Abramovich to buy: there was a platform on which he could build. The day Ranieri arrived here he told me that, as he came from the continent and wanted a continental approach, he wanted two players for every position. We tried to accommodate him, but I am sure he is now pleasantly surprised by the quality of players he has for every position. I am delighted, too. I know that, with no financial restraints, there is no limit as to what Chelsea can achieve.'

Claudio Ranieri enjoyed Bates's backing, but the chairman's influence was on the wain. The recruitment of Peter Kenyon as chief executive further diminshed his already limited power, and the cumulative friction ended with Bates walking out, even though he had a deal to remain as chairman until 2005 and was proudly looking forward to bowing out after the centenary season, at which point he would have been appointed life-president. Before the internal bickering, he had said, 'We won the title in 1955 and it would be great to win it fifty years later so that it coincided with our centenary. But, believe me, I won't have any problems if we win the Premiership this season as well. Two in a row? Yes, that would do me just fine. It seems to me that my enemies are stirring it up for me ... I am enjoying my life at Chelsea very much at the moment. I have all of the pleasure and none of the pain. I'm going nowhere. I've got a job to do and I've started it and I'll see it through to the end. I'm not on my way out. No way.'

Bates criticised the way that Birch was ousted. 'The day after the summer transfer deadline after Trevor Birch had signed eight players, Bruce Buck and Eugene Tenenbaum went into Trevor's office and told him they had just signed Peter Kenyon. Birch just burst out laughing. The acting chief executive Paul Smith had no experience of running a football club at all. He was brought in by Kenyon to act as his locum and that was a problem. I've never got on with Peter Kenyon. We have different values. He only wanted what was best for Manchester United; I wanted what was best for the whole of football. A lot of Premier League votes were 19–1 – Manchester United being the one.'

Bates warned Abramovich that success is not guaranteed: 'If you take Arsenal, Manchester United and, in the old days, Liverpool, their directors never put their hands in their pocket. They achieved everything with good business and planning. You have to admire them more than the people who just throw money at it. People have done that in the past and not been successful.'

The financial profile of Chelsea in the dying days of the Bates regime was revealed in the last set of accounts filed by Chelsea Village: they disclosed losses of more than £26.5 million in the year ending June 2003, the third biggest loss ever recorded by a British football club, exceeded only by Leeds and Fulham. The accounts filed at Companies House, revealed that the club's core football activities made a loss of £10.1 million, while the travel agency and 'leisure services' businesses were also in the red. There was also a huge and unexplained increase in 'central costs' from £1.4 million to £5.1 million. The club ended the year with debts of £79.2 million, including £74.1 million from the Eurobond. The playing squad was valued in the balance sheet at £87.1 million. The report said that £117 million had been spent on new players, slightly more than the reported figure of £111 million. With regard to reports at the time which suggested that the new regime contemplated changes to Chelsea Village, Bates responded, 'It is Roman Abramovich's toy shop now and it is up to him what he does with the toys.'

But, when Kenyon began work, Bruce Buck became the new chairman of Chelsea Village.

On his appointment, Buck announced, 'We see Manchester United with a very good brand that is reasonably well recognised around the world and we think that we can do that or better, largely because we are a London club. If Manchester United was sold today it could yield £500, £600 or £700 million depending on how the Stock Market is on any given day. That's the kind of thing we want to achieve. We want to be able to have a club with that kind of a value. You have got to have a whole new approach to marketing and brand recognition.'

Buck stressed that Chelsea would continue to be run as a cost-efficient business, despite the vast wealth provided by its owner. 'It's very important to fulfil our financial potential. This is a business and we are looking at our costs. We want to develop our football team and put money into it. In Peter we have really found the guy that can take marketing to the next level. That's what we are excited about. With his background at Umbro and United he can do things in the marketing and branding area that have not been seen in sports on this side of the Atlantic.'

Bates was shunted even further to the periphery with a shock call from Buck. Space was required in the next programme for an introductory interview with Kenyon. There would be no room for Bates's column! Bates informed me of the precise contents of his conversation with Buck. 'Bruce Buck didn't want me to write my notes. I asked him, "Why not?" He explained there was a big spread by Peter Kenyon and they wanted to give him a clear run. I said, "What's that got to do with my programme notes?" He said I can write them for the next game. I was not going to be buggered about so I suggested we call it a day. I probably said it in my usual way: "You can shove it. I won't be doing them again."'

Bates's programme notes are renowned for their hard-hitting attacks on the FA, journalists and other figures within the game and have made compulsive reading over the years.

Along with interim chief executive Paul Smith, Buck attended the most recent Premier League chairmen's meeting before Kenyon's arrival as Bates was ill, but the arrival of Kenyon would again affect Bates in his prominent role with the Premier League and the FA.

Kenyon accepts that Chelsea's development is not about a revolution. 'You get there by evolution and the foundations have to be right. This is about making the club a real European force and you don't do that overnight or in a season. There are clubs who have bought the title in the past and then nearly disappeared. That's not what we're about at Chelsea. We want to be up there with the best, not just winning once, but regularly.'

Kenyon confirmed that Bates would accompany him – not the other way around – to Premier League chairmen's meetings. 'The first thing I would acknowledge is Ken's contribution to Chelsea. Equally, he sold the club last summer and, as a consequence, he ceased to have any executive responsibilities. There's nothing unusual in that. My job as chief executive is to be responsible for the day-to-day running and the long-term strategy of the club. So, in effect, I took over those executive responsibilities. Ken remains as chairman of the football club and, as a key responsibility, he will accompany me – the representative of the club – to Premier League meetings and will continue to do that until he takes up his life-president position. There were some discussions about making some space in the programme in order to introduce the new team – Bruce Buck and myself. Ken indicated that he wasn't going to do them [his notes] any more. There wasn't a spat. I think we all recognise his contribution, but we're also moving the football club and the business on.'

I was invited to Bates's last supper at his own Chairman's Supper Club in the Charles Kingsley suite in the West Stand on 2 March 2004, during which he fired a departing broadside at Abramovich. 'Certain things were agreed when I signed the contract that handed the club over to Abramovich. A gradual fade-out is what I planned, but things have not gone the way I anticipated. It has been a clash between Eastern and Western cultures. Their values are not my values, their philosophy is not my philosophy and their standards are not my standards. Roman Abramovich now owns the toys. Let's hope that he respects the toys we brought into the club. We have to have patience and build brick by brick, not overnight.'

Bates also blasted Kenyon. 'What a great appointment! Kenyon must have thought all of his Christmases had come at once. I was asked not to write anything for the programme that introduced Kenyon. I thought that was irrelevant. They insisted – and I decided to call it a day. With Kenyon now here, it's better he operates the club his way without me being on the sidelines. I don't want to go the same way as Matt Busby at Manchester United. He never retired and intimidated many of his successors. ... I have retired as chairman of Chelsea.'

Bates is seeking a £2 million pay-off. Under the terms of a contract agreed following Abramovich's takeover, Bates was entitled to generous expenses to cover the work he would do on behalf of the club. The contract did not provide for a salary and does not contain a notice period or pay-off clause if it is terminated. Talks had been going on over the terms of his departure and Bates is now considering legal action.

When asked about any potential settlement, he said simply, 'Mind your own business.'

Bates removed his possessions from his office and it has now been taken over by Kenyon. Bates also criticised Buck for his failure to attend the Supper Club. Buck bought three tickets, but no one from the Abramovich camp was there. He said, 'I was hoping Mr Buck would be here so I could give him my resignation letter, but unfortunately he's not turned up. Perhaps that's an indication of the difference in values between the East and the West.' Bates concluded, 'The King is dead, or at least is retired, long live the King.

'We will continue to live in the penthouse and see you all. I live on top of the hotel and am not moving. I would accept half of Siberia for the penthouse. In the meantime, I'm going to spend my money on wine and song.'

Lord Attenborough urged the Russian hierarchy to make peace with Bates. The renowned film-maker, a lifelong supporter and vice-president of the club, sat with Bates at the top table. Attenborough said, 'Ken Bates is a colossus. He's the major figure who transformed this club from a good club into a great club. His devotion to the club, and therefore the devotion of the fans to him, is very special indeed. Like tens of thousands of other Chelsea supporters, I am very disappointed that he's going. But I think the decision is typical of his self-respect and dignity. He doesn't just want to be at the club in name only. I hope that Mr Abramovich, Peter Kenyon and Bruce Buck will perhaps do him the honour of asking him to be life-president.'

Among the audience – who were treated to a short video of Chelsea's greatest moments under Bates – were former players Nigel Spackman and Roberto Di Matteo. Spackman said, 'It's a very sad day for me and everyone at Chelsea, but I'm sure Ken will bounce back somewhere in the near future. He's seventy-two now, but I'm sure he has ambitions to be a successful football chairman somewhere.'

Di Matteo offered his own personal tribute. 'I'm fortunate enough to be quite close to him and feel lucky as we've always had a good relationship. He's always treated me very well and despite what people say about him they shouldn't judge him.'

In contrast, Abramovich and his aides were just glad to see the back of Bates! Among Bates's celebrated adversaries are Peter Osgood, Ron Harris and David Speedie.

Harris said, 'What goes around comes around. He called the team I played in, the one that won Chelsea the FA Cup and the European Cup-Winners' Cup for the first time, a bunch of lager louts. He should have gone a couple of years ago. He won't be missed and life goes on.'

Speedie said, 'He always has to be one up on you. If I told him I'd been to Tenerife, he'd say he'd been to Elevenerife.'

Osgood was similarly demonstrative. 'He certainly put my nose out of joint. He wasn't a nice man at times and he got lucky with Abramovich buying him out. But he has left the club in a much healthier state than he found it, so you've got to say well done to him.'

Bates hit back, 'At my Supper Club I told the audience that David Speedie exemplified the spirit of Chelsea – sadly that is no longer the case. Players like Speedie and Dixon should be remembered for their glories on the pitch. That is their problem, not mine, but it is a crying shame we cannot just think of them for their magnificent achievements at Chelsea.'

Bates recalls how Speedie dropped his shorts on the pitch and was fined £750 by the FA, and the Chelsea chairman was criticised in the Lord Justice Taylor Report, no less, for not only paying the fine but paying for a new pair of shorts!

Bates again hit out at the Abramovich regime, claiming they blocked video tributes to him on the club's television station. 'I didn't realise that Vladimir Putin had taken over Chelsea Television. He runs the television stations in Russia as well, you know.'

Among those who spoke on film were Di Matteo and Spackman. Terry Byrne, the newly appointed personal assistant to England captain David Beckham, was also present. Byrne was a masseur with Chelsea until he moved to Watford and then to Spain with Beckham, and had flown in especially from Madrid to attend the supper.

Ranieri also paid his tribute to Bates, 'He brought the team to a higher level.' But he then put the Bates era into perspective. 'And now there is a new era. Everything has changed and it is time to look forward. The future of this club is Mr Abramovich.'

Before kick-off at the Champions League tie with Stuttgart, Bates issued a writ for £2 million claiming breach of contract and threatened to subpoena Abramovich to give evidence in what would be a sensational case if it ever went to court. The writ was accepted by Buck. Although there was no salary linked to the contract, travel expenses and other allowances, are estimated to be worth around £200,000 a year.

Bates said, 'The case will be determined in the High Court and not by any spin-doctors briefing newspapers. I'm amused at the way in which they are trying to rewrite history. Mr Buck has been quoted as saying that "the owner decides everything". That will all come out in court. Unless I get my £2 million then, yes, it will end up in court. I can subpoena Mr Abramovich and Eugene Tenenbaum. I have no idea if that would be an embarrassment to Chelsea but, if it is, then it won't be of my making.'

Chelsea intend to 'vigorously defend' the legal action. The club announced, 'We are satisfied that we have behaved both responsibly and honourably in every way in our dealings with Ken Bates. Ken Bates has resigned his position as chairman of Chelsea Football Club and is no longer a director.'

C

Petr Cech and Steve Clarke

One player doesn't make a team, but a top goalkeeper makes a huge difference.

During a season in which Arsenal and Manchester United both experienced a crisis with their No. 1, Chelsea had *the* No. 1: the 6ft 5in Petr Cech from the Czech Republic.

In the week when Roy Carroll and Manuel Almunia were letting in six goals between them, Cech not only kept yet another clean sheet for Chelsea but also saved a penalty; one which was worth two points as his grateful teammates scrapped out a fractious 1–0 win at Blackburn. On Wednesday, 2 January 2005, Cech became a Chelsea legend – just seven months after signing for £7 million from Rennes.

Chelsea's 1–0 victory at Ewood Park was their eighth successive Premiership victory and their eighth consecutive clean sheet. In the process, Cech had set a new Premiership record for the most minutes without conceding a goal: 781, surpassing Peter Schmeichel's 1997 mark of 694 minutes. He had broken the previous Chelsea record, set by Carlo Cudicini between October and November 2002, of 513 minutes. Schmeichel was an early role model, but he was by no means the only one. The young man from the Bohemian brewing town of Plzen is quick to add that, in his formative years, he also looked up to, and learned from, Edwin van der Sar, in the Dutchman's Ajax days, and Gianluigi Buffon, the Italian regarded by many as the No. 1 in the world. 'I tried to take the best bits from each of them,' Cech said. 'Schmeichel was one of my greatest idols. That is why I enjoy my record even more. I wish that my career would go on as successfully as Schmeichel's did.'

He possesses precious little of Schmeichel's tendency for eyeball-to-eyeball confrontation with his own defenders. 'Everybody is different,' Cech says. 'You have to have a feeling for the players in front of you. Sometimes, if you believe someone is unlucky and he doesn't feel very good, there is no reason to scream. It depends on the situation.'

There is such cohesion within the rearguard that Cech rarely has cause to castigate them anyway. 'The important thing is that it is never just about four defenders and one goalkeeper. We are playing defensively well as a team. When we lose the ball, everybody is trying to win it back.'

He also equalled his own personal record of ten consecutive clean sheets that he set while at Sparta Prague. Cech added, 'I'd always take a 5–3 win over a 1–0. I think it is bizarre that we have such an impressive defensive record at Chelsea this season. The line-up in defence rotates quite a lot and most of our defenders also like to get forward as often as they can. The whole team does come back to help out in defence, but you would probably expect us to be winning, say, 5–3 more often than we do. Personally, there are still so many things I have to work on in my game. This defence at Chelsea is helping me a lot and, actually, the fact that they are so very good inspires me to remain focused throughout the entire ninety minutes. I know I have to be alert and on my toes the whole time, waiting for a shot which could sneak past the defence at any time.'

The record-breaking sequence came at Ewood Park: a bruising game for the 'keeper. No one was more abused than Cech, who was kicked twice, by Paul Dickov, the first after saving the striker's penalty. The record came under threat when Blackburn were awarded a penalty. 'When the referee whistled for the penalty, I took a glance at the clock and saw that there were only two minutes remaining for us to break the record. I told myself, when I've got so close to it, I must save it. But I couldn't celebrate too much when I did, because Paul Dickov kicked me in the stomach when he was going for the rebound, and I had a lot to do to recover.'

Mourinho said of Blackburn, 'I think they felt they couldn't beat us at football, so they tried to beat us with a different kind of football. I'm not saying they tried to get players injured, but they were nasty and they tried to intimidate our players. We gave a big answer here tonight; we showed we can deal with that tactic. We fought fantastically well, with everyone battling for the same cause. If I was polite, I would call it a special attitude. The blond boy in the middle, yes Robbie Savage, made twenty faults and was given no yellow card. It's difficult to control emotions. They were direct for every ball. They were aggressive, hard and nasty.'

Chelsea went eleven points clear at the top of the Premier League that night: the biggest gap they had had all season. In the forty-third minute of the second half, Savage tumbled under a challenge from Ferreira and won a penalty from Uriah Rennie. Dickov hit the penalty low to Cech's left, but the giant goalkeeper extended his remarkable unbeaten record by flinging himself to his left to parry. Cech hurled himself at the ball and got to it first, taking a hefty kick in the ribs from Dickov in the process: it provoked one of many ugly scenes.

Cech's £7 million recruitment from Rennes in 2004 was widely seen as an early example of Roman Abramovich's acquisitive extravagance. The club already had the best 'keeper in the league, Carlo Cudicini, who was playing so well that England had considered 'adopting' him through residential qualification. But the Czech's impenetrable excellence saw Cudicini consigned to the role of first choice in the Carling Cup and, even in the vital semi-final against Manchester United, Jose Mourinho opted for Cech.

He started as he meant to go on in English football, where his clean sheet against Manchester United on opening day was the first of three in little more than a week.

After Cech had broken his record, Schmeichel paid his tributes to the Chelsea 'keeper: 'I didn't know I held it until I read about Petr taking it away. But I'm not bothered, because he is such a great player. If you appreciate good goalkeeping, you enjoy watching somebody like him performing well. I heard a great story about him from behind the scenes at the Chelsea training ground. It comes from one of the club's strikers. I won't say who it is, but this guy was telling me how he's been cursing Petr Cech. The problem is, he can't score against him in training – apparently nobody can. The Chelsea players have all learned that, if they want to score in a training game, they have to go up the other end, because Carlo Cudicini does concede goals: at the rate of one a week. That tells you everything about Chelsea's strength in the goalkeeping department. It may seem no big deal, but the story demonstrates why Chelsea might be on to something big. Cech isn't just turning it on during games; even in practice his attitude is: "I'm the man and I'm not going to be beaten." It takes real hunger and desire to be like that, and those are among the attributes that make Cech so good.

'He is big and he has superb speed, both in terms of his ability to get around the box and his reactions. He can catch, he can dive, he can read the game and his kicking is good enough to take the pressure off his defence. But forget all that. Any goalkeeper who has made it to Premiership level has most, if not all, of these attributes. What separates the best goalkeepers is the mental side of things, most notably their decision-making and concentration. Cech's concentration is fantastic. You saw it with his penalty save against Blackburn, and you saw it again in the Carling Cup semi-final against Manchester United when, late in the game, he came up with a stunning save from Cristiano Ronaldo. You've seen it in countless Chelsea wins this season when, because of their fantastic defence, he's had nothing to do for eighty-nine minutes and fifty-nine seconds, yet when he is suddenly asked to do so, he has produced a vital stop. His decision-making is also good. I can't remember him making a mistake. Cech has fitted straight into the Chelsea defence as if he's been playing with John Terry and William Gallas for years. He's made Terry an even better player. Cech takes so much pressure off his defenders, Terry knows he can take a couple of steps forward and try to attack his man earlier, or he can take up a position covering one side of the goal, knowing that Cech will cover the other. In previous seasons, Terry would throw himself around trying to block everything, and you'd often see a shot go in off him or bounce off to the centre-forward. You don't see him doing that any more.

'But Terry's rich vein of form has made it easier for his goalkeeper as well. Just as my clean sheets were never down just to me, but also down to the likes of Steve Bruce, Gary Pallister and Denis Irwin, so Cech will know that Terry, Gallas, Paulo Ferreira, Wayne Bridge and Ricardo Carvalho also deserve a big share of his new record.

'How good is Cech? Well, there's no doubt that, in only his first season in the Premier League, he's established himself as the best goalkeeper. As for the best in the world, I'd be a bit more cautious about that. He's not yet twenty-three and, if he keeps playing the way he is over the next ten years, he could become one of the all-time greats. But best in the world right now? No, he's got to do it over a longer period.

'I didn't feel I reached my best until I was approaching thirty, but this kid is twenty-two and he's been playing international football since he was nineteen.

'Outfield, a Wayne Rooney comes along once in a generation. I wonder if, at Stamford Bridge, we're seeing the goalkeeping version.'

The influence of Cech was recognised by Chelsea and Arsenal goalkeeping legends Peter Bonetti and Bob Wilson. Bonetti said, 'The lad is still very young and is working hard to get better and there's no doubt he will. It is very exciting. He is already making the big difference between Chelsea and their rivals for the title, and he has such a lot going for him. Chelsea's defensive record is great this season and, in my view, Cech has to take a lot of the credit. It's been great to hear that people are now talking about him and recognising the contribution he has made. Cech has shown his quality in every game, not just when he's had a lot to do. He makes big saves in important situations and that's what gets you results and points. He's a great 'keeper, the best in the league and probably the best in the world. What has impressed me, considering his age, is that his concentration levels are so high. That's what you need as a 'keeper. You have to have communication skills as well. He is obviously talking and his organisation is good. Other teams give goals away through a lack of communication between the 'keeper and his defenders, and that doesn't seem to be happening to Chelsea. It helps that he has superb defenders in front of him: John Terry is a great man and a great leader and he will be the captain of England one day. He's a lovely lad. He reminds me of David Webb, who played to 110 per cent and gave his all. You see the number of times that Terry dives through bodies to head the ball away: that shows his commitment and his bravery.'

Wilson observed, 'Cech has looked almost faultless this season. He has made the odd mistake, but then he has made a lot fewer than anybody else.'

Mourinho paid tribute to both of his 'keepers. 'Cech is fantastic, but Cudicini is responsible for that. Every time Carlo plays, he plays so well that Petr feels if he slips he has a great goalkeeper behind him.'

England 'keeper David James added his voice to the Cech fan club. 'People I respect in the game have said he is the real deal. He is young for a goalkeeper, but he is already very accomplished. Goalkeepers go through phases and he is having a particularly good one. As part of the goalkeeping union you like to see other goalkeepers play well and I don't want to wish any bad luck on him, but all goalkeepers have sticky patches. We all make mistakes, but it is how you handle them that is interesting. He hasn't had one yet and I suppose it would be helpful if it started against us. His kicking was not particularly good against us earlier this season, and I remember Mourinho telling him, as well as our fans, so maybe he has a flaw. He is a similar age to me when I joined Liverpool, but the difference is that he walked into a winning environment. Chelsea had their period of change when Roman Abramovich first arrived. When I joined Liverpool, they were going through a transitional period and I also didn't have the same experience that Cech has had. He was an accomplished international even before he joined Chelsea. They say a goalkeeper gives the back four confidence, but it works the other way round as well. Cech has answered the questions asked of him and looks the full ticket every time I see him play, but the back four has been so consistent and solid and John Terry has been outstanding.'

In a season when Arsenal had a nightmare with their goalkeepers, Arsène Wenger missed out on signing Cech from French club Rennes. Wenger conceded that he was a player who had slipped through the Highbury net after they had monitored his progress at his previous club, Sparta Prague.

He attracted Arsenal's interest when he went over a thousand minutes before conceding a goal in any competition for the Czech club. Wenger said, 'We wanted to take him before he went to Rennes, but we could not get a work permit. At the time he had not played the necessary amount of games for his national team.

'Yes, we missed out – but these things happen. He is not the only player we have missed out on. And when he moved to France we still had David Seaman and then we had Jens Lehmann. But Cech is doing well and he is developing well. He has what you need to play in England. He has the size and that is vital.

'People don't realise how important that is. You get offered a goalkeeper of six-feet-plus who is doing well in a Latin country. He comes here and he gets slaughtered. Therefore, I feel that Cech has the ingredients you need to be successful in England.'

Where did he come by this early maturity? Cech says that it is from his father, Vaclav, who was once a leading decathlete, from his manager at Sparta Prague, Miroslav Beranek, who describes Cech as 'an intelligent young man who knows what he wants', and also from Christophe Lollichon, his goalkeeping coach at Rennes, who rid him of any lingering self-doubts.

He describes going to France, at a time when Arsenal were trying to sign him, as 'a good career move', although it didn't seem that way at the time. He explained, 'When Arsène Wenger came for me at Sparta, I was nineteen years old, I hadn't yet played for the national team and the Czech Republic wasn't in the European Union, so Arsenal couldn't get a work permit for me. That was why it didn't happen. It was probably a good thing. David Seaman, who was playing for Arsenal at the time, was a great goalkeeper, and it would have been difficult for me to become the No. 1 then. I was too young to join Arsenal, and the best thing for me was to spend the two years I had in France. That gave me valuable experience. I had to get by in another country, learning a new language and a new lifestyle. I benefited from all that, and I believe it was a big step in my career.'

When Chelsea came for him, the time was right, he had just been acclaimed as the best goalkeeper at Euro 2004, when five clean sheets helped his country to a semi-final place; his move to England quadrupled his wages. 'I had other opportunities but, as soon as I heard about this, I decided very quickly. Chelsea are now one of the biggest clubs in the world, and it was easy for me to make up my mind to go there.' The clincher was a tour of Abramovich's executive quarters at Stamford Bridge.

He was pleasantly surprised by his success in English football. 'I never expected it to go quite so well, but I've been working very hard and playing for a great team, and the two things together have enabled me to achieve this new record.'

How would he characterise the team he stands behind every week? 'First of all, everybody plays for the team, not himself. That's most important. Apart from that, we are very solid defensively and we can fight when we have to. Because we are disciplined and organised, it is difficult for any opponents to get through the block in front of me. We also have some great players up front who can decide, or turn, a game for us, in one moment. So everybody who plays us knows it is going to be very hard to get through our defence and difficult to defend against the great players we have in attack.

'It's never just about the one goalkeeper. The important thing is that we are playing well defensively as a team. When we lose the ball, everybody does his best to get it back. If you have great defenders, as we have, they help everybody on the pitch. This is our secret.'

Cech is already being acclaimed by some as the best in the world. 'Everybody has their opinion about such things and, of course, I'm pleased that some people are saying that, but I don't think I'm the best. I work as hard as I can because I want to be the best for my team. Because I'm only twenty-two, I can get better if I keep working hard. The experience of playing in England and more international games should mean I'm better in a few years.'

⚽ ⚽ ⚽

Steve Clarke's final match for Chelsea was the European Cup-Winners' Cup triumph over Stuttgart in 1998: it also marked the end of the Chelsea career of Mark Hughes, who was an unused substitute that night.

Hughes is one of the more recent Chelsea megastars, but Clarke enjoyed one of the longest careers at the Bridge: a career which is still in progress in his role as assistant to new coach Jose Mourinho. Hughes has progressed via the Welsh national manager's post to become boss at Blackburn Rovers.

Clarke stepped up from his position as youth-team coach when Mourinho took over from Claudio Ranieri. His previous coaching experience came at Newcastle when he first worked under Ruud Gullit and then Sir Bobby Robson, who was a mentor to Mourinho.

But it is as a player that he will be best remembered, even though his playing career came during an era when there were perhaps more downs than ups. Steve still remembers the night when, playing at full-back, Chelsea were humiliated by Scunthorpe (4–1) in a League Cup clash at Glanford Park back in September 1988. The Londoners fared little better in the second leg at Stamford Bridge, only managing a 2–2 draw in front of just 5,814 fans and crashing out of the second round 6–3 on aggregate.

Clarke admitted, 'I'm too embarrassed. It was a humiliating night for all of us. We'd just been relegated from the old First Division. But it was still considered a big upset. It was 1–1 up there for a long time and then the roof fell in on us, as it often did for Chelsea in those days. I think they scored three goals in five or six minutes. I remember walking off feeling so ashamed. We thought we could turn it around at Stamford Bridge, but could manage only a draw.'

Clarke's humbled side went on to win the old Second Division title in the 1988–89 season by seventeen points. The Scot also helped Chelsea lift the FA Cup in 1997.

He added, 'It was the highlight of my playing career. It was a long time since Chelsea had won a trophy and it was a wonderful day. Back then, the FA Cup was one of the few ways of winning a trophy. We didn't have the strength in depth to challenge for the league title, but times have changed for the better since my playing days. Now we are one of the major powers.'

Paul Musselwhite played in goal for Scunthorpe in that famous night for the Humbersiders. Seventeen years on, he recalls, 'Chelsea are now a team full of superstars, but they still had a very good side back then with Kerry Dixon up front. And they won the old Second Division title that season. I was a kid of nineteen playing just my ninth game for Scunny, but we were brilliant that night and battered them. We did the same in the second leg at Stamford Bridge when people down at Chelsea thought it would be easy for them to get a result. Their fans were so sure they would do it that only 5,000 turned up at the Bridge. But in the end we drew 2–2. I don't suppose many of their top players now have even heard of Scunthorpe. But Stevie Clarke will remember that game.'

Chelsea's team beaten 4–1 by Scunthorpe on 27 September 1988 was: Freestone, Clarke, Dorigo, Roberts, Pates, C Wilson, McAllister, Nicholas, Dixon, K Wilson, Bumstead.

The Men behind Mourinho

STEVE CLARKE: assistant manager
The only member of Ranieri's staff to survive. Ranked fifth in Chelsea's all-time appearance list, the defender played 421 games for the club before retiring in 1998. Clarke assisted Ruud Gullit and Sir Bobby Robson at Newcastle before returning to Stamford Bridge, originally as youth-team coach.

BALTEMAR BRITO: assistant manager
Has known Mourinho for most of his life having played under Mourinho's father Felix at Vitoria Setubal. The Brazilian moved to Portugal in 1974 and spent twelve years in the Portuguese First Division before becoming a coach, and first teamed up with Mourinho at Leiria. 'He knows what I'm thinking even before I think it,' says Mourinho.

SILVINO LOURO: goalkeeping coach
From Setubal, near Mourinho's family home. Louro played in two European Cup finals for Benfica during a lengthy career that took him around the

Portuguese leagues and into the national side. Was coaching the Portugal national team's 'keepers when Mourinho stepped in to take him to Porto.

RUI FARIA: fitness coach

The twenty-nine-year-old has worked with Mourinho at Porto and Leiria and is known for his tough, military-style training sessions. 'Of all the people I wanted to bring,' Mourinho said earlier this season, 'I told Chelsea that he was a must. No argument. We have been together since the beginning and he knows how I work.' He met Mourinho while at college studying sports science, and has also coached at Penafiel, Sao Martinho and Tirsense.

ANDRE VILLAS: scout

Still only twenty-six, Villas spent five years coaching junior teams at Porto before Mourinho's arrival, when he took over the scouting of future opponents. 'It takes me four days to put an entire dossier together,' he says, 'so it is comprehensive.' This was also Mourinho's first role back when he was working for his father and Villas also hopes to become a manager one day. 'This is not my ultimate ambition,' he says of his current job. Has an English grandmother and speaks fluent English.

MIKE BANKS: head physio

A long-term member of Chelsea's staff, whose first job in football was part time at Enfield. Has now been involved in professional football for almost ten years.

MICK MCGIVEN: reserve team manager

Former Sunderland and West Ham defender who managed Ipswich without great success. Was appointed by Ruud Gullit in June 1996 and has retained the role ever since.

NEIL BATH: academy manager

Heads a team including former Chelsea players Damian Matthew, Eddie Newton and Jason Cundy. 'We have spent time watching Mourinho's training sessions and reading up on his philosophy,' he says. 'They've given me a brief that their long-term plan is to have homegrown talent rather than to invest year after year.'

BRENDAN RODGERS: youth-team coach
Personally selected by Mourinho and purchased from Reading, where he had headed the academy. 'I've had a fantastic time at Reading,' he said after joining in September, 'but the opportunity to work with a European Cup-winning manager at a club like Chelsea was too good to turn down.'

NEIL FRAZER: club doctor
The former Queen's Park Rangers doctor was involved in catching out Adrian Mutu when staff suspected the Romanian was taking cocaine. He also broke the news of QPR's relegation from the Premiership in 1996 to their then manager (and future Chelsea coach) Ray Wilkins. 'I suppose he's used to giving bad news,' Wilkins said at the time.

BILLY MCCULLOCH: masseur
Every club needs a joker and McCulloch is Chelsea's. But good hands and a sense of humour are not his only skills – the backroom staff run a football-prediction competition, and the physio has proved to have a keener eye than his more high-profile colleagues this season.

STEWART SULLIVAN: masseur
Mauro Doimo: masseur
Joe Patterson: Under-16 team manager

D

Didier Drogba, Kerry Dixon and Tommy Docherty

Jose Mourinho convinced his record £24 million capture from Marseille that signing for Chelsea would catapult him into an elite group alongside Arsenal maestro Thierry Henry and Brazilian superstar Ronaldo. That prediction struck a chord, because Drogba idolised the French striker and envied his love affair with the Highbury faithful. He was building up the same rapport with Marseille's supporters, but recognised that he needed a bigger challenge if he was going to emulate his hero. He explained, 'What Mourinho said was simple but very effective. Marseille were a good team, yet I had to think of winning trophies first. I had to contest in the Champions League every year to make progress. He ended up saying, "For me, there is Thierry Henry, Ronaldo and you. You belong up there."'

He had a slow start to his career, scoring just fifteen goals in four seasons for Le Mans and Guingamp, but then he notched up seventeen goals in thirty-four games for Guingamp in 2002–03. Incredibly one year before his move to Chelsea, Drogba signed for Marseille from fellow French First Division club Guincamp for £3 million. He scored eighteen goals in thirty starts for the former European champions, collected the French Player of the Year award, and his prize was the big-money move to the Bridge. It was in Europe that he caught the eye, with six goals in Marseille's UEFA Cup campaign which took them past Liverpool and Newcastle before losing in the final against Valencia.

Before his first season with Chelsea he said, 'My life has been transformed in a very short space of time, but that's why I'm in the job, to savour moments like last year and I'm looking forward to learning a lot from Jose Mourinho and achieving great things with my new team-mates.'

Mourinho said, 'I wanted to sign him two years ago for Porto, but I couldn't afford him. Then I had to play against him in the Champions League and I had to watch him score against me. But I won.'

Drogba revealed that manager Jose Mourinho has banned running during training, unless the players have a ball at their feet. 'I haven't jogged a single step since I got here,' said Drogba. 'We never run, except with the ball.'

Talking about his first day of pre-season training, he added, 'I turned up with jogging trainers on. Mourinho looked at me with surprise and said, "You can put them back to the bottom of your bag. With me you'll never be needing them."'

Drogba's incredible strength and speed made him a vital component of Mourinho's most successful tactics of adopting a lone striker with two wingers in support. Drogba, though, had his setbacks with injuries, but was enjoying his first season. 'I love the Premier League. What speed the game's played at and with what passion. I don't agree with those who devalue the English championship. I belong to a team with incredible talent who are on the top of the table.'

As his reputation grew, he reflected on his decision to choose the Ivory Coast. 'I have no regrets about not playing for France. I arrived in France at the age of five. I was always a fan of the team of Platini at the time of the 1986 World Cup, but I am proud to play for Ivory Coast and to have been born in Abidjan.'

Kerry Dixon has no doubts that the centenary celebrations at the Bridge will mark a new era for the club and a complete change of image.

Dixon reflects on the past and looks forward to an ultra-bright future that he could never possibly have envisaged during his time as a goalscoring centre-forward who was much loved by the fans for his whole-hearted approach. His affection for the club remains unaltered by time.

Dixon tells me, 'Nine years at Chelsea was the greatest part of my footballing life, there can be no doubt about that. I played for other clubs, but I enjoyed a wonderful time at Chelsea, it was the pinnacle of my career and I played for England while I was there.

'Yes, I never became the club's record goalscorer, perhaps I should have been, but I never made it and Bobby Tambling retains the record that I don't think will ever be broken.

'You would need to find a goalscorer at Chelsea who could not only manage twenty a season, but who could do so for ten seasons, and that means both staying fit and staying loyal for that length of time. They seem to have managed that at Arsenal with Thierry Henry following Ian Wright, but I really don't know if it will ever happen at Chelsea. Certainly the present team still needs that one goalscorer.

'The club paid £24 million for Drogba and maybe he will do that, but I am not sure he is that type of forward. They paid that kind of money for him because he starred in Europe and for me he does give the team something different, but I am not sure he can deliver the twenty goals a season that you can guarantee from a van Nistelrooy or a Henry, or even a Hasselbaink.

'Drogba is more of a team player than Hasselbaink, as Jimmy-Floyd was more of a basic goalscorer.

'But Chelsea do not yet have that out-and-out goalscorer. Even though Gudjohnsen scored twenty-three in a season, that was the exception rather than the rule, and he is more a link player.'

But the future is most definitely bright according to Dixon, much brighter than even the goggle-eyed fans might think, still shaking their heads in disbelief following the enormity of the transformation under new owner Roman Abramovich.

Dixon says, 'I never could have imagined during my time at the club that Chelsea would be where they are today. I played in the Ken Bates era and you could see his vision for the club: he had big plans, and you always knew the club had the support, because, even in my time when we hardly did much trophy wise, apart from that silly Zenith Data trophy, we would still attract 40,000 gates.

'But how could anyone have foreseen the Abramovich era? For a start I would never have imagined Ken Bates leaving the club.

It's got to be better now than in the past. This club will challenge in Europe on a regular basis for the foreseeable future, maybe forever, with the foundations that are now being put into place.

'I don't subscribe to all those who criticise by saying that Chelsea are buying the championship. They are not; they are buying into success from here until who knows when. It's not a Jack Walker scenario: the foundations are there for the next ten years, possibly forever. In twenty years' time, who knows where this club might be?'

Dixon once shared the Golden Boot with Gary Lineker, but he fell just nine short of reaching Bobby Tambling's all-time goalscoring record. With 193 goals, however, Dixon remains one of the heroes of the trophyless years of the 1980s.

The golden boy of that era, Dixon, big, blond and full of commitment, epitomised the kind of player the fans held so dear to their hearts.

He arrived from Reading after the team had just avoided relegation in the 1982–83 season and scored twice on his debut, then once in his second game, twice in his third and four times in his fifth. He struck thirty-four goals in his first full season and was an ever-present in the side. He scored more than anyone else in the Second Division and was a major factor behind Chelsea's first Second Division championship win. The following season, in the First Division, his tally of thirty-six goals equalled that of Lineker. Not bad for a big traditional centre-forward with a wayward first touch. 'But my second touch isn't bad,' he would say.

He won eight England caps, scoring four goals for his country. Dixon tells me, 'Looking back, I suppose landmarks that stand out are the goal up at Grimsby that clinched the Second Division championship and then the next match when we were paired with Arsenal at Highbury for our opening fixture in the First Division. Arsenal had a wonderful team with Tony Woodcock and Paul Mariner, and I scored against the great Pat Jennings to level the scores, and prove to myself that I could score at that level.

'Over my period at the club, I would pick out John Neal as the best manager I played under, he gave the players immense confidence and belief. It was such a shame when heart trouble meant that he had to take a back seat.'

Gambling contributed to Dixon's downfall. He ended up selling his house and moving into a council house with his girlfriend. He was also hit by poor form on occasions: in the relegation year of 1987–88 he managed just fourteen goals in all competitions. The form returned with fifty-two goals in the next two seasons, but he ended up with Luton, where he got further in the FA Cup than he had ever managed at Chelsea, but ended up facing his old club in the semi-finals.

Dixon concludes, 'Over the years Chelsea have always promised a lot and never quite delivered, in fact, delivered a lot less than they should have done.

'But, as the club reaches its centenary, the dream is going to become reality – and lots more besides.'

Dixon retains his affection for the game and now concentrates on his role as a radio summariser after he was sacked from his post as manager of non-league Hitchin Town – because he opted for watching Chelsea on Saturdays rather than his own team. Dixon coached Southern League Premier Division side Hitchin during the week, but spent his Saturday afternoons commentating at Stamford Bridge for the Premiership table-toppers' pay-per-view channel. Hard-up Hitchin could not afford to pay Dixon enough money to convince him to attend his side's matches and give up his media commitments. So they were left without managerial direction for their league games, while Dixon sat in the press box commentating on Chelsea owner Roman Abramovich's team of millionaires. With Hitchin struggling to balance the books, managing director Andy Melvin took the decision to axe Dixon. Melvin said, 'Kerry is an excellent coach and has oceans of experience. But, as a club, our financial position didn't allow us to make it worthwhile for him to give up his media commitments in order to devote more time to us. The decision to release him was based on the club's inability to find a workable solution to balance Dixon's media commitments. It is a shame that were unable to find a solution, but we have to face the facts.'

Tommy Docherty arrived at Stamford Bridge in September 1961 as player-coach with this amazing greeting from Ted Drake. 'Congratulations, I wish you all the luck in the world, but you weren't my choice, I wanted Vic Buckingham.'

At thirty, Drake became increasingly desk bound. At the age of thirty-three, he was persuaded to return to the game briefly, with Chelsea winning their first match 6–1 against Sheffield United, and he played a further three times.

On Thursday, 27 September 1961, it was announced that Drake was leaving, and he did so with a chairman's familiar comments ringing in his ears. Joe Mears said, 'Let me say how grateful everyone at Stamford Bridge, and I am sure this includes all of you, is to Ted for the honours he has brought in the past.'

Docherty was handed control and, in January, his trial period ended when he was finally appointed team manager. But, by mid-December, the team were already bottom of the table, and Docherty did not see how he could avoid relegation. Although the signing of Eddie McCreadie, for just £5,000 from East Stirlingshire, proved a bargain.

After thirty-two years in the top flight, it was a shock to be back in the Second Division for the start of the 1962–63 season. With full-backs Ken Shillito and McCreadie and 'keeper Peter Bonetti in their ranks, promotion was clinched with a 7–0 win over Portsmouth with Bobby Tambling, at the age of twenty and captain of the side, scoring four times.

The feeling in the camp was pinpointed by trainer Harry Medhurst. 'When Tommy first came he was unpopular because of the iron discipline he imposed at the club; now we would follow him anywhere – he's won our respect.'

However, that iron discipline came into full effect when he sent eight senior players home after a breach of discipline – the infamous 'Blackpool incident'. By doing so, and with three games to go, Docherty effectively jeopardised Chelsea's chance of winning the championship.

The Doc did win the League Cup, however, in the days when the tournament didn't even warrant a Wembley final and when many of the top clubs shunned it.

The 3–2 aggregate win over Leicester in 1965 was watched over the two legs by a total of 47,647 fans, more than 20,000 less than the first Full Members Cup final twenty-one years later.

The Doc also managed a hat-trick of FA Cup semi-finals, until he eventually took them to the final where, they lost in 1967 to Spurs in the first all-London occasion. Six months later, the Doc was out. He resigned within hours of receiving a month-long suspension by the FA following an incident during Chelsea's close-season tour to Bermuda. He was succeeded by Dave Sexton after seventy whirlwind months in charge. A day later, Chelsea conceded seven goals at Leeds.

Perhaps the Doc's fate was also sealed by the tragic death of chairman Joe Mears, as a result of a heart attack suffered on 1 July 1966 while accompanying the England World Cup party in Norway; he was also chairman of the Football Association. Mears and Docherty had established such a strong relationship that the Doc once suggested he would have stayed his entire career at Chelsea had it not been for the passing of the chairman. The Doc had even rejected overtures from Athletico Madrid.

But the Doc never quite had the same rapport with Mears's successor Charles Pratt: despite all the recriminations and disagreements, however, the parting was typical of Docherty.

Having been summoned by the chairman, he was told, 'Tommy, we just can't go on like this.'

The Doc made an excuse, left the room without listening to another word and returned with some bottles of champagne. 'I knew this was going to happen, but, come on, let's have a drink!' And the Doc's parting comment: 'Good luck for the rest of the season, gentlemen.'

Dave Sexton was appointed his successor. His approach to management was the complete opposite to the Doc's flamboyance.

E

Europe

Champions of England, Chelsea were drawn against Djurgardens of Sweden in the inaugural European Cup, only to withdraw from the competition on Football League advice. The League strongly advised chairman Joe Mears not to allow Chelsea to compete, as the European Cup – an idea that evolved from French sports newspaper *L'Equipe* – was considered to be unimportant.

An indication of Chelsea's chances of success in the European Cup could only be gauged by their limited excursions into Europe during that time. The club rounded off their championship year with a short post-season tour. They drew 2–2 with the Dutch national team in front of a 55,000 crowd in the Olympic Stadium in Amsterdam with goals from Roy Bentley and Derek Saunders. They also played two games in France against Lens and Rouen. On the eve of their championship season, Chelsea travelled to New York to play in the North American Soccer tournament. They beat Fortuna Dusseldorf 3–2 in front of a 19,000 crowd at the Triboro Stadium, but lost 6–1 to Borussia Dortmund.

Real Madrid won the first European Cup beating French champions Stade de Rheims 4–3 in the final and went on to dominate the tournament in their fetching all-white strip until 1961 and the emergence of Internazionale of Milan.

Chelsea finished in third place in 1958, when, possibly, they might even have won the title, but Tommy Docherty's team's form fell away after Easter and then came the infamous Blackpool incident, when the team travelled north for a game at Burnley and stayed the night in Blackpool. The Doc was fuming when he discovered that some of the players had escaped the hotel curfew and spent the night in a club. The manager sent eight players home and Chelsea lost both to Burnley and Blackpool. Chelsea qualified for the Inter-Cities Fairs Cup.

The previous year, Jimmy Greaves and Ron Sillett had been part of a united London side that had drawn two apiece against Barcelona at Stamford Bridge before being hammered 6–0 in the return leg. It all changed the following year when it was decided that individual clubs could represent their city and Chelsea were chosen to represent the capital. Boldklubben Frem of Copenhagen were beaten in the first round and the second round was played at the end of the 1959 season: Chelsea were comprehensively beaten over two legs by Belgrade.

Chelsea played in some prestigious friendlies, none more so than when they beat West Germany in Duisberg a year before the 1966 World Cup. The 1965 German side contained such luminaries as Beckenbauer, Tilowski, Libuda, Piontek and Seeler. A Barry Bridges winner surprised the 32,000 home crowd.

Tommy Docherty's 'little diamonds' began their 1965–66 Inter-City Fairs Cup campaign beating Roma 4–1 in the first round with Terry Venables scoring a hat-trick and Eddie McCreadie being sent off. Passions were running high for the return leg in front of 40,000 in the Olympic Stadium and the Chelsea players were subjected to intolerable abuse with stones and urine-filled balloons hurled in their direction by the fans. John Boyle was struck on the head by a bottle. On the way back to the airport, the windscreen of the coach was smashed by a flying brick. At the end of the same month, Chelsea returned to Italy for a charity game against a combined AC/Inter Milan team: they lost 2–1, but received a rapturous reception! Next, it was off to frozen Vienna with only 4,000 turning out at Wienna Sk. Hinton was sent off for allegedly striking an opponent as Chelsea lost 1–0, although they won the return 2–0, the victory sealed with a memorable diving header from Osgood. Hinton was later cleared when a disciplinary committee saw a film showing that the Austrian player had dived.

Then, it was back to Italy with AC Milan and their star Gianni Rivera and a lesser light in Cesare Maldini, who was to become the Italian national coach.

Because of fog in Milan, the tie was played on a February afternoon. A crowd of just under 12,000 saw Rivera and Amarilldo score, before George Graham claimed an important away goal – although they did not count double at that time – it was a goal that kept Chelsea in the tie. A crowd of 59,541 turned out at the Bridge to see a wonderful night of European action. A majestic Osgood lob and a fierce Graham header, plus a Soramni goal, meant that a coin was tossed to determine the destination for the replay – and Chelsea were heading back to Italy. A crowd of 30,000 saw a 1–1 draw, with Chelsea's goal scored by Bridges, and not even extra-time could break the deadlock. Harris and Maldini tossed a coin and the Blues went through.

Chelsea travelled to snow-covered Munich later that month to face TSV 1860, then the top club in the city. Two Bobby Tambling goals helped them to a 2–2 draw. A stunning Osgood header twelve minutes from the end of the tie at the Bridge, sent them through.

Chelsea's next assignment was against the mighty Barcelona in the semi-final. A crowd of 70,000 saw Chelsea outclassed as they fell to a 2–0 defeat. At the end of a gruelling six games in thirteen days, and much controversy, Charlie Cooke made his debut in the return and two own goals gave Chelsea parity and another coin toss: this time it came down on the Spanish side and Chelsea were heading back to the Nou Camp once again. The unrest within the camp came to a head with a huge public argument at Heathrow on the way back to Spain. Docherty sent Bridges home. Back at the Bridge, 9,000 fans watched on a giant screen, but a tired Chelsea were crushed 5–0.

Apart from winning a prestigious charity match against Ferenc Puskas and his Real Madrid side in 1966–67, there were no more major European excursions until Dave Sexton replaced the Doc and the club had another crack at the UEFA Cup. The first trip was the far-from-exotic docks of Greenock with Morton beaten 9–3 on aggregate. Osgood, who had made a successful comeback from a broken leg, scored in the home leg, as did Tambling, to maintain the pair's impressive record in Europe. The little-known DWS Amsterdam managed two goalless draws and Chelsea were eliminated by the toss of a coin.

Chelsea would eventually return to European football with a vengence. Qualifying for the Cup-Winners' Cup after finally winning the FA Cup in 1970, the team were full of confidence: they were also boosted by the return to fitness of Alan Hudson and the £100,000 signing of Keith Weller from Millwall, who played in all but one of the matches of the European campaign.

Chelsea's first-round opponents were Greek side Aris Salonika and, after a 1–1 draw in the away leg, Chelsea triumphed 5–1 at home, with Hutchinson scoring twice. Marvin Hinton was also on target, while John Hollins collected a double, including a long-range left-footer.

CSKA Sofia of Bulgaria were beaten 1–0 home and away in the next round to set up a meeting with Bruges of Belgium. With Chelsea trailing 2–0 from the first leg, the stadium, often accused of lacking atmosphere, vibrated to the passion of the fans and when Houseman cut the deficit, and then Osgood levelled, the supporters erupted. Osgood then put Chelsea ahead in extra-time, but, until Baldwin finally put the tie beyond doubt, classy Bruges were always a threat.

The semi-final against holders Manchester City lacked the previous round's flair and entertainment. It was settled by Derek Smethhurst's goal in the first leg at the Bridge, and City 'keeper Healey's own goal in the second.

The final, in Athens on 19 May, was against the mighty Real Madrid, who had been led by Di Stefano and Puskas to five successive European Cups just a decade earlier and had been champions again in 1966. Osgood was carrying an injury and only played because of a cortizone injection. Followed by 5,000 fans, Osgood put Chelsea into a fifty-seventh-minute lead, but he had to leave the field when the cortizone wore off. Real equalised through Ignaco Zocco with seconds to go.

The replay was scheduled two nights later, with the majority of Chelsea fans forced to head home to watch the game on television, but hundreds made up all sorts of excuses to their bosses and wives to stay on! Some, who had run out of money, slept rough on the beaches.

The players headed for the bar! Osgood went out with Cooke and Baldwin the night before the replay to sample the delights of the local nightclubs and beer. What a way to prepare for a final! Osgood recalls, 'Friday came, the hangover eventually lifted, and we got out on the pitch and played a blinder.'

It was Real who had the hangover in front of a 24,000 crowd. Webb's burst from the back forced a corner, which was taken by Cooke, and, when the ball was only half-cleared, Dempsey scored with a spectacular volley – one of only seven goals he scored in more than a hundred appearances for the club. Chelsea went two-up in the thirty-eighth minute, when Harris and Baldwin combined to set up Osgood for a clever low shot into the corner from twenty yards. Again Osgood could not last the entire game but, fifteen minutes from time, Real recovered with a goal and, in the final seconds, Bonetti pulled off a flying save from Zoco's header.

The fans who stayed on embarked on a wonderful night of celebration, and the players ... well, they headed for the bar.

But the FA Cup and Cup-Winners' Cup glory was a fleeting episode, an oasis amid a lack of trophies, and Chelsea's defence of their European crown did not last long. Nor did it reflect the team's abilities.

Chelsea failed to score more than once against Swedish part-timers Atvidaberg, despite having scored twenty-one against Luxembourg part-timers Jeunesse Hautcharage in the first round. The gloom returned.

It was not until more modern times that Chelsea finally returned to the fore in Europe. In Glenn Hoddle's first season as player-manager, the club were comprehensively beaten in the FA Cup final by Manchester United, but the United team, containing Mark Hughes, won the Double, meaning that Chelsea had qualified for the Cup-Winners' Cup. It was that competition which provided most of the excitement during Hoddle's second season in charge.

Chelsea fans travelled in large numbers, first to a small town, Jablonec, near the Czech-Polish border, and on to Vienna, Bruges and Zaragoza. Against Austria Vienna, John Spencer ran eighty yards to score in a breakaway from the opposition's corner!

Despite the three-foreigners' rule and injury problems, Hoddle made amends for a disappointing domestic season by masterminding a European adventure which saw Chelsea reach the semi-finals, where they could not overcome a 3–0 drubbing by eventual winners Real Zaragoza in the first leg, despite a thrilling enough 3–1 home win.

European glory arrived again for Chelea in the final of the European Cup-Winners' Cup in May 1998 when substitute Gianfranco Zola scored a stunning winner against VFB Stuttgart.

There had been some battles en route to the final. Vicenza arrived at the Bridge with a 1–0 lead following the first leg and Chelsea looked down and out when the Italians extended their lead through Luiso: the crucial away goal meant that Chelsea needed to score three to reach the final. Although Gus Poyet pulled one back almost immediately, such a feat still looked unlikely. However, Zola scored just after the interval and substitute Mark Hughes, who had hardly played in the competition, scored one of his trademark goals that saw Chelsea take a 3–2 aggregate lead. Some outstanding late saves by Ed De Goey ensured Chelsea's place in the final.

And the final was a nervous stalemate until Zola came off the bench in the sixty-ninth minute. Moments later, he received a pass from Dennis Wise and struck a half-volley past Franz Wohlfahrt. Dan Petrescu and Gerhard Poschner were both sent off in the final minutes, but one of the club's most popular and diminutive players had clinched their second major European trophy. Chelsea had won the Cup-Winners' Cup and the UEFA Cup, but, the Champions League was the next target: it had become the most important club competition in Europe.

And Chelsea excelled in a thrilling 1999–2000 campaign which saw a number of memorable glory nights.

A phenomenal 5–0 win in Turkey was one of the club's most notable results ever in Europe. 'Welcome to Hell' read one banner that greeted Manchester United when they played two ties against Galatasaray in the Ali Sami Yen Stadium in 1993 and 1994. United had failed to win either of those games, but, when Chelsea made the same trip five years later, two goals from Tore-Andre Flo either side of half-time and another from Zola silenced the hostile crowd. Skipper Dennis Wise, who had surprisingly been left on the bench, came on to score the fourth, before Gabrielke Ambrosetti collected the fifth.

On 5 April 2000, Chelsea beat Barcelona 3–1 at the Bridge and a place in the Champions League semi-final beckoned. Having excelled in their wins over Feyenoord and Galatasaray, and despite having held both Lazio and AC Milan to draws, few gave them much hope against Barca but, in the first leg, Zola curled an unstoppable free-kick past Ruud Hesp. Zola then turned provider for Flo, who also added a third before Luis Figo grabbed a priceless away goal.

Sadly, Luca Vialli's side lost 5–1 in the Nou Camp, after having held on to a winning position until late into the two-legged tie.

Claudio Ranieri took Chelsea to their first ever Champions League semi-final, having finally ended the Arsenal jinx by beating them in the quarter-finals with a superb winner from left-back Wayne Bridge at Highbury, and by winning a group-stage game against Lazio in Rome 4–0. Hernan Crespo gave Ranieiri's team a half-time lead against his old club, but Eidur Gudjohnsen, Damien Duff and Frank Lampard all scored in the last twenty minutes. Not even the behaviour of Sinisa Mihajlovic could spoil a wonderful result. The Serb was eventually sent off for a second yellow-card offence after a foul on Duff.

Here are detailed accounts of the two amazing Champions League ties with Lazio and Arsenal.

Tuesday, 4 November 2003

LAZIO 0 CHELSEA 4

This was one of the best results of all time by an English club on Italian soil. It was a devastating performance that stunned the rest of Europe and confirmed Ranieri's team as genuine Champions League contenders. Ranieri was asked whether this was the best performance during his reign. 'I don't know. Of course, I'm very pleased tonight because Rome is my city and a little more, but it's OK. I always look forward and I hope that at the next match it will be better.'

Around 5,000 Chelsea fans witnessed the famous victory that is destined to become a part of Stamford Bridge legend. If Crespo had put away more of his chances, Chelsea would have surpassed their record 5–0 Champions League victory against Galatasaray in 1999.

Chelsea fans were understandably ecstatic, bellowing out chorus after chorus of 'Are you watching Arsenal?' and 'Are you Tottenham in disguise?' They celebrated with Zola, who had made the trip from Cagliari to see the game. Zola milked the applause of the travelling fans and his former team-mates. Lampard said, 'He was great for us and the fans – who have been amazing for us here and given us an extra edge – are showing their appreciation. It's a well-deserved result. It's testament to the lads that we kept our heads and were the better team.'

Terry said, 'Brilliant, great night, fantastic. It's good to see Franco in the dressing room, and Robbie (Di Matteo), so good to see them. We were brilliant, to be fair. We dealt with everything they had to throw at us, even though they put a lot of pressure on. Carlo made some great saves as well, but overall we dealt with it and went down the other end and scored some great goals. It just opened up, as soon as Mihajlovic was sent off. If they want to mix it, we can mix it with them and get stuck in and we showed that. In the second half, we showed just how good we are on the ball. We got on it and kept the ball, it was like a training session. There was a lot of provocation from Lazio. They are going to complain because they've just been hammered 4–0, but they've given as good as they got. We had been performing as well as we can do, but tonight I do think it all clicked. Some teams were always going to feel it, and tonight it was Lazio. We've been performing well and grinding out results, but overall, that's been our best performance.'

The stunning victory left the Blues three points clear at the top of Group

G. They needed one draw from their remaining two games to make it through to the knock-out stages.

The only blemish came when Glen Johnson was shown a second yellow card for kicking the ball away after conceding a free-kick. But the game had shown why Ranieri insists that Juan-Sebastian Veron is the world's best midfield player. This was his first game back at the Olympic Stadium since his move to Manchester United two years before, although he did not help his cause with the Blues fans when he wrapped a Lazio scarf around his shoulders when treated to a standing ovation before the kick-off. Any such feelings were dispelled by his Man of the Match performance, though.

It was his ferocious fifteenth-minute free-kick that opened the floodgates and signalled the beginning of a nightmare night for former Ipswich 'keeper Matteo Sereni, who was making his Champions League debut in place of the injured Angelo Peruzzi. The 'keeper got both of his hands to Veron's drive, but punched the ball rather than catching it, and pushed the ball on to the chin of the incoming Crespo, who literally did not know what had hit him as the ball crashed back into the empty net. Crespo should have netted a second on the stroke of half-time when he exchanged passes with the lively Mutu. This time Sereni made a fine point-blank save. It was a miss that almost came back to haunt Chelsea within two minutes of the restart, but a miraculous double save by Cudicini – first from Stankovic and then from Corradi's follow-up – ensured the Blues kept their control as Lazio totally lost theirs when they were reduced to ten men in the fifty-third minute.

Mihajlovic had got away with kicking Mutu in the shin when he was grounded. He then spat in the face of Mutu after the two had tangled as they challenged for a Duff corner. The offence was missed by the referee, but television cameras captured the event and UEFA were alerted. The referee's oversight provided the Serb with only a momentary reprieve. Booked for tripping Duff, he then left Russian referee Valentin Ivanov with little option but to reach for his red card when he repeated the offence three minutes later. He then trooped down the tunnel to get an overcoat.

Mutu showed great restraint and said that the spitting had occurred after he cracked a joke at the Lazio player's expense. Mutu said, 'Mihajlovic was trying to play mind games and lost those as well. He should concentrate on football as he needs to improve his game. It was an awful insult, but I didn't react. It was humiliating to be spat at, but I put the good of the team before my personal vendetta. It was not good and he has a very poor sense of humour. He didn't get the joke! Some exchanges were made and he couldn't take it so he got violent. It was unprovoked and he started it. It had the opposite effect as he got sent off. Mihajlovic lost his mind and didn't play well. He made a lot of mistakes. Lazio tried to be aggressive, but it didn't work. It was a fantastic result and a night to remember. Our performance was too powerful for them to handle. Everything is coming together and we're improving with every game.'

Skipper Terry said, 'He was disgusting, a disgrace. At a corner, he elbowed me a couple of times and poked me in the eye. I don't want to whinge, but you don't expect such a great player to sink to such tactics. I couldn't believe the referee wasn't doing anything about it. I didn't see him spitting, but he has let himself down. You can handle the poking and elbowing during the game, but spitting is out of order. It's not acceptable and something has to be done.'

Mihajlovic had received a two-game UEFA suspension for a racist verbal attack on Vieira three years earlier. After his latest misdemeanour, Lazio manager Roberto Mancini insisted, somewhat incredibly, 'I heard Mutu hit Sinisa with an elbow. But, if he spat, it is bad. It is serious and he will pay for that. I am sorry. Sinisa is a nice man who does not do that type of thing. If he did that, then I apologise on his behalf, but it had to be a reaction to something else. I am sure he will not pay for it and be suspended.'

The drama continued off the field at half-time when Couto and Makelele had a fight in the tunnel. They were pulled apart by the referee.

Midway through the second half, Sereni failed to hold a Lampard drive, presenting substitute Gudjohnsen with a gilt-edged opportunity which he gratefully gobbled up just three minutes after replacing Crespo. Lazio fans were already heading for the exit as Duff sliced their team apart again to score the third fifteen minutes from time. Lampard applied the finishing touch in the eightieth minute, smashing the loose ball past Sereni after the 'keeper's block from Gudjohnsen had rolled invitingly into his path.

Mancini added, 'If there was a difference between the two sides, it was the performance of the goalkeepers. Carlo Cudicini was amazing – he made excellent saves. Matteo [Sereni] had a difficult night.'

David Beckham and his superstar Real team-mates sat up and took notice of the margin of victory in Rome. Beckham said, 'They are not surprising anyone with the way they are winning games because of the players they have got. But I'm sure the result the other night surprised all of Europe because of the way they went to Lazio, which is a hard place to go to. To perform like that in Italy and to get a result like they did, you have to congratulate them for that. They are going to be a good team in the future. But, as far as the threat to other teams in Europe and in the Premiership, we will have to see at the end of the season.'

Beckham's team-mate Zinedine Zidane rued the loss to Chelsea of Claude Makelele. 'Even though we have started the season well, our team still misses Claude. He was a key element in our tactical plans, and he has not been replaced like for like, so we try to compensate for him as a team. The strength-sapping workload he got through was essential for us, but he did not think Real were paying him what he was worth. He did not want to give in, and he is now blossoming at Chelsea. All the better for him. I understand his decision very well, because I was in a similar situation before I moved to Madrid.'

Makelele said, 'It was a great victory and we are happy about it, but nothing more. The important thing for us is to keep progressing, little by little. There's no rush. We're a team of excellent players, but we still need to mature as a group. We don't yet know each other that well because we've only been together less than three months. We are still short of the number of games together that you need to reach the level of the great sides in Europe. Juventus have been playing the same team for three or four years and it shows.

'The team showed a bit more of what I was asking for. This was the first time we've seen what I've been working at. My players are linking better every day. We are improving and we are building the foundations and that's important.'

Ranieri disciplined Johnson, who had picked up a yellow card in the latter stages of the game. 'The match was finished. If the referee gives a free-kick, it doesn't matter. I admit I was angry with Glen Johnson, though. He is young, but he must improve. He is a great young player, but he must understand it is important for him to keep calm and in control. I have always told my players that the referee can make mistakes, but it is not important. They should continue to play and be calm; that is their job. He did the same thing in a friendly match once, he kicked the ball away. It is no good and he must understand that. It is a hard lesson, but he must learn quickly and he will.'

Frank Lampard added, 'The expectations are there now! The fans were the best I've ever seen travelling with us. We came out for the warm-up, we heard them and we gave them a little tinkle. They were brilliant: regardless of the money that has come into the club, those fans have been there over the years, and they deserve what's happening to Chelsea right now.'

Mihajlovic was suspended for eight matches, the second-longest punishment of its kind. In 1994, the Finnish player Anders Roth was suspended for ten matches for his behaviour in a UEFA Cup match between MyPa and Boavista.

Tuesday, 6 April 2004

ARSENAL 1 CHELSEA 2

(Chelsea win 3–2 on agg)

It was a European night to savour and was hailed as one of the greatest results in Chelsea's history. The club had qualified for the Champions League semi-finals for the first time. The team that night was: Ambrosio, Melchiot, Terry, Gallas, Bridge, Parker (Gronjkaer 46), Lampard, Makelele, Duff (Cole 82), Gudjohnsen, Hasselbaink (Crespo 82). Wayne Bridge's eighty-seventh-minute winner sealed a dramatic victory. The big question at that time was whether such a famous win would be enough to save Ranieri's job: perhaps he would yet have the last laugh.

'It's difficult to kill me,' he said. 'I may be dead, but I will continue to work. Can we win the Champions League? Why not? Anything is possible now. This can transform the season and we want to catch Arsenal in the league. Describing my joy at the final whistle is difficult, but I was mad, it was thirty seconds of delirium. Roman Abramovich was mad afterwards as well; everyone was going crazy in the dressing room as we have made history. I wanted to join my players on the pitch. People have said I am a dead man walking. But I'm not. I am still moving and I will continue to fight. What happens next season? I am focusing only on this season. That is my way. That is important for me, for the club, for everyone.'

When he was shown his exuberant celebrations at the goal, punching the air, waving his arms like pistons, he joked, 'It's a crazy man!'

There were tears in his eyes as he applauded his team before heading down the tunnel. Those tears were to provoke a national debate about grown men crying à la Gazza. It endeared him to football fans, not just Chelsea supporters, and indeed to anyone who had witnessed his show of pure emotion.

Watching from the stands was Sven-Goran Eriksson. Later, Abramovich made a rare comment: 'Chelsea played great and I think the team showed the Russian character to hold on, to fight, to win. This is a great result. We are now waiting for Monaco.'

Peter Kenyon described the match as a tremendous advert for English football. 'The timing of Arsenal's goal was horrendous for us and I don't think the (half-time) scoreline was justification for how we played. But the players came out fighting, the spirit came through and I think the win was deserved.'

There was also a shock as Monaco eliminated Real Madrid: expectations that Chelsea could actually win the Champions League were raised even higher. Former Chelsea midfielder Didier Deschamps was the Monaco coach and Kenyon added, 'Didier has done a great job there. There are no easy teams at this stage, but it will be great to play them in the semi-final.'

Ranieri got his game plan spot on. The Tinkerman even named an unchanged side which must has thrown the Gunners! Chelsea squeezed the life out of Arsenal in the middle of the park and never gave Henry or Pires any room. In the first half, though, Arsenal looked a class act. Pires almost produced a replica headed goal to the one he had collected in the first leg, from Cole's cross, but directed it into the side-netting. With virtually the last kick before the break, Reyes put Arsenal ahead. Pires swept the ball out to Lauren and, when his cross was headed down by Henry, Reyes slammed home from close range. Arsenal were in command. Ranieri stirred his team at half-time and, on fifty-one minutes, they equalised. Edu's clearance was superbly volleyed by Makelele from thirty-five yards, Lehmann spilled it, and there was Lampard to roll the ball coolly into the net. Chelsea's tails were up. Lampard, who seemed to get faster and stronger while Vieira wilted, whipped in a thirty-yarder which rattled the side-netting. Ambrosio rose to the occasion, diving to his right to push away a drive by Reyes and then sprang to tip Toure's thirty-five-yard effort over the bar. Then came the sight of Henry being substituted with a hamstring injury.

Cole's desperate clearance off the line from Gudjohnsen's close-range shot denied them, but it was only a stay of execution. Arsenal were on their knees by the time Bridge scored. The full-back exchanged passes with Gudjohnsen, burst into the box and rapped a left-footed shot into the far corner. Bridge was engulfed by joyous team-mates. The left-back was wearing No. 18: the number of games it had taken Chelsea to beat their adversaries.

Terry was outstanding, Lampard outbattled Vieira, and Gudjohnsen was a handful. Even when Ranieri started fiddling, his substitutions worked. Cole made a brief cameo appearance and found gaps.

Ranieri observed, 'In the first half we wanted to close down their space, but were very nervous. When we went 1–0 down I knew we had do something more. But I told my players at half-time that we had to stay calm and, after the break, we played much better. In the second half we were fantastic. I have players with fantastic character. They never give up, I like that.'

Parker was swiftly removed at the interval after they had been skinned so often down the right flank. There may have been a few sighs when he was replaced by the more lightweight Gronkjaer – not everyone's idea of a big match performer – yet it proved the masterstroke. Gronkjaer gave new width and enterprise and kept Ashley Cole in check. After the equaliser, the momentum of the game had changed so much that Arsenal were deflated. Ranieri's late double introduction of Joe Cole and Hernan Crespo was perfectly timed to help set up the killer blow. 'I thought it was important that we didn't allow Ashley Cole to come forward so much in the second half,' explained Ranieri.

Wayne Bridge said, 'I'm not too sure what to believe about the manager and am not sure what is going on. Maybe this result will persuade the Board that he should stay. Everyone feels for Claudio and, if there is any possibility, the club should let him stay. You can see the enjoyment in his face, but we're not just playing for Claudio. We're playing for the fans, ourselves and for the manager. He has been great for me; he's brought me to the club and keeps playing me, so I can't ask for much more. He seems to believe in me and the lads get on well with him. He deals with all the pressure and the speculation and just tells us to keep it clear of our minds, saying that it's always much worse in Italy. But he seems happy in training every day and is always laughing and joking and chatting with us.

'When Eidur Gudjohnsen had a shot cleared off the line I thought it wasn't going to be our night. But we battled right to the end, matched them for effort and I popped up with the goal.'

Frank Lampard said, 'Arsenal are one of the best teams in the world at the moment, but we've beaten them which gives us the belief we can go on and win the competition. We have to believe. It won't be easy, but, if we play like we did, we've got a good chance of reaching the final. There's an incredible feeling in the dressing room and it's the result of all our hard work since July. It was a great night for the whole of Chelsea and I'm ecstatic. It's the best night of my career and a lot of the lads are saying the same thing. A lot of us are young lads who haven't experienced much Champions League success, so this is incredible.'

Monaco's victory over Real was a bigger surprise, but Lampard was adamant that they will not take the French side lightly. 'There wasn't much of a reaction when we heard the Monaco result and we're just pleased to be in the semi-finals. People will say it's an easier draw, but there are no easy games in the semi-finals.'

Lampard also praised Ranieri. 'It's a great vindication for the manager. He's a good man and deserves a lot of credit for the way he's handled himself this season. All the speculation isn't nice and he's done a great job all season.'

In the hour of his most crushing disappointment, Wenger was asked whether he could feel just a touch of pleasure for Ranieri. It says much about his grace that he just smiled ruefully. 'You will understand if I cannot jump to the roof because he is happy.'

Monaco manager Didier Deschamps was confident that he would come away from Stamford Bridge with happier memories than those he had accrued during his time there as a player. He unexpectedly became a bit-part player under his old friend and manager Vialli and left acrimoniously with their relationship shattered. Deschamps famously complained that the problem with England was that it was dark when he dropped his young son off at school in the morning and dark when he picked him up in the afternoon. He said, 'There is no reason to be afraid of going to Chelsea. It will be special to go back to Stamford Bridge and see a few old friends. People like Marcel Desailly are still around and I am already looking forward to it. Everyone thought it would be Arsenal against Real and Chelsea have caused an upset, too. But, while I respect them, we have no reason to fear them. Our victory made history for football in Monaco, but now we have to make sure that we come away with something at the end of the season.'

Ranieri claimed that he was not pleased to be meeting Monaco. 'It's not good news because I know Real Madrid very well. If Monaco won, it is because they have very good players, a good coach and a good fitness coach.'

Chelsea departed for Monaco with Ranieri stressing how important the game was to his career. 'This has been my first time in the Champions League and the first time in the semi-final. It is all new to me, even though I have a lot of experience in the Italian, Spanish and English Cups.'

He found himself in the unusual position of having most of England behind him. 'Yes, I realise I am probably the most popular coach in England at the moment. It is nice, it is good and I thank the people. The fans at Villa

Park applauded me last week, and on Saturday, when the final whistle went, a gentleman from the Everton bench, I don't know who he was, shook my hand and said, "All Liverpool is with you – go and win the European Cup." It is a like a big vitamin for me, but we are not there yet; first we must beat Monaco and that will not be easy. I want to achieve something important for Chelsea, that is my goal.'

A London club has never won the premier club competition in Europe before and Ranieri admitted, 'This is strange because London has had some very good teams.'

But Monaco could not be underestimated. 'Only a good team would beat Deportivo La Coruna 8–3 and then Real Madrid in the quarter-finals – and that is what Monaco have done. All four clubs left in the competition have an equal chance. The true favourites have gone. Now there are four surprises.'

In the build-up to the semi-final, Ranieri was tipped off that Abramovich and Kenyon had travelled to Vigo to hold talks with Jose Mourinho, who was also preparing for a Champions League semi-final. The visit lasted seven hours before Chelsea's power-brokers arrived in Nice at 7pm, with the squad arriving at 1pm. Mourinho conducted his media conference later that day and dropped a hint. 'The English league is seen as one of the world's finest. When chances come along, they should be grabbed with both hands.' Victory over Deportivo might see his Porto side pitched against Chelsea. Mourinho watched his words. 'I don't think there will be a big win for either side in either of the semi-final games.'

There were more eve-of-game headaches as the Spanish newspaper *Marca* published a Q&A interview in which Ranieri says, 'Abramovich knows nothing about football.' Ranieri was quoted as saying, 'Ever since he arrived at the club, Abramovich wanted Eriksson. From the very start. They even met in the summer. But Eriksson said he couldn't leave the England team and so the next day Abramovich met me and told me, "OK, you've done a good job these last few years and you are going to carry on, and take them into the Champions League."'

But Ranieri claimed that even victory in the final would not save him. 'Look I already have the Abramovich sword embedded in me. I'm convinced that even if I win the Champions League I will be sacked.'

Ranieri said that, when Abramovich took over, he had little understanding of the work he had done the previous season. 'Abramovich knows nothing about football. That's the real shame. If he had understood what my side had achieved that season, he would have valued me more highly. We did it all without any money.'

He also accused Abramovich of having no appreciation of how difficult a job it had been to make the team gel. 'It was a very tough job to sign so many players and get them to play together. Abramovich didn't realise that. He thought, I'll sign that one and that one and then we will win. Since he arrived he has signed eleven players, it's crazy. Moreover, Abramovich's people are not yet convinced about me and for this the public are on my side, but I haven't had any time to digest it all, I have only had time to work, work and work. It's true the people love me: it's my spontaneous character; what I feel I say, and they like this mixture of curiosity and positivity. They see Italians as strange, moving their arms about and not very diplomatic, whereas the English are always politically correct. For that, I have gained affection from a lot of people. Mostly they love me out of feelings of compassion. How can it be Abramovich is thinking of changing the manager if this Italian is working well?'

Ranieri was shocked at the timing of publication, as he had been interviewed on 8 April, and felt that it had been grossly misinterpreted.

Abramovich played host to Ranieri and the players aboard his yacht moored in Monte Carlo harbour in the afternoon, but it was Ranieri who was all at sea with his substitutions on the night: his reputation sank to an all-time low following a 3–1 defeat.

The small group of Chelsea fans who had made the trip were determined to make themselves heard. They chanted, 'Are you watching Arsenal?' but once again the match ended up being a big let-down, as Ranieiri's status, which following the Highbury win had soared to unprecedented levels, now nose-dived.

Ranieri tried out Veron on the left in training, but plumped for Gronkjaer in the absence of Duff. He wanted the Dane to get at the opposition early on and try to rattle them. Instead, his team were the ones who were rattled from the start. Rothen got away down the left, Melchiot took him out with a scything challenge and the full-back could not argue about the yellow card. Monaco scored from the seventeenth-minute free-kick. Rothen whipped the ball in. Crespo tried to clear but missed with an elaborate diving header and, as the ball bounced, Prso climbed above Melchiot to head it firmly into the top left corner. Within five minutes, Lampard fooled the defence with a delightful ball over the top and Parker collected it on the right. He played it in to Gudjohnsen, who fell over but managed to push the ball on to Crespo, who shot low into the bottom corner from eight yards. Crespo was there again to meet Lampard's cross minutes later but, at full stretch, he put the ball just over the bar. Chelsea were in the groove, with Lampard pulling all the strings, and Crespo proving a point. But Ranieri's tinkering from the start of the second half cost them a winning position.

Ranieri hauled off Gronkjaer at half-time and replaced him with Veron: it was a misjudgement. It got worse.

A turning point, which should have been in Chelsea's favour, ended up being an advantage for Monaco. After fifty-two minutes, Makelele held off Zikos, allowing Ambrosio to slide out to collect the ball. Makelele touched his opponent on the side of the face, and Zikos reacted by slapping him gently on the top of the head. Makelele had time to glance around for a split-second before going down. Referee Meier reached straight for the red card.

Chelsea instantly looked like getting a second. Gudjohnsen was denied by the legs of the 'keeper and also put a free header over the top from Veron's corner.

Ranieri got all excited and, sensing more goals, replaced defender Melchiot with Hasselbaink. Puzzlingly, Huth was sent on for Parker.

The ten men seized two goals through Morientes in the seventy-eighth minute and substitute Nonda on eighty-three minutes.

Hasselbaink fluffed a headed chance at the far post from Bridge's cross, the 'keeper played the ball out swiftly and Morientes raced away down the right to smash a half-volley beyond the despairing Ambrosio. Substitute Nando scored at the near post, but Ambrosio should have stopped it.

Ranieri said that his players had lost the plot in the last fifteen minutes. But what exactly was the plot? From the moment Veron came on, no one knew. Deschamps said that coaches get 10 per cent of the credit when their team wins and 90 per cent of the blame when it loses.

Ranieri believes it all turned following the sending-off. 'I wanted to take advantage of our extra man, so I sent on another forward to win the match. But the last forty-five minutes were without doubt the worst I have experienced since I have been manager of Chelsea. It was like we had ten players against Monaco's eleven. It was my fault because I was too committed to winning the game. The problem was all the players suddenly wanted to do something extra. They all tried to run with the ball instead of passing it quickly to our three forwards. But after thirty years in football I know it is the manager who is the guilty one and the one who must always take the blame.

'Only our very best performance can save us now. We have only a 20 per cent chance of going through, but it will not be easy to get two goals or maybe more against a Monaco team who are used to scoring. We have very good defenders and a good defensive line, but Monaco still scored three times. It is very difficult to lose a match like this 3–1. How can I feel good after this?'

Ranieri's bizarre tactical changes left his players utterly bewildered, but Gudjohnsen insisted that they should take responsibility. 'It's disappointing because we slacked off and lost our shape. We lost because of our own wrongdoing rather than their inspiration. It's unacceptable, really. You can't fault the work-rate, but we were working as individuals rather than as a team in the second half. When you lose your shape as a team, you can do all the running you want, but it won't make any difference. The fact that we didn't score when they were under pressure was crucial and their second goal gave us all a shock. It's disappointing to have lost the game, because coming in at half-time we felt confident and as though we had the game under control. We responded well after their goal and came in confident of getting a good result. We had a couple of chances at the start of the second half – I had a shot blocked and a header that went just wide.'

The worst moment came when Hasselbaink missed at the far post with a header: the 'keeper began a move with Hasselbaink still throwing his arms up in the air in disbelief, and Bridge was caught out of position. 'We were a bit gutted,' said Bridge. 'When they went down to ten men we didn't capitalise. We should have played the ball around and kept possession, but we weren't doing that. They caught us on two counter-attacks. This was a wasted opportunity, from being at 1–1 against ten men, it was a great chance. It's uphill from now. By the time the return game comes along we have to make sure we don't concede any goals. We can't be afraid of the game.'

Ranieri played down the impact of the press interview in Spain in which he accused Abramovich of knowing nothing about football. 'I have said the same things since July, but maybe in another country they understand my comments in a different way. One year ago, Mr Abramovich didn't know anything about football, but he wanted to buy a team. Now he understands everything very well. I've always said I don't know what will happen in the summer. I have been working this way for the past eleven months. Nothing has changed.'

While Chelsea had never previously reached this stage of the Champions League, their opponents were playing in their third semi-final. Deschamps was seeking to succeed where Wenger and Tigana had failed and guide them past the last hurdle.

The Russian billionaire invited Ranieri on to his yacht, *Le Grand Bleu*, to discuss the game. Ranieri declined and told Abramovich he was going back to the hotel to talk with his team. But the manager was almost silent as the players discussed reasons for the defeat.

There was no mistaking the discontent that had developed within the dressing room, as one international made plain: 'Claudio made a complete cock-up.' A text message from another player was even more derogatory.

Abramovich, who had been cheered by the fans in the stadium, was said to be in tears and endured a sleepless night. He had tears in his eyes as he walked across the pitch for a post-match meeting with Ranieri, but had recovered his composure by the time he entered the dressing room. Ranieri explained the reasons for his bizarre substitutions and apologised for comments attributed to him in a Spanish newspaper, but was told there was no need to apologise. Abramovich returned to his yacht for an informal gathering with friends, but after they left he found himself unable to sleep. So at 2am he went to the team hotel, La Port Palace, for a meeting with Kenyon, Buck and Shvidler. Abramovich had a drink in the hotel bar and discussed the match with several players, including Hasselbaink, Lampard and Desailly, before returning to his yacht in the small hours.

Ranieri joked, 'It's not true that he was crying. Roman Abramovich was a fantastic man after the defeat. He invited me on to his yacht – because he wanted to use me as his anchor!'

The fall-out for Ranieri was devasating. One star demanded, 'What the f*** was that all about?' in an otherwise silent dressing room after the match. Ranieri did not respond and stood with his head bowed. Confused players were left without a clue about who was supposed to be playing where.

When Ranieri told Veron to replace Gronkjaer at half-time, the Argentine said he was not fit to take part in such an important match after five months out injured. Ranieri surprised his players by instructing Veron to play on the left side of midfield. It was the first of a series of tactical blunders. Veron had only managed forty-five minutes in Chelsea's game against Middlesbrough twelve days earlier, but then pulled a thigh muscle at Aston Villa. Ranieri admitted in the build-up he needed him to be100 per cent fit. His supporters were dismayed by his blunders.

Hasselbaink confessed, 'I don't think a single one of us slept on Tuesday night. We are all disgusted about what happened. We can't believe it. It is a massive missed opportunity and everybody is feeling s**t. Roman Abramovich spoke to us after the game and what he said is private. But he felt the defeat just like us. I bet he feels as s**t as we do. Maybe we feel a little bit worse, because it really was the chance of a lifetime. Words can't really describe what happened in the second half. In the first half, we felt very comfortable and often looked like scoring. But, after the break, we didn't play at all and our passing went altogether. We were playing against ten men and everybody thought, OK, we have got them. But it wasn't to be. It was not about tactics. It was not about who stands where. We all had a job to do and we were in it together. I don't want to go into whose fault it was, because we are professionals. It's not only about one man. Everybody in the team knows who to blame and we all have to look in the mirror for the answers. Yet it won't change anything. The result is still 3–1 and now we have to win 2–0 at Stamford Bridge.

'We are not throwing in the towel, though it is going to be a massive task to turn this tie round now. Miracles are not out of the question, but it will be very hard. We will fight and fight in the return game and everything is still possible. Yet we know we have put ourselves in a situation that we didn't have to be in.'

Supporters had finally had enough of Ranieri's tinkering. One fan wrote on the club's official website, 'I've really tried to be supportive of our manager over the past few years, but Monaco is the last straw. The team changes were an embarrassment. To say we were like headless chickens is an insult to headless chickens.'

Another said, 'Ranieri has been exposed for what he is – a bloke trying his best but who is tactically inept at this level. He has got away with his tinkering in some games and been lucky.' The criticism continues, 'Maybe now the "Keep Ranieri Brigade" will shut up. I was in Monaco and the second half was embarrassing.'

Ranieri borrowed a line from Frank Sinatra: 'I did it my way... I cannot change my ways now. If I do not tinker, then people will have nothing to write about. I learn lessons from every defeat and, yes, it was all my fault, but you cannot always win.

'At every club, there are bad moments. But at Chelsea we are still in a great moment. We can still finish second and reach the Champions League final. I'm still enjoying a great moment in my career. I'm down after the defeat, but I still remain positive that we can reach the final. If we finish second in the league, it will be a great achievement. It's not easy to link together ten players who are used to the Champions League with another new ten or eleven players and make a good team. But I'm sure that I've built a good team.

'I told the players everything I did in the Monaco game was wrong. I changed things to win the match – but we lost and I was thinking, Oh f*** Claudio, why, why? Bad Tinkerman!

'There were specific reasons why I made certain decisions. At half-time, the score was level and the mood was excellent in the dressing room. The lads were telling me, "We can win this; we can beat these guys tonight!" I thought we had done well, but Monaco were well organised defensively and I felt that we needed something different to break them down. Hugo Ibarra, their right-back, was having an excellent game against Jesper Gronkjaer. Gronkjaer's strength is running at people and creating width, but, on this night, Ibarra was shutting him down. So I replaced him with Juan-Sebastian Veron. I knew he was coming back from a long injury, but, in his first outing, against Middlesbrough, he looked sharp after coming on as a substitute.

'Veron is a different sort of player from Gronkjaer. He is capable of providing the defence-splitting pass and creating chances from deeper positions. I thought that, by putting him in, Ibarra would have to adjust to a different type of threat and this could cause Monaco problems. It was a mistake to play him and every change was made for the right reasons, but when you lose a game no one is interested in that.

'The sending-off of Akis Zikos a few minutes later changed the game. All of a sudden we had the man advantage, and it felt as if the pendulum had swung in our direction. That's when I made the decision to go for it, to try to close out the tie that night. I thought that by sending on another striker we could pin them back and create the chance for a winning goal. Yes, it was a gamble, but a calculated risk. I had two strikers on the bench, Jimmy-Floyd Hasselbaink and Adrian Mutu. I picked Hasselbaink because Mutu was not 100 per cent fit and I thought that, by playing him on the right of the front three, he could use his superior physical presence against Patrice Evra, their left-back, who is small and quick. Of course, this meant I had to take somebody off. It was not an easy choice, but the logical candidate to me seemed to be Mario Melchiot. I knew that Scott Parker had the intelligence and versatility to fill in as an emergency right-back and I was a little concerned because Melchiot had already been booked, and I could tell the referee was watching him closely. We could not afford to have a man sent off as well. The plan worked for a while. We created two good chances for Hasselbaink and he was unlucky not to score. But Parker was struggling. I wasn't sure if it was a muscular problem or if he had picked up a knock, but he was not 100 per cent. With William Gallas and Glen Johnson injured, I had to ask Robert Huth, a central defender, to come on at right-back.

'I don't need to remind anybody that Monaco scored twice in the last twelve minutes. My strategy had backfired. We spent too much time on the ball, everybody tried to do too much and they took advantage. That's football. You make a decision, you formulate a strategy and everything can go wrong.'

Ranieri refuted the absurd accusation that he deliberately sabotaged the tie to get revenge on Abramovich. 'Whoever says these things doesn't know me. We still have a chance to win the Champions League. Madrid, AC Milan and Arsenal would love to be in our place. If Arsenal, Real Madrid or AC Milan were in our position, they would go for it and believe. I expect Chelsea to do the same. Monaco have the advantage, but the tie is still open. Had we lost 1–0, most would say we still had a good chance of reversing the result. Yet a 1–0 deficit would mean that we needed to score two goals. Which is exactly what we need to do now. A 2–0 victory will get us to the final. In that sense, while the 3–1 defeat hurt, it is not insurmountable. Do we have the strength – mental and physical – to overturn this result? My players have shown it before. After the 1–1 home draw against Arsenal in the quarter-finals, many said we were out. Instead, we believed in ourselves, went to Highbury and won 2–1. That's the kind of spirit we will need on Wednesday week at Stamford Bridge. We have done it before. We can do it again.'

Ranieri's agent Morabito rounded on Hasselbaink. 'I heard he was saying the tie was over. Well, for the return leg Chelsea need eleven very committed and motivated players. Hasselbaink should think more about his own performance, especially as he is one of the highest-paid players at the club, rather than create a negative atmosphere. He was a major cause of the bad result. If he had done his job and scored with the great chance he had, Monaco would have been mentally broken at 2–1 down. Instead, he missed and they went straight down the other end and scored.'

Sir Bobby Robson sympathised with the Chelsea coach. 'Ranieri has done well at Chelsea. He first had to learn our language, but he has done a good job for the club. This is something that has been recognised by his players and the fans. He is under pressure after losing in Monaco. They have one foot in the Champions League and one foot out. But he will still think that winning 2–0 is a possibility – and I agree.'

But Chelsea found it too tough to reverse at the Bridge, and with their exit Ranieiri's fate was sealed.

Chelsea' s 2004/2005 Champions League campaign couldn't have started with a more controversial and intriguing draw. Jose Mourinho began the defence of the Champions League he had won with Porto, the group stage games including a Russian team sponsored by Roman Abramovich! The other teams in the group were Paris St Germain and Porto.

Jeered by PSG fans from the moment his name was announced, Drogba's two goals secured a 3–0 away victory. Mischief in the fixture calendar next brought FC Porto to Stamford Bridge, four months after Mourinho had led Porto to the European Cup. Chelsea beat them 3–1

In an entertaining and yet comfortable 2–0 victory over CKSA Moscow, Gudjohnsen made the first goal for Terry and scored the second on the stroke of half-time. Then Chelsea won 1-0 in Moscow with Mourinho describing Robben as his 'extra dimension' after the Dutchman's first goal enabled Chelsea to became the first team to qualify for the last 16 – with two games to spare.

In the knock-out stages, Chelsea began with a 2–1 defeat in the Nou Camp, that turned into one of the most controversial ties in the history of the Champions League. Mourinho refused to take part in any post-match interviews, a violation of Uefa regulations. It was the manner of the defeat, and the harsh dismissal of Drogba that had pushed the manager into hyper-drive. After Belletti's own goal had rocked Barcelona in the 33rd minute, Drogba missed a golden chance to put the tie beyond doubt shooting wide with only the keeper to beat. Then, shortly after the interval, Drogba was red carded for going for the ball fractionally ahead of the keeper but the pair clattered into each other. Substitute Gaston Maxi Lopez equalised and Eto'o pounced as the 10 men just about held on.

It one of the most thrilling European nights, on Tuesday 8 March, 2005 Chelsea beat Barcelona 4-2 to go through 5-4 on aggregate. Mourinho danced along the touch line and flung himself into an ecstatic sea of players at the final whistle. Terry's 76th-minute header sent the Blues roaring into the last eight.

Mourinho's men surged into an unbelievable three-goal lead after just 20 minutes thanks to strikes from Gudjohnsen, Lampard and Duff. Ronaldinho's double, the first from the penalty spot, gave Barca the advantage on away goals. Cech had to produce a string of outstanding saves. With time running out, Terry popped up from a corner to head home, although Carvalho impeded Valdes on the goal-line. Having been accused of negative tactics in the Nou Camp, Mourinho bravely fielded Kezman just ahead of Gudjohnsen.

Chelsea beat Bayern 4-2 at the Bridge. At the return match, Lampard and Drogba gave them a 2-1 lead with 11 minutes to play. Bayern, who had equalised earlier through Pizarro, went on to win the game with goals from their two substitutes Guerrero and Scholl in injury-time.

Next it was an all-English semi, versus Liverpool. Despite a goalless home draw Mourinho was convinced Chelsea would secure passage to the final. But he was left frustrated, claiming the 'best team lost' as Benitez's side had benefited from a controversial refereeing decision when Luis Garcia's fourth-minute goal was allowed to stand, even though Gallas cleared the ball before it crossed the line. Mourinho insisted that linesman Roman Slysko had been intimidated by the fever-pitch Anfield crowd, but maintained he was still proud of his team.

The captain John Terry said: 'We're gutted. We've reached the semi-finals for the second year running and not made the final. The fact that we've won the league doesn't make it better, in fact it's even worse. We threw it away because overall we were the better side and over the two legs we just deserved it. We dominated the second half but couldn't get a goal. We've beaten them three times this season but they defended well in both legs. Jamie Carragher threw himself in front of every shot that went on target. He was magnificent. We're disappointed but overall for Chelsea it has been a great season. This will put a downer on things for the next couple of days but we've still won a cup and the Premiership. I'm really gutted for the fans.'

F

Football League Champions in 1955 and 2005

Bill Haley and his Comets were rocking around the clock, a pint of beer cost one shilling and three pence (6p) and the world lost Albert Einstein as well as James Dean who died at the age of twenty-four in a car crash. The board game Scrabble went on sale, and Elvis Presley made his first television appearance in the States. It was also the year that Winston Churchill resigned.

In terms of sporting milestones, Ian Botham was born and Rocky Marciano retained the heavyweight crown.

Ted Drake, the former Arsenal and England centre-forward, was a Hampshire man; Jose Mourinho, the fourth successive foreign coach, was never a player of any note. Mourinho has Roman Abramovich's boundless millions to spend; Drake plucked his players from the Third Division – Johnny McNichol and Les Stubbs, the inside-forwards, from Brighton and Hove Albion and Southend United, respectively; precocious Frank Blunstone, later an England outside-left, from Crewe Alexandra; and Derek Saunders, a left-half, from Walthamstow Avenue, the London amateurs. The big star was Roy Bentley, the elegant England centre-forward, who cost £11,000 from Newcastle United. That Chelsea team won the title by the skin of their teeth.

Mourinho's team is packed with expensive foreign stars and the only player to have emerged through the club's ranks is their captain John Terry.

While Mourinho was hired on a lavish £4-million-a-year salary after wining the Champions League with Porto FC, Drake arrived at the Bridge having won three championship medals with Arsenal as a player before the war and scored seven times in a single league match against Aston Villa. He hit four against Chelsea at the Bridge in November 1934 and built his reputation as a manager at Reading.

But there are also similarities between Mourinho and Drake. They were both innovators. Drake tore down the traditions and removed the most famous of Chelsea's Pensioners, the one on their badge. Drake did not like the Pensioners image and replaced it with a lion. He also wanted the fans to roar; he felt that the crowd was too genteel. He made the point in his first programme: 'You folk may be rightly proud of your title "Football's Fairest Crowd", but for my part I would like to see not a little, but a lot more partisanship in favour of Chelsea. All too many people come to Stamford Bridge to see a football match – instead of to cheer Chelsea. Please prove me wrong, but it's my opinion that over the years too many bystanders have gone out of their way to grouse, jibe and grumble, to pull the club down rather than to say a good word for Chelsea. And for years now, the players must have been thoroughly sick of all the Music Hall publicity that has gone on before. Let's have more people eating, sleeping and drinking Chelsea. Let's spread the spirit of Chelsea across London ... don't tell me the crowd can't make a difference.'

Another key strategy was to assemble a squad that was later to become known as 'Drake's Ducklings' as he turned to youth.

'I knew that in time I wanted to come around to a young side, that was always my ambition,' he recalls. 'You've got to get the crowd behind youngsters, haven't you?'

Drake abandoned the suit, tie and bowler hat, to become one of the new breed of tracksuit managers. Nothing too subtle, just a lot of hard work and running. He also put a medical team into place who sorted out Eric Parson's knee injury, enabling him to play every game in the title season. Drake introduced a version of the mid-season break in 1955. Not the modern-day sunshine trip to La Manga, but three visits to the costal town of Broadstairs in Kent. Jack Oxberry took over as head trainer and former goalkeeper Harry Medhurst became his assistant.

'When I arrived at Chelsea I had the feeling that they were very Cup minded,' recalled Drake. 'I said to the players that I would like to win the Cup

: centre-forward who captained Chelsea in their 1955 league championship win.
y Bentley was the first Chelsea captain to lift a major trophy.

Above: Bentley scoring another goal – he was the first player to score 150 goals for Chelsea Football Club.

Below: The Chelsea league championship winning side of 1955.

ove: John Harris played in all but eleven games in the 1955 season. Having only ıed Chelsea as a guest player during the war, Harris went on to appear in 500 games the club.

low left: Jimmy Greaves, nicknamed 'The Goal', rose through the ranks at Chelsea. his first full season in the youth side, he scored an astonishing 114 goals. As he ›gressed to the senior side, Greaves became a goalscoring sensation.

low right: Tommy Docherty arrived at Stamford Bridge as a player-coach in 1961. soon took on the full-time manager's role when Ted Drake left the club.

Above: Alan Hudson, *left*, and Charlie Cooke, *right*, along with Peter Osgood, became synonymous with the King's Road set of the 1970s.

Below: Chelsea Captain, Terry Venables, celebrates their 1965 League Cup win with his team-mates Barry Bridges, Eddie McCreadie, John Boyle, Frank Upton and Bert Murr Chelsea beat Leicester City to win the trophy.

e of the highest profile products of the Chelsea youth team, Terry Venables went to captain the team and eventually moved into one of the most prominent jobs in tball – managing England.

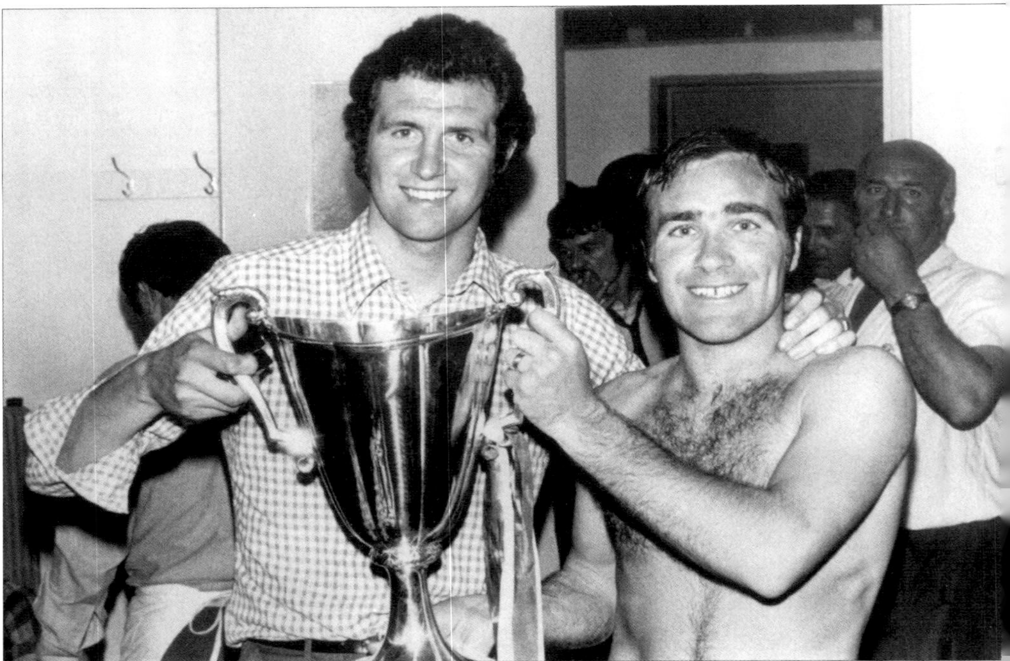

Above: Peter Osgood – the George Best of Chelsea.

Below: Peter Osgood and Ron 'Chopper' Harris with the European Cup-Winners' Cup in 1971.

ove: John Neal became the seventh Chelsea manager in seven years when he joined in 1. He revolutionised the team with a batch of new signings but his reign was short-d as he retired in 1984 due to ill-health.

ow left: Pat Nevin was one of Neal's signings. He entertained the fans and played in games for the club.

ow right: Kerry Dixon scored twice on his debut for Chelsea and became the golden of his era. He described his time at Chelsea as 'the pinnacle of my career.'

Glenn Hoddle was player-manager at Chelsea. He managed the side for three seasons and, in his final season, he signed Ruud Gullit who succeeded him in the managerial r

of course, but would dearly love to win the league. They looked at me and gave me the impression that they thought they had no chance.'

Drake asked the fans for patience, and three years to win the title. The club approached fifty years without a trophy, one FA Cup final defeat in 1915 and three semi-finals without success; their highest league position had been third in 1920. He addressed the fans with a 'Heart-to-Heart' in the official programme: 'Greetings to you all! ... I wish to express my delight at being appointed manager of Chelsea. From my days as a player, I have had a great admiration for this club ... I have felt that the club deserved to do itself fuller justice than it has ever done in the past.' He stated that his intention was to make Chelsea 'one happy family'.

Drake's reign began with a 2–0 defeat at Old Trafford, but eight goals without reply in just four days against Blackpool and Aston Villa gave a rather different complexion to the start of the season. However, seven consecutive defeats through November and leading up to Boxing Day had the fans wondering whether there would be yet more inconsistencies through the Drake years. Only a 3–1 final-day win enabled the club to leapfrog over Stoke City to safety.

On Saturday, 24 October 1953, Drake spotted encouraging signs in a 5–2 defeat at West Brom and, seven days later, Chelsea dispatched Liverpool with a 5–2 win, and began a run to eighth in the league, their best place since 1920.

There was renewed optimism for the start of the 1954–55 season, which was reflected in Drake's opening remarks: 'Everyone tells me we are going to have a good season in this the fiftieth year of Chelsea Football Club, and I believe so, too. The spirit is here that I have always wanted, not only inside the club but among you, the supporters ... and that's great ... I am confident that we can match the best ... the lads are the happiest and nicest bunch I could wish to have with me.'

After a five-game unbeaten start to the season – a run that equalled the club's best ever start – it was a bleak October that yielded just a single point from five games and left them languishing in twelfth place in the table. A 6–5 defeat at the Bridge against Manchester United hardly suggested a title in the making and Chelsea slid to mid-table.

But it proved to be the turning point, as they went on to lose just three more games in the rest of the season. Bentley recalls, 'As the season reached the halfway stage, the players were looking forward to every game, and we started to believe we were the best side around. There was an inner belief that emerged and I knew the lads were up for it – Ted Drake believed in us all, too.'

November was inspired. Two goals down at Roker Park, the team fought back to earn a draw against Sunderland and might have won, but Bentley's header struck the underside of the bar. It set the tone, and during the next six months, apart from a single-goal defeat at Highbury on Christmas Day, only Manchester City and Aston Villa could beat a team that surged to the top. Of the other twenty-one games, only six points were dropped. In November and December, the team hit twelve goals against Portsmouth, Wolves and Villa in just fifteen days.

The New Year was even better, with seventeen scored against Bolton, Newcastle, Huddersfield and West Brom.

Saunders recalls, 'To me the championship season really ebbed and flowed. Things were never really going badly and there was a belief in the squad.'

Despite eventually winning the league by four points – in the days of two points for a win – Chelsea never actually topped the table until March, just fifteen days before actually lifting the title. After being knocked out of the FA Cup by Notts County in February, Chelsea went on a twelve-match unbeaten run that culminated in two crucial games against Wolves and Portsmouth.

A record total of 1,017,451 fans flocked to the Bridge that season and the gates often had to be closed. The glorious day finally arrived, Saturday, 9 April, when Wolves arrived at the Bridge in second place knowing that only a win would prevent the championship from going to Chelsea. Fans arrived soon after breakfast; the turnstiles opened at midday and closed two hours later with hundreds spilling on to the greyhound track. Wolves tried to cling to the point which might have kept their hopes, albeit slim, alive but with a quarter of an hour remaining, Seamus O'Connell struck a shot towards the top left-hand corner; after the 'keeper Williams had been beaten, the legendary England captain, Billy Wright, punched the ball away ... the ref signalled for a corner! Swamped by the Chelsea players, the ref finally consulted his linesman and pointed to the penalty spot.

Step forward dead-ball expert Peter Sillett who, years later, admitted he wished the penalty had never being given. He described it as 'the most terrifying moment of my career'.

The nerves never showed as he hit the spot kick under the 'keeper's diving body. Several players had turned their backs – they could not bear to watch!

Wolves struck the post just before the end, but Chelsea were virtually home and dry: they had a lead of five points with three games to play, although, mathematically at least, there were five other clubs still in the chase.

Next stop Fratton Park: Stubbs had a goal disallowed, but the goalless draw was enough, barring a miracle, to remove Portsmouth – one of the five outsiders – from the equation.

Doomed to relegation, Sheffield Wednesday were next up at the Bridge. Little Eric Parsons, known as the 'Rabbit', sped down the right wing before heading the first goal just before half-time. Sillett scored again from the penalty spot and added a third with a shot under the hands of the deputy 'keeper.

With a kick-off fifteen minutes later than this game at the Bridge, only Pompey still had an outside mathematical chance: it all depended on the outcome of their game at Ninian Park. Before that result came through, though, the Chelsea crowd thought that it was a foregone conclusion and swarmed on to the pitch forming a semi-circle in front of the directors' box.

The announcement – Cardiff City 1, Portsmouth 1 – signalled that the championship had been concluded. Emotions ran high. A microphone was produced as the team filed into the front row of the stand, followed by Drake.

Chairman Joe Mears made a brief address: 'You want to hear from Roy and the boys and from the one and only Ted.'

'The happiest moment of my life,' said Ted. 'At the start of the season I was asked if we could win the FA Cup. I thought we might, but I thought we had a greater chance of winning the championship. I congratulate all the boys and every one of my staff – office, training and playing. Right throughout they are one and all – Chelsea.'

But the fans wanted to hear from their favourite. Sitting astride the ledge at the front of the stand, with a towel draped around his shoulders, was the Rabbit.

'We want the Rabbit,' chorused the fans repeatedly, but he took off with his usual turn of speed!

Behind the scenes the champagne flowed in the directors' private room. Chelsea actually clinched the title with a game to spare; the final match took place at Old Trafford with warm applause from the Manchester United fans and the band played 'See the Conquering Heroes Come'.

Much like Mourinho, Drake had the respect of the players. As Saunders says, 'We all admired Ted Drake. If he believed it, then so did we.'

The players' affinity with the club was rock solid. Ken Armstrong's ashes were transported from New Zealand where he lived to be spread at Stamford Bridge when he died in 1984; Ken was the right-back in the championship-winning side. He was Bradford born, but the club that he had played for 402 times meant everything to him.

Key Men

TED DRAKE. Manager. 426 games in charge: won 156, drew 103, lost 167. Won the title and Charity Shield in 1955.

ROY BENTLEY. Captain. 128 goals in 324 games. Started as a defender averaging a goal every other game with Newcastle. When he signed for Chelsea in 1948 he was switched to a striker. Top scorer in the title season with twenty-one goals, scoring a memorable hat-trick in the 4–3 win over Newcastle in February that year.

STAN WICKS. Played under Drake at Reading and followed his manager to Chelsea in January 1954. Impressed in reserves and came in after Chelsea lost 6–5 at home to Manchester United. He turned the tide after poor results in October, demonstrating their new defensive stability by marking Jackie Milburn out of the game in Chelsea's 4–3 win over Newcastle at the Bridge in Febuary. Played eighty games, one goal.

JOHNNIE MCNICHOL. Drake's first signing, and the manager built the side around this scorer and creator. He finished second-top scorer with fourteen in the title season: his two goals in the 3–3 draw against Sunderland at Roker Park, coupled with his winner in the 2–1 victory over Preston North End at Deepdale, earned vital points for the championship success. Played 181 games, sixty goals.

ERIC PARSONS. A tricky winger, called the 'Rabbit' because of his quick bursts of speed. Along with Saunders, the only ever-present in the title campaign. Scored eleven goals in-title season, including two in the win over Sheffield Wednesday to secure the championship. Played 158 games, thirty-seven goals.

DEREK SAUNDERS. Tenacious defender who rarely crossed the halfway line, but never pulled back from a tackle. Played in every league game in the title season. Played 202 games, nine goals.

Key Games

Chelsea 5 Manchester United 6: 16 October 1954

Jim Lewis gave Chelsea a 2–1 lead, but Tommy Taylor put United ahead at 4–2. Dennis Viollet completed his hat-trick, 5–2. Ken Armstrong got one back before Jackie Blanchflower restored United's three-goal dominance. Even a hat-trick from O'Connell was not enough.

Wolves 3 Chelsea 4: 4 December 1954

Wolves had hammered Chelsea 8–1 at Molyneux the year before. This time Roy Bentley scored the first two goals, but Chelsea surrendered a 2–1 lead to go 3–2 behind in just three minutes. Les Stubbs and Johnnie McNichol also scored, while John Hancocks, Peter Broadbent and Roy Swinbourne got the goals for Wolves.

Bolton 2 Chelsea 5: 1 January 1955

Chelsea had missed their previous five penalties, but Peter Sillett ended the jinx to give Chelsea a New Year's Day lead. Goals from O'Connell, Bentley and an own goal from John Higgins produced a stirring result.

Chelsea 4 Newcastle 3: 12 February 1955

Bentley stole the headlines from Jackie Milburn after he scored his first hat-trick. McNichol also scored to give Chelsea a commanding 4–0 lead. Newcastle staged a comeback in the last twelve minutes, with Vic Keeble scoring twice and Milburn finally getting one.

Chelsea 3 Sheffield Wednesday 0: 23 April 1955

The win at the Bridge, coupled with Pompey's failure to beat Cardiff, brought the championship to the club for the first time in fifty years. Parsons put Chelsea ahead, Sillett added a second from the penalty spot and Parsons scored again after the Wednesday 'keeper fumbled a shot. Chelsea were champions at long last!

Jose Mourinho began to plot Chelsea's first title win for fifty years as the priority trophy. He asked the players which honour they wanted the most, and it was the Barclays Premiership. He delivered.

This was a season never to be forgotten, arguably one of the best – if not the best – in the club's career, and that made it all the more frustrating not to round it off in the Champions League final, falling at the semi-final hurdle against Liverpool. But this was a rollercoaster season of emotions, controversy, rows, accusations and disciplinary hearings.

The highly charged Mourinho, likened to the late Brian Clough, was never far from the back-page headlines. Not only that, but the Carling Cup was his first piece of silverware and, after concluding the title in April at Bolton, a few days later just missed out on the Champions League final because of a linesman who was sure the ball crossed the line at Anfield when perhaps it didn't.

The self-proclaimed 'special one' spent money wisely on a squad he considered instantly capable of winning all four major trophies, not just the Premiership crown. Robbed of the services of one of his main assets – flying Dutch winger Arjen Robben – first the Quadruple disappeared and then the Treble. Anyone asked at the start of the season if they would have been satisfied with a league and Cup Double would have accepted it.

Robben's ankle injury in a pre-season game in America prevented Chelsea from reaching the heights they scaled when he finally returned to action in October. Up until that point, Chelsea's Premiership campaign had only been relatively successful and, while their third successive victory of the campaign, a 2–0 away success at Crystal Palace, briefly put them on top of the pile, it did not last. Four days later, they were back in second spot even though they overcame Southampton 2–1 at home. But, while they remained unbeaten, the critics were already gunning for them. Chelsea's penchant for narrow 1–0 victories brought with it a 'boring' tag they found hard to shift until that man Robben finally recovered from his ankle injury.

On 23 October, Robben's impact as a second-half substitute could not be ignored as Chelsea blasted Blackburn 4–0 at home. It was the beginning of a goal-filled spree which put the Londoners on top by 6 November. Wins over Fulham and West Brom by the same 4–1 scoreline helped Chelsea to finally shake off their 'boring' label and maintain their lead at the top of the league. It was the perfect response to those critics who has suggested their bubble would burst following the only defeat of the season away at Manchester City on 16 October.

Off the pitch, though, Mourinho's ruthless streak had begun to show itself among the players. Hugely suspicious that Romanian striker Adrian Mutu was taking cocaine, the Portuguese coach ordered a drug test to be carried out on the player. It proved positive and Chelsea immediately sacked a striker they bought from Parma for £15.8m in August 2003.

On the pitch, Mourinho was still quietly confident but already playing the mind games he would use to such devastating effect in Europe later in the season. He said, 'In England, it is different because everyone can take points from the big teams. It is more complicated. The signals in the Premiership at the moment are that there will be a big fight for the title. I would say until the end of the season there will be a question mark over who will win it. But I still feel Arsenal are a team with years of work and still at a higher level than we are. I have not changed my mind yet.'

Yet Chelsea never relinquished their grip on the leadership from the moment their 1–0 home victory over Everton, courtesy of Robben, put them ahead of everyone else. On 18 December, their 4–0 win over Norwich at Stamford Bridge was to herald the start of another amazing sequence of events in a season that will never be forgotten by Chelsea fans. Goals from Frank Lampard, Didier Drogba, Damien Duff and Arjen Robben may have grabbed the headlines but it was at the other end where the plaudits would eventually come to rest.

Petr Cech was a relatively unknown goalkeeper when he joined the club from Rennes in July 2004. The Czech international, still only twenty-two, soon made his mark behind the meanest defence the top flight had seen for years. Nine league games later, Cech had still not conceded a goal in the league. He was eventually beaten again in the return game with Norwich at Carrow Road on 5 March – a week after Chelsea had lifted the Carling Cup by beating Liverpool 3–2 in extra-time at Cardiff's Millennium Stadium.

Even an FA Cup exit to Newcastle in February failed to deflect Chelsea from their main aim of winning the title. By this time, Chelsea were in pole position with a lead which fluctuated weekly between five and eight points over their nearest rivals. But still the ever cautious Mourinho refused to tempt fate. He said, 'Chelsea haven't won the league for fifty years and this Chelsea side hasn't won it yet in 2005. I came to Chelsea because of ambition, to manage a big club with the chance to win major trophies on a regular basis. I am really happy with Chelsea. We have a group of people so close in spirit, so strong and united in ambition, that tiredness, little injuries and occasional setbacks cannot knock us from our path.'

It was an insight into Mourinho's working methods and there was no doubting the winning mentality that he had instilled into his players over the course of their amazing season. The coach had succeeded in raising the quality of English stars like Frank Lampard, Joe Cole and skipper John Terry. In Terry, he had the perfect captain – a leader who had come through the ranks.

His coaching style also turned Lampard into one of the world's top midfielders, as the former West Ham player added creativity, guile and non-stop energy to his game. The spirit and togetherness of the squad remained the biggest factor in their favour and eventually the gap at the top became unsurpassable.

These are the main men who made it happen, the first title in fifty years, the perfect symmetry in the Club's Centenary ...

PETR CECH (goalkeeper): The inspiration behind Chelsea's title success. A record ten consecutive clean sheets – from December to March – came in a season when the Czech international was rightly nominated for the PFA Player of the Year award.

PAULO FERREIRA (right-back): Considered by Mourinho to be the best right-back in the world, Ferreira rewarded that faith with a string of consistent performances before a broken foot forced him to miss out on the run-in.

WILLIAM GALLAS (centre-back/left-back): The French defender played a starring role alongside Terry when first-choice centre-back Carvalho was out with a broken toe. Gallas was switched to left-back when Wayne Bridge broke his ankle and, even though he was playing out of position, the defender continued to produce solid performances.

JOHN TERRY (centre-back, captain): The Chelsea skipper enjoyed a phenomenal season. Under Mourinho, Terry matured into a commanding defender who is surely destined for an illustrious career with club and country. Led by example all season and received personal recognition with the PFA's Footballer of the Year award.

RICARDO CARVALHO (centre-back): His season was interrupted by a broken toe, but the former Porto defender played a major part in Chelsea's success in the Champions League, Carling Cup and Premiership. Voted Europe's most valuable defender by UEFA last season, Carvalho lived up to his billing in the Premiership with some outstanding displays in a season when Chelsea's defence showed their mean streak on the way to the title.

FRANK LAMPARD (central midfield): Enjoyed the best season of his career and, for many, it was hard to pick between himself and Terry for the PFA award. With a flurry of timely goals, and consistently dynamic displays, Lampard is now on the brink of becoming one of the best midfielders in the world.

CLAUDE MAKELELE (central midfield): The midfield 'enforcer' with the no-nonsense style. The part played by Makelele cannot be underestimated. Quietly efficient, and Mourinho says he is among the best in the Premiership.

JOE COLE (midfield): Took time to get into the side and had to curb his natural attacking tendencies, but the increasingly mature former West Ham captain showed during the second half of the season that he has a solid all-round game to accompany his many tricks.

TIAGO (midfield): One of the unsung heroes. Clever and efficient on the ball, the former Benfica midfielder has benefited from Mourinho's guidance after initially finding the physical aspects of English football a little hard to come to terms with.

DAMIEN DUFF (winger): Pace, wing wizardry, an eye for goal and a hardworking ethic have turned Duff into one of the Premiership's most feared players. Duff has matured superbly in a Chelsea team which used Duff, Robben and Cole to terrorise defences. The Republic of Ireland international has enjoyed the best season of his career.

ARJEN ROBBEN (winger): Although his season was interrupted by two serious injuries to his ankle, Robben's electrifying pace and goalscoring skills still played a major part in helping Chelsea to land the title.

Unstoppable once in the groove, Robben took the Premiership by storm when he first burst on to the scene as a substitute in the 4–0 demolition of Blackburn back in October.

DIDIER DROGBA (striker): At £24m, some felt the Ivory Coast striker was overpriced, but he won many over with some superb displays. Drogba showed he had the physical ability to handle the Premiership's toughest defenders and quickly found Chelsea's 4–3–3 system suited him as he gained from the pace and trickery of Duff and Robben.

EIDUR GUDJOHNSEN (striker): The Icelandic striker is one of the elder statesmen at the club, as Mourinho got the best out of him. Often asked to drop deep into midfield, Gudjohnsen's work ethic and goals were a significant factor in Chelsea's magnificent season.

Chelsea's Premiership Season – Match-by-Match

15 August – Chelsea 1 Manchester United 0

Gudjohnsen's first-half winner gets Mourinho's reign off to the perfect start.

21 August – Birmingham 0 Chelsea 1

A lacklustre performance is saved by a sixty-eighth-minute strike by substitute Cole.

24 August – Crystal Palace 0 Chelsea 2

Drogba scores his first Premiership goal and Tiago follows suit to seal the victory at Selhurst Park.

28 August – Chelsea 2 Southampton 1

Chelsea concede their first goal and need a James Beattie own goal and Lampard penalty to overcome the Saints.

11 September – Aston Villa 0 Chelsea 0

Chelsea miss out on a fifth-successive victory as Villa hold them to a goalless draw.

19 September – Tottenham 0 Chelsea 0

Another 0–0 draw prompts Mourinho to accuse Spurs of parking the bus in front of the goal.

25 September – Middlesbrough 0 Chelsea 1

Back to winning ways with another narrow victory, though this time Drogba had to wait eighty-one minutes before finding the net.

3 October – Chelsea 1 Liverpool 0

Chelsea's 'boring' reputation grows apace with another 1–0 win. Cole once again comes off the bench to steer his side to victory.

16 October – Manchester City 1 Chelsea 0

An Anelka penalty hands Mourinho his first defeat as Chelsea look stagnant while struggling to salvage a point.

23 October – Chelsa 4 Blackburn 0

Back to winning ways as Gudjohnsen hits a hat-trick and in-form Duff sparkles against his old club.

30 October – West Brom 1 Chelsea 4

Gera equalises after Gallas's opener but the Blues romp home, Gudjohnsen, Duff and Lampard destroying the Black Country strugglers.

6 November – Chelsea 1 Everton 0

Robben announces his arrival in English football with a stunning performance capped off with the winning goal.

13 November – Fulham 1 Chelsea 4

Lampard, Robben, Gallas and Tiago all beat goalkeeper Mark Crossley as the Blues win the west London derby with ease.

20 November – Chelsea 2 Bolton 2

Jaidi snatches a late draw with three minutes to go after Chelsea had led 2–0 through goals by Duff and Tiago.

27 November – Charlton 0 Chelsea 4

Chelsea take out their frustration on the Addicks with Terry scoring twice and Duff and Gudjohnsen netting either side.

4 December – Chelsea 4 Newcastle 0

Kezman hits his first league goal, an injury-time penalty, following goals by Lampard, Drogba and Robben.

12 December– Arsenal 2 Chelsea 2

Terry cancels out Henry's opener but Henry scores again, only for Gudjohnsen to spare Chelsea's blushes.

18 December – Chelsea 4 Norwich 0

Another 4–0 rout for Chelsea, the free-scoring quartet of Duff, Lampard, Robben and Drogba adding to their season's tally.

26 December – Chelsea 1 Aston Villa 0

Duff's thirtieth-minute winner ensures the Chelsea faithful enjoy a happy Christmas.

28 December – Porstmouth 0 Chelsea 2

The Blues leave it late with Robben clinching three points with 11 minutes remaining and Cole doubling the lead in added time.

1 January – Liverpool 0 Chelsea 1

Cole is once again on hand to provide the vital killer touch, silencing Anfield after eighty minutes shortly after his introduction from the bench.

4 January – Chelsea 2 Middlesbrough 0

Two Drogba strikes in three first-half minutes sent Boro back to Teesside empty-handed.

15 January– Tottenham 0 Chelsea 2

Lampard does the business with a penalty before half-time and a late second.

22 January – Chelsea 3 Portsmouth 0

Drogba scores a brace and Robben also finds the net as Chelsea cruise past Pompey.

2 February – Blackburn 0 Chelsea 1

Chelsea have to scrape their way to victory after Robben's early breakthrough as a physical Rovers side put the Blues to the test.

6 February – Chelsea 0 Manchester City 0

City take more points off Chelsea than any other team following their defeat at Eastlands as they struggle to find a way through without Drogba.

12 February – Everton 0 Chelsea 1

Chelsea have to fight their way to victory, aided by the sending off of Toffees striker James Beattie in the first ten minutes.

5 March – Norwich 1 Chelsea 3

McKenzie cancelled out Cole's opener but Kezman and defender Carvalho score in the seventy-first and seventy-ninth minute respectively.

15 March – Chelsea 1 West Brom 0

Drogba nets in the first half to deny a gallant Albion side a draw.

19 March – Chelsea 4 Crystal Palace 1

Another four-goal rout at the Bridge – Lampard, Cole and a Kezman double securing another home win.

2 April – Southampton 1 Chelsea 3

Lampard makes the breakthrough before Gudjohnsen scores either side of the break to crush Harry Redknapp's Saints.

9 April – Chelsea 1 Birmingham 1

Chelsea are stunned by Pandiani's goal but Drogba rescues his team-mates with a late leveller.

20 April – Chelsea 0 Arsenal 0

A cautious approach sees the Blues keep an important clean sheet against title rivals Arsenal to keep themselves on course for the Premiership trophy.

23 April – Chelsea 3 Fulham 1

Victory over west London rivals Fulham, with goals by Cole, Lampard and Gudjohnsen, means a loss or draw for Arsenal against Tottenham two days later will seal the title for Chelsea.

30 April – Bolton 0 Chelsea 2

Two goals from Frank Lampard take the title to Stamford Bridge.

G

Jimmy Greaves and Ruud Gullit

Ruud Gullit's dreads and sexy football; Jimmy Greaves's goals in the days of laced footballs and ankle-high boots. Greaves and Gullit are as much a part of Chelsea's folklore as Osgood, Hudson and Harris – the players synonymous with the King's Road set of the early 1970s. Gullit and Greaves represent everything that Chelsea fans would want to be associated with.

Greaves is also associated with some great football during his glory years at Spurs, but, in recognition of Chelsea's centenary, Greaves looks back at his time with the club and contemplates his hopes and desires for the future.

He tells me, 'I hope I am just as synonymous with Chelsea as I am with Tottenham. I had a good few years at Chelsea and joined them straight from school. They are as much a part of my life as Tottenham, and I have a great affection for both clubs. I had seven years at Chelsea and nine years at Tottenham. I had great times at Chelsea, and that club was very much a part of my young life.'

Greaves 'The Goal' rose through the Chelsea ranks and commanded media attention even before his debut in 1957. In his first full season in the youth side, he scored 114 goals. Chelsea had won the title for the first time in 1955, but the following season they finished sixteenth! But along came Greaves to lessen the sense of frustration, scoring on his debut against Spurs on the opening day of the 1957–58 season, at the tender age of seventeen. He scored six in his first nine games, took a break back in the reserves, before returning at Christmas to smash four past Portsmouth. Chelsea's average gate rose by 7,000, as they flocked to see the new goalscoring sensation of his generation: average attendances hit 38,000 that season, during which Greaves struck twenty-two goals in thirty-seven games including a hat-trick in the 3–2 win over Sheffield Wednesday. Yet Chelsea still only finished eleventh.

Still the fans kept flocking to the Bridge: the following season, the gate rose by another 1,500 to an average of nearly 40,000 as Greaves amassed thirty-seven goals in forty-seven games. He made his debut for England that year, scoring in the 4–1 defeat in Peru.

In his third season, he scored thirty in forty-two games and Chelsea still finished eighteenth!

By the time he was twenty-one, Greaves had already collected a century of league goals – the youngest player ever to do so.

Greaves scored five goals in a game on three occasions and collected thirteen hat-tricks. In December 1959, he scored all five at Preston in a 5–4 win. He didn't stop scoring until his final game for the Blues, at home to Nottingham Forest in 1961, when he scored four times; as the club knew he was leaving, they made him captain for the day. He was carried from the pitch on the supporters' shoulders. It ranks as one of the biggest errors in the club's history that he was allowed to leave for AC Milan.

Greaves scored 127 goals in 167 games. Unfortunately, the defence let in more goals than even Greaves could manage at the other end! In his final season, Chelsea finished twelfth having scored ninety-eight goals only to concede 100. Greaves also scored thirteen goals for his country that season, including two hat-tricks.

In his final season, Greaves created a record by scoring forty-one league goals which, of course, still stands today. Remarkably, he only played in forty games. In consecutive home games, he scored three against Manchester City, five against West Brom and two against Aston Villa. The end of the Greaves reign also marked the end of the Drake era.

The game at that time was gripped by the battle to end the maximum wage of £20 a week and Milan moved in with fortunes.

He scored regularly for AC Milan, but did not like the move and, despite Chelsea's attempts to buy him back, he moved to Spurs where he became part of the side that made history as the first British club to win a European trophy.

Greaves tells me, 'Without question, the Tottenham years were the best football wise. I had a much better time than I had had at Chelsea because I achieved so much more from a footballing point of view. From a personal viewpoint, I had enormous enjoyment at both clubs.

'That's not to say that we didn't have a good team at Chelsea; we did. I loved coming through the ranks and playing with such talents as Sillett and Brabrook.'

Greaves enjoyed two decades of goalscoring success, but also some astonishing lows – such as being left out of the World Cup-winning side in 1966. He became a popular television presenter – *The Saint and Greavise Show* was the peak – and he continues to write an established newspaper column in the *Sun*.

Reflecting on his era at the club and looking to the future, he told me, 'Chelsea have always threatened to be a bit of what they are not. Everybody really expected great things from Chelsea: we always thought they would have a great team and would be a great club. It had everything going for it: it had the ambience of being in the right place, the West End of London, and we all know location means everything. All right, Manchester United are a great club, but their ground is on an industrial site! And Arsenal, well, King's Cross, for goodness sake.'

But did Jimmy ever envisage the Chelsea of today? 'Good Lord, no. Well, who would ever have imagined a Russian billionaire? For the fifty years I've been associated with Chelsea, since leaving school and joining the club as a youngster to this very day in a journalistic capacity, I would never have imagined what is going on there now.

'I'm simply fascinated, from a personal as well as professional interest. It has finally become the club it has always wanted to be and I would not have thought that possible five years ago, let alone fifty years ago. They are in a unique situation: a Russian billionaire, who would have thought it?

'So how can I possibly imagine what the club will be like in twenty years' time? I would like to think that it will establish itself in the next few years and carry on as one of the powerhouses of European football. Chelsea will roll off the tongue in the same way as Real Madrid, Manchester United, Arsenal, Barcelona, AC Milan, Juventus.

'Tottenham never quite did that. We should have won the European Cup, but we were refereed out of it in the semi-final against Benfica. I did play for AC Milan, but they were not the AC Milan of today until Silvio Berlusconi arrived and did similar things to what Roman Abramovich is doing with Chelsea today.

'Regardless of whatever anyone says, and whatever anyone thinks of Ken Bates, he kept Chelsea Football Club alive and kept them at Stamford Bridge. But Abramovich is Chelsea's Berlusconi. When I played at AC Milan they were a great club, but they didn't become the legends they are now until the new owner arrived.

'It's amazing to think that Abramovich looked at Spurs before he bought Chelsea, but if you have no geographical intimacy with London and you are flying over the city in a helicopter and you see the north end of the place and then the West End, there's little wonder he chose to go to Chelsea. He clearly fancied a football club and the fact that he opted for Chelsea is wonderful for every single Chelsea fan.'

It is clearly a vastly different Chelsea to the one he joined straight from school. 'Chelsea won the championship the season I joined them, and that was their fiftieth anniversary. It was a well-run club, with Ted Drake the manager, but it was run in a vastly different fashion to the modern game. For a start you never saw the Board of directors, Joe Mears was the chairman of the club and he was also the chairman of the Football Association.

'It was a professionally run club, but nothing of the intensity that the game generates now.

'Jimmy Thompson was their chief scout and he was the reason I joined the club: he sold it to me, just as he did with a number of boys from the East End. I was really under the influence of one man at that time and that was Jimmy. The club owes an unbelievable debt to him, to this very day.

'I went to Chelsea because of him and because my mates had also gone to the club, not because the club were champions. Funnily enough, I didn't support anybody, I was too busy playing. Everyone tries to worm it out of me: "Who did you support, who do you support ... Tottenham, Chelsea, West Ham?" The truth is I didn't have a favourite team, and no one really believes me!

'I did have a favourite player, though: it was Len Shakleton. Don't ask me why, although I did love Sir Stanley [Matthews] as well.'

Greaves finally looks back on the glittering start to his career at the Bridge. 'I remember I was a fairly useful player! I used to get a fair amount of goals, but the only trouble was that we would let more in at the other end. But the Bridge was a lovely stadium, it was a lovely pitch. There was a high bank of terracing where they could pack in 45,000 alone, then there was that dog track around the pitch. I enjoyed fantastic times, it was a fabulous place to be, with dear old friends like Peter Sillett and old snoz, John Sillett. Yes, it was lovely, wonderful.'

⚽ ⚽ ⚽

There is no ready-made link between the Brylcreem era of Greaves and the more modern times of Ruud's dreadlocks, other than the fact that both players would figure in any Chelsea All Time Greatest XI.

Gullit became the first black manager to win a major trophy in English football, and it was the highly prestigious FA Cup that he brought to the Bridge to end a quarter of a century without a trophy. At the age of thirty-five, he was also the youngest manager in the Premiership.

It was an inspired choice plucking Gullit from the dressing room to succeed Glenn Hoddle, who had come to the end of his contract and, despite the personal intervention of Matthew Harding, had opted to coach his country.

Among the more experienced media-hyped candidates was George Graham, but in the final match of the season, during the defeat by Blackburn Rovers, the fans chanted, 'You can stick George Graham up your arse.'

It was followed by a chorus of: 'We want Ruddy, we want Ruddy.' Chief executive Colin Hutchinson had been put in charge of recruitment by chairman Ken Bates, and it was Ruddy they got.

Under his reign, sexy football gripped not only the Bridge but the entire nation. It was enthralling to watch.

Gullit arrived at the Bridge as a player in 1995, attracted to west London by Hoddle from Sampdoria on a free transfer, two months before his thirty-third birthday. The one-time World Footballer of the Year, who had captained Holland to the European Championships in 1988 and who had been involved in two European Cup triumphs with AC Milan, was generally regarded to be past his peak because of a succession of serious knee injures. Hoddle was seeking an inspirational figure and had enquired about Paul Gascoigne, but was impressed when he met Gullit: the conversation had centred on the playing side rather than merely the finances. At the press conference to unveil Gullit, the club also announced the signing of Mark Hughes from Manchester United.

Gullit started his illustrious career as a sweeper, before successfully switching to a roaming striker, and then becoming a right-sided midfielder. At the Bridge, he would revert back to the role from the beginning of his career – as a sweeper. Even so, the prestige of capturing Gullit raised Chelsea's profile globally for the first time. It also raised Chelsea's wage bill, as he signed a £750,000-a-year contract – one of the biggest ever at the time in English football.

On his debut against Everton, he breezed through the game as a sweeper with such aplomb that he was already a candidate for Player of the Season! His sweeper role didn't last long, though. He returned from injury to play in central midfield and it proved an inspired move by Hoddle. Although Gullit had never played in that position before, he revelled in it: he became an inspiration on the field, while Hoddle revolutionised the club off it. Chelsea reached the FA Cup semi-final, only to fall to Manchester United, 2–1. The Dutchman became only Chelsea's second-ever runner-up in the Footballer of the Year vote and, after just one year, he became the club's player-manager. But such was his impact in such a short space of time that you could well argue that he was Chelsea's best ever player.

When Gullit took over from Hoddle, Chelsea had finished the previous four seasons eleventh, fourteenth, eleventh and fourteenth respectively. In his first season in charge, Gullit returned as a sweeper, but soon left himself out in favour of one of his key signings Frank Leboeuf, and he took Chelsea to sixth in the league and the FA Cup final.

He had recruited three world-class players: Gianluca Vialli, captain of Champions League winners Juventus; Roberto Di Matteo, the first current Italian international ever to move to English football when he switched from Lazio and he was the first current international of a major nation to sign for Chelsea in more than forty years; and, a little later, Gianfranco Zola from Parma. Frank Leboeuf had also arrived from French club Strasbourg.

Gullit promoted Graham Rix from youth-team coach to his right-hand man with the first team and continued playing. Administrative duties were handed to Gwyn Williams, while fitness trainer and Olympic sprinter Ade Mafe was recruited as part of the backroom staff. Hutchinson negotiated the transfers, while Gullit utilised his worldwide net of contacts to promote the signings and, at times, to sell the club to the players he wanted to buy.

The route to the final contained one particular match that will live in the memory. Gullit left out Hughes, the fans' Player of the Year, for the third-round tie with Liverpool at the Bridge: the Welshman was joined by Vialli on the bench. Liverpool majestically took advantage as they strolled to a 2–0 half-time lead. A couple of the Liverpool players made cigar signs to the Chelsea players in the tunnel, but Gullit brought on Hughes for the second half and took off left-wing-back Scott Minto. Goals from Hughes and Zola levelled the tie, and then Vialli gave them the lead, and then made it four with a header. The brilliance of Chelsea's football was captured in the live television game on BBC.

A touch of luck against Leicester with a penalty decider, a 4–1 win over Portsmouth and victory in the semi at Highbury over Wimbledon with an exquisite Zola goal, propelled them into the final.

Gullit's Cup final line up consisted of Norwegian 'keeper Frode Grodas, with Frank Sinclair and Scott Minto alongside Scotsman Steve Clarke and Leboeuf. In midfield were Wise and Eddie Newton alongside Di Matteo and Romanian Dan Petrescu. Zola and Hughes were the forwards.

Although Vialli and Craig Burley played such vital roles in helping the team to reach the final, they were left out. Vialli started the season as first choice, but was then injured and struggled to regain that status. The Gullit–Vialli situation was one of the big talking points, but other outspoken stars, such as John Spencer, opted to leave.

Roberto Di Matteo collected the fastest Wembley goal in history and, late in the game, Eddie Newton ensured the trophy went to the Bridge. Two minutes after the goal, Gullit took Vialli off the bench to replace Zola for the final couple of minutes. It was hard for Vialli to know whether it was a tribute or an insult!

'Blue Day' rang out at Wembley: the party went on long into the night at the Waldorf Hotel for the players. Tens of thousands turned out for the open-bus parade the next day in the streets of Fulham.

At the celebration dinner at the Wardorf Hotel that night, Gullit stunned his audience when he announced that his partner Estelle was pregnant. He would be a dad for the fifth time. He had just as colourful a private life as he did on the pitch!

Mark Hughes had set his own piece of history by becoming the first player in the twentieth century to win the FA Cup four times: three of those times with Manchester United.

Between 60,000 and 100,000 fans paid tribute to the team as the players rode aboard the traditional open-top bus to the Fulham and Hammersmith

Town Hall. Gullit told the fans, 'We're happy to make your dream come true. We love you all.'

All that troubled him now was his perception that everyone in England assumed that he put style before substance as a manager – an image due, perhaps, to the continued reference to a phrase of his own making. 'Ach, yes, sexy football,' he laughs. 'That's a phrase that has totally been taken out of perspective. I said it once. Honestly. Once. It was an international game I was commentating on, I think it was the Czech Republic against Portugal, and it's followed me through my career since then. People repeat it to me wherever I go. They say there are some things you wish you'd never said in life – well, that is mine. It was never my idea as a manager to play sexy football. I never use that instruction to players; I just want to win matches, because that's what this job entails. I think sometimes that maybe this "sexy football" comment is haunting me.'

Everything started for him as a player at Feyenoord. Where better for him to restart as a coach? At forty-one, he still looks youthful, even if the dreadlocks have long gone. These days the hair may be short, but it is as spiky.

Gullit assumed control during the close season. The one criterion he had for accepting Feyenoord's offer was that the job description, to borrow a Dutch phrase, should be 'total football'. There was to be no deskwork with his post. 'It's a good feeling to be back in management again,' he says. 'It's the little things about football that you miss: the smell of the grease and the oils; the tapping of the studs on the pavement ... things like that.'

Nobody ever doubted Gullit as a player. He signed for Feyenoord as a teenager in 1982 from Haarlem, joining Johan Cruyff in midfield to claim a Dutch championship, before a two-year stay at PSV Eindhoven, and then a £5.5 million transfer to AC Milan in 1987.

In his debut season, Milan won their first league title for a decade and went on to claim consecutive European Cups in 1989 and 1990. The first of those two finals, in which Gullit scored twice for Milan in a 4–0 victory over Steaua Bucharest in Barcelona, is still considered one of football's all-time great team performances.

When Glenn Hoddle left Chelsea for the England job in the summer of 1996, Gullit was invited to become player-manager at Stamford Bridge. Did it come too early for him? 'Well, perhaps, but you have to understand that I was asked,' he replies. 'They came to me and made the offer, so I said yes. I hadn't really expected it, but I just tried to do my best. I still feel that I managed to do things I'm proud of, things I could never have imagined myself doing. It was all new for me, so maybe some mistakes were made, but I tried to do as well as I could without any experience.'

Chelsea won the FA Cup in his first full season, but an unpopular squad-rotation policy finally saw Gullit encircled by his detractors. When discussions began about a contract renewal in February 1998, as manager only, he seemed to talk himself out of a job with his opening demand of £2 million a year 'netto' (after tax).

He called the theory that it was all about money a 'smokescreen', but the manner of his departure has not clouded his memories. 'I view Chelsea as a good experience,' he insists. 'And it's that experience I've taken with me to use in management. I realise now that you do have ups and downs as a coach, and I'm better prepared for that.'

His departure from Newcastle United in August 1999 was more amicable in terms of his relations with the Board – he declined to take any compensation for the rest of his contract – but the way he handled the players at St James' Park had been criticised. With the omission of Alan Shearer, Gullit finally dropped himself in it, although he still believes it was the right decision. When he returned to St James' Park for a pre-season tournament, Gullit remarked, 'The moment I chose to move to Newcastle, it was for all the wrong reasons, and perhaps I made the choice too soon after Chelsea.' However, he points out that there was still some success on Tyneside, notably reaching an FA Cup final.

During his enforced time out after his dismissal by Newcastle, Gullit hosted a television chat show in Holland, with his surname as its title. Rather than let guests come to him, he went to them, visiting and interviewing a broad range of celebrities worldwide, from Victoria Beckham to Nelson Mandela. 'I want to see how famous people really are,' he said at the time. His only coaching work was with the Holland Under-19 team – the Jong Oranje – but the Dutch Football Federation did not block the move to Feyenoord, where he succeeded Bert van Marwijk. 'The fact that it was Feyenoord who wanted me was what made the difference,' Gullit says. 'This is the club of my heart, you know.'

Always a regular churchgoer in England, he was christened by the Franciscans in 2001 and remains a religious man, but it is his football beliefs that are central to him again now.

H

Glenn Hoddle and Matthew Harding ... John Harris and Ron Harris

Glenn Hoddle made two pivotal signings in his third and final season as Chelsea manager before he left at the end of his contract to become the England coach. Hoddle revolutionised the playing style of the team, but did more for the club's global profile when he captured Ruud Gullit and Mark Hughes.

Chelsea's league form saw them finish in a disappointing twelfth, but an FA Cup run promised so much, with victories over Newcastle, QPR, Grimsby and Wimbledon to set up a semi-final clash at Villa Park against the side that had beaten them in the previous season's final, Manchester United. They lost 2–1, though, with Gullit scoring Chelsea's goal.

Despite the efforts of director Matthew Harding to persuade Hoddle otherwise, the call from the FA was too great a temptation for Hoddle to resist as he took over from Terry Venables as England coach.

Hoddle had been one of the most gifted individuals of his generation as a Spurs player and, in two seasons at unfashionable Swindon, had earned a reputation that attracted Bates to bring him to the Bridge. He left to take over the England team, only to leave in controversial circumstances and end up at Southampton and then back at his beloved Spurs, then losing that job before resurfacing at Wolves.

Hoddle was the eighteenth manager in Chelsea's history and, arguably, their most famous. Hoddle had Peter Shreeves and Graham Rix, as youth-team coach, as his back-up team.

Now leading a revival in the Midlands with Championship side Wolves, the manager credited with beginning the transformation of the Blues talks about his Chelsea experience.

Hoddle tells me, 'They were good years at Chelsea and whenever I have gone back, whether it be as England manager, with Southampton, even with Tottenham, the Chelsea fans have wanted to come over and shake my hand to show their appreciation.

'If you look at where the club was at before I arrived, it is easy to see why it needed foundations. The facilities were poorer than the club I had just left, Swindon! The attitude and the outlook were all wrong and the players felt that the club was dragging its heels. The vibe about the place was not right and it was essential to lift the standards.

'In order to attract the right type of player, the priority was to upgrade the training facilities, which we did: we introduced a gym – even the detail of ripping out the showers and putting in baths for the players; it was just imperative to change the standards at the training ground. We also brought in a better standard of hotel when we travelled and, as I had learned from my time abroad, I introduced a higher standard of food at the training ground and brought in dietary experts to oversee it.'

Hoddle reflects on his three years in control of the team. 'The first year we reached the Cup final on a shoestring. Perhaps, yes, that was the proudest moment of my Chelsea career: walking out with the team for the Cup final after having only been there for twelve months, and against such a fantastic team as Manchester United. We faced one of the best sides of all time in the final, a really top-notch Manchester United team. Oddly enough, though, Manchester United were only a minute away from the biggest shock of the season, losing to Oldham in the semi-final, but they made it to Wembley. Maybe we would have beaten Oldham and set the fuse for the transition at Chelsea even earlier, but Manchester United were far too strong. Even so, they got two second-half penalties, and two penalties in a Wembley final was unheard of. Gavin Peacock also hit the bar in the first half and if that had gone it might have been a different story.

'The second year we reached the semi-finals of the European Cup-Winners' Cup and I must say that ranks as perhaps my greatest achievement in such a short space of time, given the difficulties that existed for English clubs in Europe at that time. Remember, the Scots, Welsh and Irish were then classed as foreigners and you were only permitted to have three, which meant we had to play eight English players. It was a handicap for all the English teams in Europe, and it didn't hinder anyone else in Europe. It was so ludicrous that I had to register Graham Rix, who was our youth-team coach at the time, and he actually ended up playing, because we were so short of English players. So reaching the semi-finals under those circumstances was one hell of a feat.

'The third season was significant because we moved up a notch when we signed players of the calibre of Ruud Gullit, Mark Hughes and Dan Petrescu, all of whom became hugely popular with the fans and who raised the club's profile to an unprecedented level.'

Hoddle's reign coincided with one of the most controversial periods in the club's history. A power struggle of momentous proportions was being played out, first behind the scenes and then in the full glare of publicity, between chairman Ken Bates and the man who he had brought into the club to help save it, Matthew Harding.

Harding loaned the club £5 million to build a new North Stand. Whatever the intricacies of the row and the counter-arguments, Harding was hugely popular with Hoddle, and Bates perceived an allegiance he felt was harmful to his cause. Hoddle, for the first time, talks about his personal relationship with Harding, who met with a tragic death in a helicopter crash on his way back from a midweek game, and indeed Bates.

'Matthew brought a big change within the club and behind the scenes there was an awful lot going. Matthew and I hit it off straight away and I shared his vision for the club; his dreams for Chelsea were the dreams of a genuine fan and benefactor. He had designs to take the club to an even higher level. But I also got on well with Ken Bates and, despite what anyone might say, Bates left you alone to get on with the job of running the team. Ken Bates and his chief executive, Colin Hutchinson, were as good a combination as you could find in football, and together we lifted the perception of Chelsea.

'Perhaps I got on better with Matthew because the age gap was not so pronounced as it was between myself and Ken. Ken was very supportive, but Ken is Ken, while Matthew and I gelled; we were a lot closer and had more common ground, more to talk about, and I could relate to the dream he wanted for Chelsea.

'It was difficult for everyone at the club when there became this open hostility between Ken and Matthew, and Ken perceived that I was in Matthew's camp because I got on so well with him. But all the plotting that Ken thought was going on behind his back, as far as I was concerned, didn't exist.'

Harding tried to persuade Hoddle to change his mind about accepting the England job, and Hoddle reveals, 'Surprisingly enough it was a tough decision, even though everyone thought that it was a done deal and my mind was instantly turned by the England job. The last thing on my mind was leaving Chelsea when the England job arose.'

In conclusion, Hoddle retains enormous affection for the club and wishes them well in their centenary. 'I have really, really good memories of the club. They really do mean something to me, and I hope I brought something to them, even before anyone had even heard of Roman Abramovich, who, to my mind, is a one-off.

'I am really delighted about what is happening at Chelsea, and it is fantastic to think that I helped lay the foundations for it; all their supporters deserve the success that is coming their way now with Abramovich in charge. I could smell that success was long overdue and all the players and supporters could also smell success was on its way to the Bridge. I had a very big decision to make with the England job, believe it or not, but I weighed it up and felt that perhaps it might never come along again and I would spend the rest of my life kicking myself if I didn't take it. But who knows what might have happened if I had stayed for another three years at Chelsea?

'They have got the success they deserve, and I am sure Matthew is looking down and delighted as well, even though it is someone else who has put it all together. It is certainly Matthew's dream fulfilled to see such a successful and vibrant Chelsea.'

Matthew Harding tragically died in a helicopter accident and never fulfilled his dream of witnessing Chelsea pick up silverware as they did at the end of that season.

His spiritual presence was felt at the Wembley final. His widow Ruth, dressed in emerald green, even shared a kiss with Ken Bates's other half Susannah, as Chelsea won the FA Cup. Ruth was one of the official party of twenty-nine FA guests: the list was provided by the club. Ruth also joined the all-night party at London's Waldorf Hotel. She said, 'The final would have been the best day in Matthew's life, and it was the best day of mine. I felt as though he was upstairs looking down on the occasion.'

Matthew's girlfriend Vicky was not on the official list, but she, too, was at the final. She decorated the outside of her leafy home with a Chelsea flag and balloons. They both heard the fans chant his name: 'Matthew Harding's Blue and White Army.'

⚽ ⚽ ⚽

John Harris played in all but eleven of the championship games in 1955. Two years earlier, at the age of thirty-six, he lost his place first to Ron Greenwood and then to Stan Wicks. Early in 1954, when Peter Sillett was injured, he was recalled by manager Ted Drake to play at right-back. When Chelsea lifted the championship, Harris spoke to the cheering fans from the directors' box. First chairman Joe Mears addressed the emotional crowd gathered in front of the stand, next Drake, and then captain Roy Bentley. But Harris had topped 500 appearances, having arrived at the Bridge as a guest player at the height of the war in August 1943. It was a moving occasion for Harris, perhaps more so than any other player. He was summoned by Bentley to speak.

'I am so happy to be with all the boys on this the happiest day of my life now that the championship has come to Chelsea ...'

Even though he was just 5ft 10in, he was a stopper centre-half. The well-travelled Scotsman had played for Swindon, Swansea, Tottenham and Wolves before the outbreak of the Second World War. Stationed in the south during 1943, he played for Chelsea and captained them from his first game. He led by example, even though he was a quiet man.

He twice led Chelsea to Wembley in the war years for Football League Cup South finals, but these were unofficial teams. Chelsea lost the first before 85,000 fans and won the second in front of 90,000. He collected the trophy from Winston Churchill.

When the war ended, he was twenty-nine and had played over 100 games for Chelsea which did not count towards his official total.

After 1945–46, he skippered Chelsea for another six years, including the 1950 FA Cup semi-final with Arsenal and the escape from relegation in 1951. He also played in the side that reached the 1952 FA Cup semi-final.

But, just when it seemed as though his Chelsea career was over, he came back and contributed marvellously to their championship season.

Seamus O'Connell was another unusual character in the title-winning side. He scored twelve goals in twenty games, including the one at Cardiff that put Chelsea on top of the league. It was his shot against Wolves that was fisted over the bar for the penalty that just about assured the championship. He only appeared a handful of times after the title-winning season when he actually joined the team direct on away trips in the north. He played a few games for Carlisle, continued his amateur game with Crook Town and successfully ran his business until the mid-1980s when he sold out and retired to golf and Spain. He actually began as an amateur with Bishop Auckland, winning the FA Amateur Cup four times. He worked in the cattle-importing firm which had made his family wealthy. His father opposed him turning professional with Manchester United but, in 1954, he joined Chelsea. The cows his company imported from Ireland were sold at market in Northumbria on a Friday, and when the work was completed he took the night train to London, where he stayed until Tuesday before travelling back north to prepare for the next market. While he was up there, he trained with Carlisle – who were managed by Bill Shankly.

He scored a hat-trick on his Chelsea debut at the Bridge, only to finish on the losing side 5–6, and didn't even get the match ball.

Ron Harris was the first Chelsea captain to lift two major trophies – the FA Cup and the European Cup-Winners' Cup. He arrived as an uncompromising defender and, 795 games later, that's how he finished. He played 655 league games for Chelsea – a figure that is unlikely ever to be broken. The players called him 'Buller', but the fans nicknamed him 'Chopper'.

When a fashion promotion photo shoot was organised for George Best in flowing action at Old Trafford, the pictures were useless because the photographer discovered that in virtually every shot Chopper, who had been shadowing the star mercilessly, cropped up alongside him. So, there was handsome George, with his long hair flowing; over his shoulder was the scowling, cropped-hair Chopper.

Ron remembers it well. 'I was marking him; that was my job. I didn't know there was some fancy photo shoot going on. But George tells me it was ruined because I was in fifty of the fifty-two frames.'

The pair have been pretty close since they stopped playing as Chopper tells me. 'Myself, Greavsie and George used to tour the country doing shows together. Now it's just Greavsie and me, as George dropped out for a variety of reasons. One of the last shows we did together was in Plymouth and he was done for drink-driving. We did one in Southampton, but it was around the time he was having trouble with his missus, and he didn't do another.'

The FA Cup final replay against Leeds was one of the highlights of his career. He switched from centre-half to right-back to tame Eddie Gray who had been giving David Webb a torrid time. Leeds took the lead after a tough challenge on Peter Bonetti that had left the 'keeper limping. Next time Gray received the ball, Ron's tackle was even harder: the Leeds winger was anonymous for the rest of the game.

Chopper had his rows with former chairman Ken Bates and still resents the fact that his name is not recognised at the club along with some of the other greats.

'I go to the ground and see Roy Bentley remembered, Bobby Tambling, Kerry Dixon, Zola and Dennis Wise. There's even a Nigel Spackman entrance. But me, nothing. If I'd been a pain in the arse I could understand it, but ...'

During the Bates era, Chopper, like several other distinguished Chelsea old boys, was told that he was not welcome at the Bridge. His crime, like theirs, was to be quoted in the media venturing criticism of chairman Ken.

He rarely got into trouble off the pitch while a player, so he hardly expected to get into trouble as an ex-player. He is still in love with the club as his mobile phone ringtone will testify: it is the 1970 Chelsea anthem 'Blue is the Colour'.

If anyone other than Chelsea should win the league, however, he would like it to be Arsenal. This you might not expect of a man with a 'Blue is the Colour' ringtone, but as a boy, growing up in Stamford Hill, north London, Harris was a devotee of the Arsenal. He started going to Highbury in 1952, when he was eight, and, significantly, his hero was not a fancy striker but the uncompromising left-back Wally Barnes. In 1959, he joined Chelsea as a fifteen-year-old and had to shelve his affection for the Gunners. 'But theirs is still the second result I look for.' Harris owned up to his old Highbury habit in his autobiography *Chopper: A Chelsea Legend*.

Of Micky Droy, the gigantic centre-half who played alongside him in his latter years at Stamford Bridge, he says, 'We bought him from Slough, and he looked useless. For such a big lad he couldn't even head the ball. He was a gentle giant, a big baby. If someone was going to fail a fitness test, you could bet it was going to be him.'

Terry Venables is everything Chopper wasn't. 'I've no axe to grind with Terry, but I do think he was overrated as a player. There were fellas around him at Chelsea, like Bobby Tambling and George Graham, who were far better players. Off the field it was, "Come on, lads, let's do this or that," and everybody followed. But as soon as he went to Spurs, fellas like Jimmy Greaves, Alan Mullery and Dave Mackay didn't want to know.'

Chopper's brother Allan, who also played for Chelsea, was one of Tel's closest friends. 'My brother worked with him wherever he went,' Chopper says.

Following a brief coaching spell at Brentford, Chopper decided not to stay in football. But he has done allright for himself in the property market. Even though the taxman recently tackled him from behind, he is, at sixty, fairly comfortable; not on his uppers like his old mate Hudson.

He has met Roman Abramovich, and talked to him, through an interpreter, for an hour. He liked him, and liked the fact that Abramovich seemed to value his opinions. 'I've heard that Russians are very good at picking other people's brains.' Then he sent out a warning: 'Money doesn't always buy success. Mind you, Blackburn won the title with Jack Walker's money and, if you gave Sam Allardyce £90 million, he'd probably win it at Bolton. I must admit, I would like a limit on foreign players. Chelsea have only got one homegrown player, John Terry. He's similar to me in the way he plays, although the difference is that, when he tackles someone, the guy gets up afterwards. John Terry would run through a brick wall for Chelsea, but, if you look at some of the foreign players, I don't think you can say that. If you talk to some of the older supporters, there's not the same excitement as there would have been if three or four John Terrys were coming through. And I do think these foreigners deprive English lads of opportunities. If my own lads had a chance of going to Chelsea or a lower-league club, I'd send them to the lower-league club. I mean, this boy Huth has played for Germany. He's lucky to be a sub at Chelsea. And Scott Parker, if he had the opportunity of still playing regularly at Charlton or one in ten at Chelsea, which do you think he'd take? The other thing is the stuff that's come into the game since the foreign players came in, things like spitting. That never happened in my day. And manhandling in the area at free-kicks and corners. They always

y Wilkins, *left*, and Dennis Wise, *right*, both captained the side in different eras. til recently, they worked alongside one another as manager and coach at Millwall otball Club, *below*.

Gianfranco Zola spent seven seasons with the club. He was awarded with the ultimate accolade of being voted Chelsea's greatest ever player by the club's fans.

ınluca Vialli played under Ruud Gullit before eventually taking over as manager of elsea. He was controversially sacked by chairman, Ken Bates, yet he remains one of the st successful managers at the club. He is pictured with his European Cup-Winners' Cup dal, *below left*, and with the Coca Cola Cup, *below right*.

Another star who graced both the pitch and the sidelines is Ruud Gullit. He is picture
here in action, *above left*, and proudly holding the FA Cup in 1997, *above right* and *belo*

lsea beat Middlesbrough 2–0 in the FA Cup Final in 1997.

ove: A triumphant Dennis Wise clutches the trophy.

ow: The Chelsea squad celebrate their success.

Graeme Le Saux made more than 300 appearances for Chelsea in two spells at the cl

der the management of 'the Tinkerman', Chelsea stunned Europe when they played
io in the Champions League in 2003. Ranieri's team beat the Italian side 4–0.

Chelsea faced premiership rivals, Arsenal, in the 2004 Champions League Quarter Fin As Claudio Ranieri's future was in the balance, his spot-on tactics saw Chelsea beat th Gunners and qualify for the semi finals of the competition for the first time. A dejecte Arsenal are pictured, *below*.

used to do that in Serie A and we'd laugh at it. Now it's become the norm. And the national side has gone down the pan since the foreign players arrived. Where are all the top English goalkeepers now?'

Chopper explained his approach to playing. 'I seldom used to speak to anyone before or during a game. But my manager at Chelsea, Tommy Docherty, gave me a fantastic tip about man-marking. He told me to larrup somebody in the first few minutes, and after that just to stay behind them and cough every now and then, to show them I was not too far away.'

The tactic worked: Jimmy Greaves, who was marked nineteen times by Chopper, scored only once. Such is the respect that Greaves has for him, he wrote the foreword to his autobiography. It begins: 'I've been acquainted with Ron Harris, better known as "Chopper", for longer than I care to remember – and for most of that time I thought he was an evil git.'

Like Smith, Hunter and Stiles, however, Chopper could do more than chop, but it is for his toughness that he will always be remembered. He had his adversaries, though ... 'The toughest fella was a big Scotch geezer, broken nose, called Andy Lochhead. I knew if I got stuck into him I would get one back; that instead of me winning forty-love, it'd be deuce. Denis Law was the same. But only one fella ever got the better of me. A geezer called Mike Barnard, who played for Stoke and Everton. He came right over the top of the ball, and that was the only time I ever lay on the ground. My father used to say, "Never show 'em you're hurt," and, apart from that one time, I never did.'

After he retired, Harris tried management at Brentford, bought and developed a golf course and became a millionaire ... with Roy Bentley looking after his books!

Inception as Football League Club in 1905

Chelsea's history is synonymous with the club's love of exciting, big-name, free-scoring centre-forwards, and an affection for flamboyant goalkeepers. From Tommy Lawton to Jimmy Greaves to Peter Osgood, there have been big signings, big names and plenty of goals. In 1930, Chelsea paid out the huge sum of £10,000 on centre-forward Hughie Gallacher, while these days, of course, the record signing is striker Didier Drogba who cost £24 million, and whose wages come to more than £10,000 *a day*!

Trouble is that the club have always had problems in preventing goals at the other end, and have hired all shapes and sizes, from a variety of counties to keep goal.

The first Chelsea side was captained by an England and FA Cup-winning goalkeeper, the twenty-two-stone Willie Foulke, as Chelsea started life in the Second Division of the Football League with crowds occasionally topping 60,000. But there was not an instant surge of interest, with a mere 6,000 turning up for the very first game against Hull City in September 1905. Crowds ranged from the 3,000 that saw Chelsea play Lincoln to the 67,000 that crammed in for the Easter clash with Manchester United. At the end of the first season, the average gate at Stamford Bridge was over 13,000, with Newcastle top of the attendance league with an average crowd of over 22,000.

Foulke only played for just less than one season; it was rumoured that he once ate the entire pre-match meal for the whole team before his team-mates arrived at the hotel! He was a big attraction in every sense, but he died aged forty, after contracting pneumonia while making a living on Blackpool Sands facing penalties for a penny a time, and returning threepence to anyone who could beat him.

John Tait Robertson was signed from Southampton to become Chelsea's first player-manager. James Robertson, Bob McRoberts and Jimmy Windridge – an England international in the making – all signed from Small Heath for a combined fee of £340. Windridge went on to score more than fifty goals in seven years and played more games for the club than anyone else of his era. Ten further signings were made before the crucial vote from the Football League was made to admit Chelsea.

Despite misgivings about their lack of footballing pedigree, the number of signings, the stadium and stable finances swayed the vote, which took place just three weeks after the club was formed. Fred Parker also offered compensation for some of the travelling expenses incurred by Chelsea's opponents making the long journey to London.

Ground season tickets were sold at half a guinea for men and five shillings for women and children.

The club's baptism in the Football League ended on 2 September 1905 in a 1–0 defeat at Stockport County. Two days later, though, they beat Liverpool 4–0 in a friendly: match receipts for the game at the Bridge came to £102. Chelsea's opening two away fixtures in the league realised record receipts for Stockport County and Blackpool.

A crowd of only 6,000 turned up for the first league game at the Bridge, a 5–1 win over Hull City that included a Jimmy Windridge hat-trick, but then again the game was played on a Monday afternoon. Twelve days later, 20,000 turned out for the match against West Bromwich Albion, a big crowd in those days for a Second Division game. A quotation from *Football Chat Mag* was reproduced in that game's programme, which asked, 'It would be interesting to know if Chelsea's popularity is brought about by newspaper booming, Foulke's name, or curiosity to see the team who are being provided with the most palatial home of any club playing football.'

Chelsea finished third in their first season in the Second Divison and were in contention for promotion for a long time until Manchester United pulled away and finished nine points clear. Crowds increased as the new boys collected fifty-eight goals in nineteen home games, until 67,000 watched the match with Manchester United on Boxing Day. The popular *Chelsea Chronicle* programme sold 11,000 copies that day.

The club took just two seasons to reach the top flight as more signings were made before their second season. Bob Whiting replaced Foulke in goal, but the biggest impact was made by George Hilsdon, who was signed on a free transfer from West Ham United reserves. He scored five times on his debut, in a 9–2 win over Glossop North End on the opening day of the season. No one has achieved such a feat in the Football League since. He finished with twenty-seven goals as Chelsea romped to promotion, winning every game bar one, against eventual champions Nottingham Forest.

Season-ticket prices were now hiked up: the most expensive cost £220. Average gates were 17,000, with the highest at 45,000 for the Easter Sunday game with Hull. Among the visitors to Stamford Bridge that season were the Prince and Princess of Wales, who attended the annual fixture between the Army and the Royal Navy that was being staged at the ground.

The crowds were a fascinating mixture of the prosperous middle classes, the artistic bohemians of Chelsea and the working classes from Fulham and Battersea.

Relations between manager John Tait Robertson and the Board became strained, however; once he turned up drunk for training. The Board assumed team selection and, when Robertson failed to attend a Board meeting, he offered his resignation, asked for a free transfer and moved to Glossop. Remarkably, considering the circumstances, Chelsea had gained promotion only seventy-six league games after their formation.

David Calderhead joined from Lincoln City and remained as manager for twenty-six years. After one win in their opening eight games, Chelsea were bottom, but eventually rallied to finish in thirteenth – attendances topped 50,000 in two games, against Woolwich Arsenal and Manchester City. Next season they improved to finish in eleventh, though the threat of relegation hovered over them until the penultimate game.

Despite investing in star names, including the amateur Vivian Woodward – a veteran of the famous Corinthians side – Chelsea were relegated in 1910 after losing a crucial game to Tottenham Hotspur, whose winning goal was scored by Percy Humphreys, a player who had left the Bridge just four months earlier. Chelsea tried to buy their way out of relegation with four late signings, but the Football League took great exception to such unsporting behaviour and introduced the transfer deadline. Relegation was hard to take, particularly as gates were soaring – 70,000 turned out for the Christmas fixture against Newcastle United, a record for a fixture in England at the time.

While still fighting to return to the big time, Chelsea did reach the FA Cup semi-finals, although they lost 3–0 against Newcastle United. And, although Chelsea returned to the big time two years later, and struggled, their best performances were reserved for the FA Cup.

Chelsea's FA Cup history began with a 7–1 defeat at the hands of Crystal Palace – but it clashed with a league game on the same date, so Chelsea fielded a reserve side for the Cup tie. The FA immediately introduced a rule that clubs must field their strongest possible sides in their competitions. Chelsea reached the semi-final as a Second Division club in 1911, without facing a team from the higher league and, in the quarter-final against Swindon Town, attracted a 78,000 Bridge crowd: not only was it a ground record, it was also the highest attendance for any FA Cup tie outside the final.

However, Chelsea reached their first FA Cup final within ten years of the club's formation. In 1914, the club had crashed out of the competition in a first-round replay against Southern League side Millwall – who wouldn't be elected to the Football League until they became a founding member of the Third Division South in 1920. A year later, in 1915, Chelsea reached the final, despite having endured a dreadful league season where they finished one from the bottom of the First Division and were relegated. The stars of the Cup run were Harold Halse, who scored three in each half against Manchester City in the first Charity Shield match at the Bridge, Bob Thompson, a one-eyed centre-forward, and Bob McNeil, the first of many tricky Scottish wingers to become favourites at the Bridge. Unfortunately, Chelsea lost the final against Sheffield United at Old Trafford. Lieutenant Vivian Woodward was given leave from his war duties to play in the final, but, despite the pleadings of the directors, he refused to play, insisting that the players who had been successful in the earlier rounds deserved to participate. Chelsea lost 3–0.

The team stayed in the north for their final two league games, both of which they had to win to stay up: they failed to do so, and were relegated for the second time in the first decade of their existence.

When normal football resumed in August 1919, Chelsea were reinstated into the top flight in unusual circumstances. A Football League inquiry in December 1915 judged that the game on the previous Good Friday between

Manchester United and Liverpool had been fixed in United's favour. United had won the game 2–0 and the win had seen them finish one place and one point above Chelsea. However, the Football League felt that United had been the victim of an act by an individual so took no action against them. There was great sympathy for Chelsea though, and, when they opted to stay loyal to the Football League following the threat of a London breakaway, they were rewarded by being voted back into the top division. So, four years after being relegated, Chelsea were back – and they had not played a single game! They celebrated by finishing third in the league and reaching the FA Cup semi-finals.

Royalty began to frequent the Bridge: King Alphonso of Spain attended a game in November and he was followed by a visit from His Majesty King George V, who attended the FA Cup tie against Leicester. The team reached the FA Cup semi-finals, but defeat by Villa saved the FA's blushes: the final was due to be played at Stamford Bridge for the first three years after the war as Crystal Palace was unavailable after being used as a supply depot.

Scottish international Andy Wilson was signed for £6,500 in November 1923, but he failed to steer the club away from relegation and the forward went on to spend six seasons with Chelsea in the Second Division.

With only two teams going up, Chelsea's six-year stint in the Second Division was the longest they had been out of the top flight. They still attracted healthy crowds, however, with attendances continuing to average 30,000. The club finally gained promotion in 1930. The drive to promotion was inspried after a trend-setting tour to Argentina – even though the journey took a fortnight's sea voyage in those days!

Half of the Scottish forward line was bought when Chelsea returned to Division One, including £10,000 crazy centre-forward Hughie Gallacher, Newcastle's demon goalscorer, who never contemplated leaving his beloved North-East where he had become a hero. The first he knew of the deal came when Chelsea chairman Claude Kirby and chief scout Jack Fraser knocked on his door only a few hours after he had returned to his native Scotland for the summer break. Newcastle buckled to the big-money deal, the first five-figure transfer in the history of the game! Other big-name signings brought the fans out in droves – the first five home gates were all in excess of 50,000 – but a sixth-round FA Cup exit and a twelfth-place finish in the league was a big let-down.

Gallacher collected thirty goals in forty-one games the following year.

Chelsea reached the FA Cup semi-final, where they lost to Newcastle. During the Cup run, Gallacher scored five goals, including the winner at Liverpool to book the semi-final showdown with his old club. He scored again, but it was not enough to prevent a 2–1 defeat. Gallacher managed nineteen goals the following season, but relegation was only avoided with a 4–1 win at Manchester City in the penultimate game, with the Scot bagging a hat-trick.

Leslie Knighton succeeded Calderhead as manager and had problems controlling Gallacher: the Scot had a notoriously short fuse and did not like the training regime. After scoring eighty-one goals in 144 games, Gallagher was sold to Derby: his career total of 387 goals is the fourth highest of any British player. Sadly he committed suicide by throwing himself under a train following domestic problems several years after the Second World War.

Despite Chelsea's star-studded sides, the team only finished higher than tenth once in the 1930s and, although always avoiding relegation, they finished in the bottom five three times.

The 1930s were dominated by Herbert Chapman's Arsenal, but Chelsea usually made some spectacular signings in this era without having much success. The Football League's record gate (82,905) was attained when Arsenal visited the Bridge in 1935. Only Manchester United, playing at Maine Road in 1948, also against Arsenal, would break that record. Knighton handed over the reigns to Billy Birrell from QPR, but the 1939–40 season was only three games old when the start of the Second World War brought a halt to proceedings.

Goalscorers always added some light relief to the comical showbusiness aura that surrounded the underachievers. Joe Payne was recruited from Luton, where he set the Football League record by scoring ten goals in a game.

George Hilsdon became the first Chelsea player to score 100 goals. He won eight England caps, scoring fourteen, including four in a 7–0 win over Hungary. Nicknamed the 'Gatling Gun' because of his prodigious strike rate, he scored five on his debut against Glossop in 1906. He also became a frequent visitor to the inns and taverns of Fulham and Battersea: his enjoyment of beer and women's company seemed to slow him down somewhat – his form deserted him and he moved to West Ham on a free transfer. He never recovered from an illness he contracted as a result of a mustard gas attack in Arras during the First World War and, when he died in 1941, only four people attended his funeral. He had been popular in his day, however, to the extent that the club erected a weather vane in his image over the only stand, the East Stand, in his memory. In recent years, the vane could be seen on the West Stand, but in the summer of 1997 with the demolition of that side, it was moved across back to the East Stand – and was given another coat of paint. Other stars of that time included right-back George Barber – a free transfer from Luton who made 294 appearances – and, after the Second World War, Tommy Lawton, who was signed from Everton for £11,500. A crowd of 53,000 watched his two-goal debut, and his second appearance came in the famous match against Moscow Dynamo just three days later.

The prestigious friendly attracted an official crowd of 74,496 supplemented by an estimated additional 25,000. It finished 3–3 when referee Lieutenant Commander George Clark allowed an offside goal to stand, but has gone down in Chelsea's history as one of the most endearing and enduring memories. Chelsea went two up, the Russians levelled and Lawton scored the third. Lawton said, 'For their third goal, this small bloke was ten yards offside and the referee told me he's given it for diplomatic reasons. Diplomatic reasons ... you've just done us out of our win bonus.'

A million fans flocked to the Bridge in season 1946–47 as Lawton amassed thirty goals in thirty-nine games, but the following season he wanted to leave. Lawton managed a final tally of thirty-five goals in fifty-three games, but was sold off to Third Division South side Notts County for a then British record fee of £20,000. Chelsea went on to finish eighteenth without him.

Roy Bentley arrived from Newcastle to become the next goalscoring icon. The club survived relegation by 0.044 of a goal in the year that Spurs won their first championship. Birrell retired and, although he had taken the club to two FA Cup semi-finals in his thirteen-year reign, he had still not collected any silverware, despite the big-name signings he had made for the club. The mould was finally broken in 1955 under Ted Drake, an era dealt with in greater detail in other parts of this book.

But fifteen barren years followed the championship success, until the Glory Days of the King's Road set in the 1970s, when the team was inspired by Osgood, Hudson and Cooke: the side won both the FA Cup and Cup-Winners' Cup.

But the love affair with goalscorers and goalkeepers continued throughout the barren years.

Chelsea signed Reg Matthews in 1956 for £20,000 – a then record fee for a goalkeeper, but he ended up losing his place to eighteen-year-old youth product Peter Bonetti, who went on to play 729 games. During Bonetti's formidable nineteen-year reign, Alex Stepney was signed for a world record fee for a 'keeper at the time, £50,000 in 1968, but he played just one game before being sold for the same sum.

Chelsea did win the League Cup in 1965, but in those days it was not regarded as one of the major tournaments. Left-back Eddie McCreadie was used as a centre-forward, and ran seventy yards through the mud to score the winning goal in five against Leicester and England 'keeper Gordon Banks. As it was then a two-legged final, Chelsea won the Cup deploying Inter Milan tactics and earning a goalless draw. McCreadie went on to play in the '67 and '70 FA Cup finals, but was unfit for the Cup-Winners' Cup final, and, by the time of the 1975 League Cup final, he was out of favour. Although he then became club captain, he never managed to hold down a regular place again. After 410 games he became youth coach and, when relegation arrived in 1975, he was appointed first-team manager. Chelsea gained promotion in 1977, but McCreadie walked out before a ball was kicked in the First Division. An argument over his contract and a club car was to blame. He overcame his fear of flying to move to the US, but his obsessive drinking caused him to miss two years from his working life. He recovered to settle in Memphis.

Off-the-field activities broke up the Osgood, Hudson, Cooke era, and the search for a new team brought a profusion of hit-and-miss signings.

Robert Fleck was signed for a new club record £2.1 million, half a million more than the previous highest, but he managed only four goals in forty-eight games before being sold back to Norwich for £650,000. In his last full season, he was not selected once.

Relegated in 1987, Bobby Campbell steered the club back in 1989: they also won the Full Members Cup before a huge Wembley crowd of 76,369. Campbell was replaced by Ian Porterfield, but Chelsea were fighting relegation to the Second Division.

David Speedie was another of Chelsea's fiery Scottish strikers. He scored a wonderful hat-trick in the Full Members Cup Final at Wembley in 1986. Speedie and Kerry Dixon formed one of the brightest strike partnerships in the league, but Speedie fell out with new manager John Hollins and was 'barred' from first team training for a spell, and was then moved on to Coventry.

Managers were also soon becoming big-name signings and Chelsea joined the trend when they signed Glenn Hoddle from Swindon Town: the new manager changed Chelsea's image and brought a style of football which lightened the mood of the fans. Twice Hoddle led the club to Wembley but, more importantly, he stabilised the team, headed off relegation and began a transitional period, a familiar term for teams going through a bad time in the hope of coming through at the end of it.

J

Glen Johnson: The First of the Roman Abramovich Signings

A spoof email circulated around the inner sanctum of the Stamford Bridge hierarchy just twenty-four hours after Roman Abramovich's shock takeover: 'Now we are owned by a man with £5.4 billion, we are in the market to buy just about any top player in the world ... and the first one he's bought is Emile Heskey.'

Ken Bates and his chief executive Trevor Birch had set up options for Scott Parker and Joe Cole at £6 million each pre-Abramovich. But the takeover provided Claudio Ranieri with an unprecedented choice of any of the world's top midfielders and that was initially a bitter blow to Cole and Parker. However, the major problem lay in convincing a number of those players that Chelsea would become the dominant force within European football.

So, although the wish list may have contained some luminaries from all over the world, including such Premiership leading lights as Thierry Henry, Patrick Vieira and Steven Gerrard, it was the little-known England Under-21 right-back Glen Johnson who has the remarkable distinction of being the first of the £250 million worth of Abramovich's signings.

The ramifications of the Russian multi-billionaire's takeover were still sinking in and the expectancy arose of all manner of world-class star signings, including Ronaldo: imagine the surprise when the first player to sign up was a virtual unknown from West Ham.

His first season under Claudio Ranieri was a learning curve for the youngster, but then came the arrival of Champions League winner Jose Mourinho from Porto which triggered a new regime that saw Chelsea catapult to the top of the Premiership. Along with Mourinho came a £14 million right-back in Paulo Ferreira and limited chances for Johnson.

But Johnson was impressed with the Mourinho regime, as he observed, 'You can go out and buy the best players in the world, but it doesn't mean you are going to win anything if everybody doesn't get on and they are not willing to work for each other. The main difference between now and last season is team spirit. Everyone is willing to work for each other and put their neck on the line. The other day, sixteen of us went round to John Terry's house to play an ISS Pro computer game tournament on the PlayStation. We had loads of TVs set up and games going at once. We do loads of things like that and we went paintballing for our Christmas party as well.

'We've definitely got a team to dominate for years. The players we have here are the best in the world – it's like a dream team – and I like the feeling we're almost unbeatable.'

Johnson could hardly believe it when the Abramovich takeover went through and he was heading off in early July to Roccaporena – Ranieri's favoured training camp – as the club reached agreement on their first signing. Johnson signed a five-year contract following his surprise £6 million move from West Ham. A right-back to replace Albert Ferrer was sorted. The eighteen-year-old was 'gobsmacked' to be the first of so many new arrivals. His initial reaction: 'I just want to get out there and to get to know everybody. They are a great club. There are lots of internationals here and I can't wait to play with all the players.'

He had become the most expensive teenager in Chelsea's history. 'This is a massive step for me, a big learning curve. It was hard for me to leave West Ham, but I couldn't let this chance slip. This time last year I was still in West Ham's reserve team and now I'm looking at playing in the Champions League. It's hard to take in how quickly everything has happened. My only target this season is to secure a first-team place.'

There was time for a change of lifestyle as well. 'I'm at Dartford at the moment and I'm buying another place not far away with my mum.'

Johnson rates his assets as both attacking and defending, but he confessed, 'When I was younger I was a striker and then, when I changed to defender, I had a bit of both in me. I was in the Under-14s and my manager said he was going to try me out as a centre-back, and that was it, I never played centre-forward again for a few years.' Johnson's move triggered a frenzy in the transfer market. Chelsea tried to sign Henry and would have probably paid a world-record £50 million, eclipsing Zidane's £46.5 million move from Juventus to Real Madrid two years earlier. Peter Hill-Wood and David Dein made it clear, when Chelsea put the feelers out, that neither Henry nor Vieira was for sale at any price.

Ranieri made light of some of the more glamorous and outrageous names linked with his club. 'Raul tonight, tomorrow it is Rivaldo,' said Ranieri. 'Maybe Raul must renew his contract.'

Speaking at their training camp in southern Italy, the manager went on to say, 'Throughout my career I've had to fight on my feet at clubs where the situations have been tough, really tough. But at Chelsea, with Mr Abramovich, the expectations are now very different and we have to start winning big trophies very soon before getting to the top of European football. I started in football management fifteen years ago at the very bottom, but now I think we have the chance to go right to the summit. Abramovich told me and the players that he wants to be the top club in Europe.

'In my opinion, Mr Abramovich represents a gigantic opportunity for this club and Chelsea have to make the very most of it. I can even say that, if Roma offered me the manager's job today, I'd tell them, "No, I want to win every trophy possible with Chelsea and then we will talk about it!"'

Ranieri believed that Abramovich was another Silvio Berlusconi – the Italian millionaire who bought a bankrupt AC Milan, who were then in Italy's Second Division, and turned them into the club which dominated Europe for a decade. Ranieri said, beaming: 'I met Mr Abramovich only a day or two after he bought the club and, the truth is, everything I see of him reminds me of Berlusconi when he arrived in football and decided to make Milan great. Our meeting was in Chelsea's offices and, although there was an interpreter, Mr Abramovich told me to speak in English because he could understand me well enough. He spoke in Russian and the meeting lasted about one hour during which I told him straight that I saw no reason for him to get rid of me. I simply told him the truth; that last season people called us no-hopers but we made it into the Champions League and that, like us, he should be proud of that.

'But I also told the new owner that it was already in my plans that we should do much better this season. The thing was, he knows everything in real detail and was obviously well informed before he bought the club. I don't know how he made his millions and it doesn't matter to me compared to the knowledge that he wants great things for Chelsea.'

He observed, 'How much better is it this summer compared to the last one? I can tell you last summer I put my list to the club and not one of the players ended up joining because Chelsea had financial problems. For sure we'll do better in the market this time. In fact, I think it will be totally different. Mr Abramovich has already signed Geremi and I think that is fantastic for Chelsea. I've tried to get him for two seasons without success. I want his power and ability, plus he can play comfortably in right midfield, centre midfield, right-back and centre defence. As for young Glen Johnson, I think he is a phenomenon, fast and skilful.'

The players kept on arriving: Wayne Bridge for £7 million, and Blackburn finally accepted a £17 million offer for the twenty-four-year-old Republic of Ireland winger Damien Duff, after they had rejected three bids. The bid triggered a get-out clause in his contract.

Duff arrived at the Bridge in a black cab and admitted that he had thought long and hard for days over the deal. He said, 'This was probably the biggest decision of my life and I didn't want to rush it. I had seven great years at Blackburn and there was no big reason to move. It was just a matter of thinking everything through. It looks as though great things are going to happen at Chelsea. It just feels right. It is a big, big chance and I can't wait.'

Duff would have to carry the highest price tag ever attached to an Irishman, but he was determined not to let it weigh him down. 'It is a great honour for myself and my family. But the most important thing is to do it on the pitch now and, hopefully, I can do it all for Chelsea. All the talk about money doesn't really bother me at all. All I like to do is to get on with my football. Of course, people are expecting huge things from us, especially after the money that has been spent. Every year, Chelsea are expected to do well and even more so now. So we hope that we can do it. But we won't feel that extra pressure down at the training ground or, hopefully, on match days. We are just worried about playing football and getting the right results.'

Before the Abramovich takeover, Liverpool were always regarded as favourites to sign Duff, but Houllier was told that £10 million did not come close to activating the release clause. Duff had made a name for himself in the 2002 World Cup and had acquired a liking for the big stage. He admitted, 'I know I'm more than capable of holding my own among the best players in the world. I've always been confident in the ability and talent I have.'

Former Ewood Park boss Kenny Dalglish said, 'Damien has developed into one of the most entertaining players in the game. He is a smashing lad off the pitch and I'm sure a high-profile move won't affect him in any way. Certainly, I have seen no change in him as his career has developed from an unknown into one of the most famous names in the Premier League.'

With Duff and Bridge signing within hours of each other, Abramovich took his summer spending spree to £36.5 million in just twenty-one days, and Ranieri continued to deliver on his pledge to keep a British backbone to the side. Bridge said, 'You need a certain number of British players if you are going to succeed in the Premier League and Chelsea now have more than they have had for quite a few years. You hear talk of the new owner coming in and drawing up lists of players, but the players Chelsea have brought in are clearly people that Claudio Ranieri has spotted and liked the look of. I've played quite a bit alongside John Terry with the England Under-21s and he is a real leader. He is so composed on the ball, he always seems to have time and he is the sort of player you want to play alongside. Like most people, I haven't seen much of Glen Johnson – but I have seen enough to know he is a very promising player. I played against him at St Mary's last season and he's a player who gets up and down well and seems comfortable when he is going forward as well as being a strong tackler. Both are players I would like to play alongside for England as well as Chelsea, although you don't like to look too far ahead.'

The left-back had been ribbed by his former Southampton team-mates ever since Abramovich's arrival when his name was first linked with the impending spending spree. Bridge acquired a new Russian nickname. 'As soon as Mr Abramovich came in, it was obvious that Chelsea were going to be able to buy the sort of players they could only have dreamed of in the past. Since the rumours started about me, my Southampton team-mates have given me a few new nicknames. James Beattie has called me "Stamford" and "Bridgeovski". And he also reckons I'm going to have a daughter called "Chelsea".'

Asked what had finally made up his mind, Duff responded, 'I suppose it was the gut feeling I had when I came down here. In the past week, I've flown down about three times. It just feels right. It's time to move on to a big new challenge for me. The easy thing would have been to have stayed at Blackburn where I was happy and played every week. Here I'm not guaranteed my place, but it's a big challenge that I couldn't turn down.'

Duff was just ten minutes away from taking off on Blackburn's flight to the United States for a pre-season training camp when the call came through that a fee had been agreed with Chelsea. He took a further week to make up his mind after consulting friends, family and colleagues. Graeme Souness told him in the departure lounge at Manchester Airport that Chelsea had raised their offer to meet the buy-out clause.

'I'd heard snippets all week, but I was getting on the plane when the gaffer said that Blackburn had accepted an offer and, with ten minutes to go, I'd better make my mind up! After I missed the flight, it took me about a week to make the final decision as I rang everybody I knew. I wasn't going to make a snap decision as it was the biggest decision of my life. But I think I've made the right one and, hopefully, that will show on the pitch. Who knows who we'll be bringing in over the next couple of weeks, but the squad already looks strong and we're just looking forward to the season starting.'

His rise to one of the most highly prized footballers of his generation has naturally meant that he's had to cope with an intense interest both in his professional and his private life. In the 2002 World Cup, he was mortified when his mother Mary revealed to the Irish nation that her son played with a Padre Pio medal stitched inside his sock.

After having exchanged a country cottage in the Ribble Valley for the frenzy and noise of the King's Road, he said, 'People seem to think that I'm some kind of country hick who spent all my time in the hills above Blackburn. That's just rubbish. I'm an Irishman and I enjoy a good night out and what have you ... but only at the right time. I've come here to play football. Everything else can wait its turn.'

Graeme Le Saux flew back from Roccaporena to become the first big-name casualty of the takeover, shipped off to Southampton as Gordon Strachan made it clear that no deal for Bridge would have taken place otherwise. The then Saints manager said, 'We may have lost one of the best young full-backs in the country, but we have one of the most experienced around as a replacement. Le Saux falls into the category immediately behind Bridge and Ashley Cole. There would certainly not have been a deal with Chelsea if Le Saux had not been a part of it.'

Le Saux moved on a free transfer and also received a 'leaving present', rather than the reported solution that Chelsea would continue to pay half of his salary – it amounted to the same sum. Chelsea also paid the fees of Le

Saux's agent and those of Bridge to raise the costs by a further £1 million. After signing a two-year deal, Le Saux said, 'There is some sadness in leaving Chelsea after eleven years, but the flip side is the buzz of joining a club where I have always felt at home. I used to come over from Jersey for soccer camps here when I was a teenager. The move happened quickly, but these things often do.'

Le Saux made more than 300 appearances for Chelsea in two spells and won the Premiership title with Blackburn in between. He also played thirty-six times for England.

Saints chairman Rupert Lowe, who beat off competition from rivals Portsmouth to nab Le Saux, believed the player's immense experience could make up for the loss of Bridge. Lowe moaned, 'If someone insists on going and hands in a transfer request, we have to decide what is in the best interests of the club. You can't make someone play if they don't want to be here – but, if Roman Abramovich had not taken over at Chelsea, Bridge would still be a Southampton player.'

Even before Abramovich arrived, Le Saux was deep in contract talks that were not progressing very well. He had a year to run and the club were in no mood for improved terms to keep him. 'It didn't come as a shock at all,' Le Saux said. 'I realised it was time to move on. I was never in a position to leave myself open to regret. I don't make decisions lightly.'

Like Zola, he conducted his departure with dignity. 'I have good friends who are Chelsea supporters and I still speak to some of the players. Like everyone who's interested in the sport, I'm looking at what's happening there from a general perspective – whether they are going to gel or not, whether it's a risk – although, when a man's that wealthy, it's not really a risk. Chelsea have suddenly inherited huge wealth and are spending at an excessive rate. But it's taken Manchester United, and other teams like Arsenal and Newcastle, a long time to build a successful team; a team not just of expensive players but of quality and based on camaraderie. It undervalues what United have achieved over the past few years just to say that success is based on wealth. There's far more to it than that. You need a spirit and money can't buy you that.'

Le Saux knows how money can construct a championship side, having been part of the Blackburn Rovers team which won the Premier League in 1995 with the assistance of Sir Jack Walker's millions. He dismisses direct parallels, pointing out that the investment at Blackburn was less sudden and that some of the buys – himself included – were hardly expensive. His hope is that Abramovich's wealth does not harm the game.

'That's something we will have to find out. It is potentially a concern for football in England when the sport is going through a difficult time financially. We all hope that it doesn't destabilise an already fragile market. It is naive to say that money brings success, because football has a nasty habit of disproving that philosophy. It will be interesting to see what happens, but there is no tinge of regret that I am not in there.'

Before the Champions League tie in Rome with Lazio, Johnson said, 'I have to pinch myself when I look back on the last twelve months. If you had told me how my professional career would unfold, I would have fallen about laughing. I look around at all these World Cup stars and, of course, I'm enjoying everything about it. I feel I'm improving as a player every minute I spend here. To think I played just fourteen games for West Ham last season – it was bound to surprise me how quickly everything happened. It's exciting – I'm sure there are a lot of players who would like to find themselves in my shoes. I didn't really know what to expect. I'd been at West Ham all my life and I didn't have a clue how other clubs worked. Seeing them and watching them training blows you away. Don't get me wrong, I'm not star-struck – I'm just excited about being around all of this. The sky really is the limit for me. I'm playing for the England Under-21s and I look at the full national side and I want to be part of it as well.

'The spending brings its own pressure, I guess. It's got nothing to do with me how much money Roman Abramovich has got or how he spends it. I don't pay much attention to it. But good luck to him. It's blatantly obvious that everyone will want to beat us this season, but I can tell you we are all up for it. We have more than enough good players to cope with that. People talk about all the individuals and whether they can play as a team. But of course they can play as a team – of course they can win the title. They're good enough players and once they get to know each other and how they like to play, they are just going to get better.

'I use to watch Desailly on television as a kid. He's a model professional, a great example of what you want to aspire to. If there is one player I look up to, it's Marcel. His attitude is incredible. Despite everything he has won in the game, he still has the hunger and attitude to go on and win more. He gets involved in everything. He has such enthusiasm for the game and if he makes a mistake he's not too big to hold his hands up. He's always talking to me, he's just a top man. He's one of the best defenders in the world and he's just so down to earth. He says to me, "If I make a mistake, don't be too frightened to tell me I've done something wrong." Can you believe that? I've done nothing in the game and he's won everything there is to win.'

Johnson maintained that the move will never change his outlook on life. 'It's nice, but I haven't forgotten where I've come from or how much I have to learn. It's not hard for me to keep my feet on the ground. I'm not that sort of boy anyway, I won't let things go to my head. I have the right sort of people around me who won't let that happen – particularly my mum.'

For many of the existing players, it was a huge challenge to adapt to the mushrooming squad. Gudjohnsen praised his dad Arnor, a winger with Anderlecht during their heyday in the 1980s, for convincing him to stay and contest a place. 'No one was expecting the transformation that went on at Chelsea in the summer. On a personal level, it's not easy when you're not playing regularly or involved. We all know that we can be brilliant in one game and still be on the bench or watching from the stands for the next. It's difficult, but we all know the situation. I saw my name was being thrown around in the papers and I was being linked with other clubs. But I called my dad at the start of the season and we had a long chat. He told me it is a matter of rising to the challenge. He said you couldn't find a top team in Europe now that hasn't got three or four top strikers in the squad. He said if I play to my best I'll have nothing to worry about. He faced a similar situation when he was a player. In his day, Anderlecht were a big, big side and he stayed there for seven years and fought for his place. So he understood precisely how I felt. It made me feel a lot better. It's great to have your family supporting you. I feel privileged that my dad really understands what the situation is.

'I was reminded of how it had been when I joined Chelsea. I arrived at the same time as Jimmy-Floyd Hasselbaink, and Gianfranco Zola and Tore-Andre Flo were already here, so there were four top strikers then, just as there are now. It's basically the same situation. There was a period, in pre-season, when there was a lot of uncertainty, a lot of rumours flying about, but now that the new players have been signed, the atmosphere is less feverish and everything has settled down. Mr Abramovich has made clear his intentions to make this club the biggest and best and so has Ranieri. He wants a big squad to enable him to change things around and constantly to have fresh legs in the team. At the moment, it's working very well. Sometimes it is hard to sit in the stand and watch the game but, to be fair, Ranieri made it clear before the season started that it would be like this. He told us that, if people couldn't handle it, they could go to him and say, "I need to play every week," in which case they'd be allowed to try somewhere else. That offer was there for everyone.'

Had Gudjohnsen been tempted by it? 'No, I want to be here. That's why I signed a new contract. If you want to be at a top club, you are always going to have to face up to big competition and, after thinking about it, I decided that this was what I wanted to do. I want to compete for a place in a team like this. I feel I've got a lot more to show the Chelsea fans, and I know that, when I play at my best, the team benefits.'

As the recently appointed captain of his country, he felt in no way inferior as part of the Stamford Bridge galaxy. 'The other strikers here are very good players, with big reputations, but I think I've built my own reputation in England, and we all have great respect for each other. We're all aiming for silverware this season and, if we can hold up a trophy at the end, we'll all be happy with the part we've played.'

It wasn't long before Johnson made the grade to his first England call-up. Bridge said at the time, 'Glen definitely deserves a chance and Gary Neville now has a contender for his place. Some people may say he's too young, but he's going to learn a lot this year. He's definitely got a chance and it'd be great to see us playing in the same England team. I'd like to think he'll get his chance in this friendly.'

Chelsea were delighted when it became official, even though it meant a bonus for West Ham should he play for his country at senior level. Johnson said, 'Mr Ranieri told me straight after the game about England. He said, "Congratulations, Sven has picked you. Enjoy it." It was just minutes after the whistle went. Everyone was there waiting to shake my hand – all the players. They said "congratulations" and "hopefully you will be there for years". Obviously I have achieved something being in the squad, but I have a lot of work to do. I have certainly not made it. Gary Neville has played at right-back for years and deservedly so. There is nobody better than him. I am still learning, so I have to be patient. After all, I have only played five times for the Under-21s. Or rather four-and-a-half as I got sent off against

Turkey! But, after being picked for England, I have received lots of calls and text messages, particularly from my old team-mates at West Ham. Sunday could not have gone better. I was not aware I was the only non-international playing outfield. I look round the dressing room and see the famous faces. But not being an international like the others was hardly a question I asked myself. But hopefully that situation will change soon. I will certainly not be put off by all the big names. I find it exciting. I will just enjoy it playing at Old Trafford. I played for West Ham last season when we lost 6–0. I came on for ten minutes, so I do not exactly have fond memories of the place.

'I have mates who are Chelsea fans who cannot believe what has happened. They were certainly shocked when I joined. Actually, they didn't believe me – they thought I was winding them up. When they finally believed me, they were so happy. They come and watch me all the time. I always sort my mates out for tickets. But some people rang and said, "Remember when we used to play football out the front when we were ten." When I arrived I did not know whether I would be in the first team or in the reserves, but I would like to think that I have established myself.'

The club captain at the time of his England call-up, Marcel Desailly, said, 'Glen Johnson has great quality for the future. He is still making small mistakes, but you can feel he's going to be one of the best right-backs in the world.'

Johnson had two sendings-off already that season – one for England Under-21s and the other at Lazio. Bridge said, 'I only saw one of the yellow cards against Turkey and I thought it was a bit harsh. He's young so he's still learning. He'll learn from the one against Lazio and I doubt he'll do it again. He knows he made a little mistake and he can put it behind him. He's big enough and man enough not to do it again. He's growing up quick. He's down to earth and works hard and has got his head screwed on.'

Ranieri said, 'I hoped Glen would be in the England squad. He has a very good future and now he must improve more. And I'm sure he's an intelligent man, so he will improve. He has a very bright future. His skill is fantastic. Physically he can run for two matches and never stands still. When I chose him I remembered when he played against us – he was fantastic. I also looked at videos of him and was very impressed.' Johnson joined up with Terry, Lampard and Cole in the England squad.

Hernan Crespo urged Eriksson to select Johnson. 'He is one of the best young players in his position that I have ever seen. He has a great future and

I am really happy to know he will play in the England national team. He must play in Portugal. He has come from West Ham, so he is still trying to adapt himself to a bigger club, but he is growing up and he is in the right lane. Considering he is so young, he has already shown that he can play well in a big team. If he plays for England, he will perform well because he has a lot of confidence.'

Johnson came on in the first half for the injured Gary Neville, while Joe Cole played all but the last fifteen minutes of the 3–2 defeat by Denmark and scored his second international goal. Cole said, 'I loved it. We were disappointed with the result, but if I keep on scoring and making goals I'll get a run in the team, I'm sure.'

Eriksson was impressed. 'Joe is another great talent. He is getting better and better and his quality is incredible.'

But Cole was dispossessed in the move which led to Denmark's first goal. Eriksson said, 'He still has things to learn about the game. I can talk to him and I'm sure I'm not the only one talking to him. Claudio Ranieri does the same. It's more or less the only thing he still has to learn. He can change a game offensively. Unfortunately, in football it's not only going that way [attacking]. You have to take positions and not give your opponents the opportunity to counter-attack easily. He will learn a lot during the next six to seven months. Maybe you have to expect he will lose the ball and that it's the price you pay for having him in, but today I think that if you want to be a complete player you have to learn a lot. If you try to create you have to be careful. You can't afford to lose the ball in midfield. You don't meet many teams today with slow strikers. They all have pace, so it's important.'

Cole was not too perturbed. 'I was a long way up the pitch and you're going to lose the ball sometimes.'

Cole was one of six Chelsea players on the Old Trafford pitch at one stage, with Lampard, Terry, Bridge and Johnson for England and Gronkjaer in the Denmark team.

Terry remarked, 'I was saying the day before the Denmark game that it is usually Manchester United who are the ones with four, five or six players in the squad. But with the takeover we've managed to get some good players in – and thankfully they are English as well. It is a massive change. I remember a couple of years ago when there wasn't one English player in the Chelsea starting line-up. Then you look around at Old Trafford on Sunday and saw five of the Chelsea players in an England shirt. Five is a hell of a lot, but it's great, fantastic. It just goes to show how well we've been doing this year ... Are Chelsea the new power in the land? Maybe. We will have to see, but our target is to keep our places. We've got to take our opportunities in the friendlies.'

Johnson is not lacking in confidence. 'Playing with Chelsea in the Champions League must help me have a chance of reaching Euro 2004. I have no fear: I have never been afraid of taking my chance and that's what I want to do. It is exciting being around England, there are a lot of great young players, and I think the future looks bright with Rooney and Cole and players like that. I'm just on a roller-coaster ride and enjoying every minute of it.'

K

Peter Kenyon and the New Chelsea Badge

Peter Kenyon is the highest-paid chief executive in football, and since his arrival at the Bridge he has been by far the most controversial.

Snapped courting Sven-Goran Eriksson and accused of tapping Ashley Cole, he's been targeted for just about everything, but there is little doubt that he is also masterminding a Russian revolution of enormous significance in west London.

Kenyon is masterminding a five-year vision under Roman Abramovich. Initial heavy spending, borne out by the publication of record losses for a British club, was quickly followed by Kenyon's declaration that the intention was to become a profitable business. Kenyon says, 'Clearly by not buying as many players, that has a significant impact. I think, if you look at the trend in 2003–04, we spent a massive £175 million; in 2004–05 we spent £88 million; and in 2005–06 it will be considerably less.'

For the year to 30 June 2004 – Abramovich's first year at the helm – Chelsea made losses of £87.8 million. Such a figure dwarfs the previous highest losses posted by a British club – the £49.5 million announced by Leeds in 2003.

But Kenyon maintains that, behind the heavy spending on players, there is a prudent approach that will reap long-term success and ensure stability for Chelsea. 'I think that's where we've been responsible, looking at the long-term view on Chelsea. Chelsea will be around long after myself and Mr

Abramovich have gone, so it is our job not to just look after Chelsea this year but to ensure that Chelsea are in good shape for years to come. And there's no better way of doing that than ensuring the long-term viability of the club to make sure that, even if it's not making massive profits, it's not losing lots of money.

'The ultimate security for Chelsea is that we run this as a business. It has been portrayed as though this is some sort of hobby. It's not a hobby. Roman is at Chelsea for the long run. He has bought in completely to the vision of making this club one of the biggest and best in Europe. This was not a vanity purchase for the owner. It is a serious investment with a long-term business plan.'

The Adidas deal is part of that. 'We believe a global partnership with Adidas will be a huge step in helping the club achieve its long-term strategic goals. Two years ago, we were seen as streets paved with gold. That is over. Chelsea is now being run properly.'

Kenyon set 'some aggressive targets' for reducing the club's payroll and one of those was that Mourinho was happy to work with a squad of twenty-four players. Kenyon admitted, 'Our squad was too large and too expensive.'

Chelsea hope to target key geographical areas, including America and China, in order to expand their fan base and income. With accounts like today's, they might need it.

Chelsea are also top of the league for salaries, with its annual wage bill having soared from £55 million to a staggering £115.5 million – dwarfing the £76.9 million spent on wages by Manchester United, the world's richest club.

The full scale of the transformation of the club from middle-ranking mediocrity to big-spending hot shots under the ownership of Abramovich, emerged when the club submitted its accounts to Companies House. The scale of Abramovich's investment into the club in the first year of his ownership was just under £300 million.

The accounts, for the twelve months to the end of June 2004, show that, in addition to paying £60 million for the club and taking on £80 million of its debt, Abramovich spent £175 million on new players.

Even by football's standards, Chelsea pay vast salaries: thirty-five Chelsea employees are paid more than £2 million a year. One of those, Peter Kenyon, the club's chief executive, earned £3.53 million, a sum that will be looked on with envy by most FTSE-100 bosses. Kenyon's salary is higher, for example, than the £3.2 million pocketed by Fred Goodwin, the chief executive of the Royal Bank of Scotland, which has 45,000 employees in the UK and which made a £7.1 billion profit in 2004. The highest-paid players include Frank Lampard and John Terry, England internationals who are both on £60,000 a week. But, as the figures relate to the previous year, they have both had salary hikes to go with extended contracts.

Another £20 million was spent on severance payments to players discarded as not being good enough for the new Chelsea, and on Claudio Ranieri. The cost of assembling such a talented collection of footballers left the club with their massive loss, despite an increase in revenue from £108.6 million to £152.1 million.

Kenyon believes that the club will break even by 2010, as less money is spent on players and the club's commercial activities increase with its new celebrity status and expected successes on the pitch. He aims to reduce the club's wage bill to 55 percent of turnover, from the current figure of 76 per cent. The break-even target will only be reached if Chelsea continue to qualify for the lucrative Champions League every season. Kenyon said, 'Given the resources at this club; that is not an unreasonable expectation.'

Chelsea's accounts also reveal that Abramovich's millions come with strings attached: he has loaned the club £115 million, interest-free, and expects to be paid back. Chelsea also has an outstanding Eurobond of £35.9 million, bringing its total debts to £151 million.

Vinay Bedi, a football analyst at City firm Brewin Dolphin, said, 'Breaking even in five years will be one hell of a task and getting into the Champions League every year will be essential.'

In financial terms, Chelsea is still significantly smaller than its main rivals and would not be able to outspend the likes of Arsenal and Manchester United without Abramovich's assistance. Manchester United's turnover for 2004 was £169 million, and the club made an operating profit of £29 million. Real Madrid, Europe's most successful club, had an income of £130 million last year.

According to its own accounts, Chelsea is valued at £225.2 million, about a third of Manchester United's £668 million market capitalisation. The club significantly boosted its income through a new sponsorship agreement with Adidas, worth £12 million a year to Chelsea over the next eight years. Chelsea paid £24.5 million to end their sponsorship deal with kit-maker Umbro, who released a statement to the Stock Exchange saying that the deal had been terminated by 'mutual agreement'. Manchester United currently have comfortably the biggest kit deal in British football. Kenyon, then at United, agreed a £300 million fifteen-year contract with Nike in 2000 after also dispensing with the services of Umbro. Chelsea's four-year £24 million deal with shirt sponsors Emirates ends this season.

Umbro have supplied Chelsea with playing and training kit and the sale and distribution of replica products since 1995. In 2001, the club signed a further ten-year deal with Umbro which was worth around £50 million. The contract now ends in June 2006, five years ahead of the original date. Umbro continue to be the kit-maker during the club's centenary season. Kenyon said, 'Umbro have made a major contribution to the Chelsea of today. However, we believe this decision will help us achieve our strategic long-term goals.'

The club were considering not having a shirt sponsor in their centenary season. The deal with Adidas is not set to begin until 2006 and the club may decide not to carry a sponsor's logo on their shirts during the 2005–06 season. Kenyon explained, 'We've been discussing that for a significant amount of time and we are in the latter stages with several big blue-chip international consumer brands. We have to be in a position to resolve it by the end of February. But one of things we are debating internally is whether the new sponsorship will start in 2005, when the deal with Emirates finishes, or in 2006, when the Adidas contract starts. That also means we are having a discussion as to whether our centenary year will carry a sponsor or not. So there are discussions over who the sponsor is and when it starts and a key component of that is really around our centenary celebrations.'

Chelsea had already revealed that the club's famous blue shirt will sport a more traditional badge and deciding to go without a sponsor would be another radical step – but one they could probably afford. It would also bring back memories of another famous Stamford Bridge side from the early 1970s, which included Peter Osgood, Ian Hutchison, Charlie Cooke, Alan Hudson and Ron Harris.

Chelsea were forced to scrap plans to launch their centenary season with a tournament involving Arsenal, Tottenham and Fulham because of police worries about crowd trouble. Both the police and local authorities in Hammersmith, Kensington and Chelsea were against the idea of a 'London Cup' being staged at Stamford Bridge at the end of July. A police spokeswoman confirmed that there were concerns about 'potential public disorder and disruption' around the tournament, which had been pencilled in for the weekend of 30–31 July.

Chelsea felt that the project would have been a fitting way to start their season of centenary celebrations, given that leading clubs in the capital used to play in a prestigious 'London Seniors Cup' 100 years ago. The competition would also have attracted huge interest from broadcasters. Stamford Bridge officials, however, accepted the advice that the four-team tournament had to be a non-starter because of security reasons.

They were working on replacing the July event with a friendly against a high-profile foreign club, with talks already taking place with Real Madrid and Argentina's Boca Juniors. The club are expected to play several centenary fixtures before and during next season and it is believed that other prestigious foreign clubs have offered to take part in the friendlies.

Kenyon changed the company's name back to Chelsea Football Club from Chelsea Village.

The name was created by former chairman, Ken Bates, who developed a leisure complex consisting of two hotels and various restaurants, as well as a nightclub and fitness centre, at Stamford Bridge. Kenyon wants the club to move away from leisure and back towards being a more football-centred business. He is reviewing the future of the complex and is in talks with a number of operators about taking over the running of the non-football businesses. Hilton and Marriott are both in discussions about operating the hotels, while fish-and-chip-shop chain Harry Ramsden's could run at least one of the restaurants. Catering giant Compass has also been brought in to advise on concourse and catering facilities.

Naming rights for the stadium was ruled out. 'I don't think it's appropriate for Chelsea, and it's not a revenue stream that we expect to get into,' said Kenyon.

Kenyon is confident that he will be able to match Manchester United's profits, the world's most profitable football club, by growing revenues by 10 per cent per annum. 'We know that a football club run properly can be profitable,' he said. 'We want to be the number-one club in Europe, both on and off the field. It's about ensuring that we're more professionally run and profitable. Today we are not profitable – we will be within five years. I don't think it's prudent today to run a football club on the basis of a benefactor. Part of our job is to leave it in good shape and good shape means self-sufficient. There are too many examples of clubs running themselves inefficiently and getting themselves into trouble. Roman will continue to invest, so I'm not concerned about that at all, but our job is to make ourselves successful and start repaying that investment.'

As part of the push towards profitability, the club will try to increase its membership base from 40,000 to more than 100,000 globally in the next three years. Target markets are China and North America, though the US has proved a tough market for English clubs to crack. Manchester United has been trying for several years with only limited success.

Chelsea responded to supporters' pleas by unveiling a new club crest. Fans lobbied the club to change the badge, which has been in place since 1986. The new crest is based on one used by the club in the 1950s. It is largely blue, but also includes red and gold trimming. There will be two versions of the badge that will be effective from May, a permanent one and another especially designed for Chelsea's centenary season.

Mourinho was happy with a new crest that showed the lion as being more aggressive; a symbol of his approach. He said, 'I cannot forget what happened in the US when we went there in pre-season, dressed in tracksuits and people asked, "Who are you?" We want to make sure we become one of the biggest clubs in the world and have a connection with fans all around the world. I like our new crest because the lion is arrogant, aggressive and also powerful. It is proud to be a Chelsea lion and my players also feel a big responsibility to be successful and this makes us even more aware of our ambition this season.'

Plans for a new £20 million training complex were advanced, as Abramovich poured his personal fortune into turning the Londoners into a major Premiership and European force, but it was the recruitment of Kenyon to oversee those plans that created so much media attention.

Kenyon's appointment was a controversial defection from Old Trafford orchestrated by Israeli superagent Pini Zahavi. The first transfer window might have elapsed once Abramovich arrived with a huge spending spree on players, but Zahavi's recruitment drive didn't just involve the players as he set up the move for Kenyon.

Abramovich's brief was: 'Find the best man there is', and Zahavi turned to someone who, three times in his three-year tenure as Sir Alex Ferguson's immediate boss, had signed cheques that broke the British transfer record.

Just twenty-four hours after the Abramovich takeover, in Les Ambassadeurs, the upmarket Park Lane casino-restaurant, Kenyon was deep in conversation with Zahavi. That was not unusual, as Zahavi and Kenyon had completed many transfers together and were attempting to secure Ronaldinho's services for Manchester United. The Manchester United chief executive made a quick exit when he was spotted by a couple of City journalists he knew. Normally, he wouldn't have been so jumpy, but the seeds of Kenyon's appointment began there.

To fulfil Abramovich's long-term strategy to develop Chelsea into a worldwide brand, Zahavi told him there was no one better than 'my friend Peter'.

Once Zahavi brokered the deal, Kenyon called an unscheduled meeting in London with Sir Roy Gardner, chairman of United's Plc, to tell him that he was resigning. At about the same time, two of Abramovich's right-hand men, Tenenbaum and Buck, called the exisiting chief executive, Trevor Birch, to tell him they were hiring Kenyon, but that they still wanted him to stay.

United's directors, as well as Ferguson, were unaware of Kenyon's proposed move; Bates and Birch were also kept in the dark. 'Within football circles, it was more unexpected than any of the Russian billionaire's dressing-room signings' was an observation in *The Times*.

Birch performed an efficient job supervising the initial surge of purchases of players for Abramovich, but his expertise came in taking care of companies in financial difficulties.

Birch's departure was cushioned by a £2.9 million pay-off, far more generous by Abramovich than he needed to be as the severance settlement was written into his contract at £2.25 million.

Kenyon was a United employee for six years who had become a fan when he was taken to the 1968 European Cup final as a thirteen-year-old. He trained as an accountant after attending the local grammar school and gained a reputation for turning around troubled companies. In 1986, he joined Umbro International, the loss-making sports retailer, and helped to sell it to an American group before joining United in 1997, where he became football's highest-paid administrator. He joined as deputy chief executive at Old Trafford before succeeding Martin Edwards as chief executive three years later. Since then, Kenyon had secured Nike as sponsor, bringing in £303 million over thirteen years, and has been instrumental in numerous other deals with the likes of Vodafone, netting the club more than £100 million a year, and a ground-breaking agreement with the New York Yankees.

Kenyon turned the club into the world's biggest football brand, with an estimated 53 million fans. Kenyon recognised the needed to expand Old Trafford, which now has 15,000 more seats than the next largest stadium in the country, bringing in £1.5 million per match. He earned £625,000 in 2002, including bonuses, and he doubled his salary to join Abramovich.

When Ferguson was intent on retiring, he offered the job to Eriksson. Kenyon's move heightened speculation that the England coach would follow him to Chelsea.

Ironically, when Abramovich launched his takeover, Kenyon questioned whether all the investment could guarantee success. 'We are not worried,' he said from a United perspective. 'Why should we be? Having money is not necessarily a route to automatic success. In some ways, a "buy everything" policy can create problems.'

Kenyon's departure was felt by Ferguson, who could always rely on Kenyon for support. Kenyon orchestrated the £28.1 million purchase of Seba Veron and the £30 million for Rio Ferdinand. Zahavi was instrumental in both transactions.

Kenyon's decision was strongly criticised by Oliver Houston, a spokesman for Shareholders United, an influential lobby group, who accused him of turning his back on the club for money. 'He is going to Chelsea, one of our major rivals. We can only speculate on the remuneration package which would be needed to take him from one of the world's biggest clubs to one with very little international reach and profile. He has always made a great play of his loyalty to the club and his alleged dyed-in-the-wool support for United. How sad that his loyalty appears to have been so easily bought.' Kenyon's solicitors issued a statement saying 'the new opportunity represents a challenge that Mr Kenyon feels is right to take at this stage in his career'.

United moved swiftly to install David Gill in his place. Gill remarked that Kenyon's departure had been 'like a bolt from the blue'. Gill warned him against trying to 'poach' key personnel from United. 'I know there are concerns about Peter returning to poach people. All we can do is make sure we recognise them. Besides, Peter is precluded from his contract against deliberate poaching but, knowing the man as I do, there will be a lot of that.'

Gill was also dismissive of suggestions of a shift of power, pointing out that Kenyon may find it difficult to repeat the commercial success he enjoyed with United. 'Peter is an able businessman and he will have ideas to take Chelsea forward. But we have 54 million fans around the globe, 11 million in the UK, and these fans are with us from cradle to grave. With all due respect to Chelsea, they won't change. Some are fickle and some youngsters might choose Chelsea if they are much, much more successful, but the majority are here for life.

'I am sure Peter will do a very good job at Chelsea. I am sure they will be competitive on and off the field, but we have so many strengths they can't replicate.'

Kenyon was hired on a three-year £1.5-million-a-year, plus bonuses and incentives, package worth £7.5 million plus, to include a one-off £2 million 'golden hello' – more than most signing-on fees agreed by the world's top footballers. A £500,000 payment was to compensate Kenyon for giving up benefits including highly lucrative share options worth £222,262, plus £150,000 bonuses for even more profits for Manchester United. No commission was sought by Zahavi as he is a close friend of both Kenyon and Abramovich.

Alan Hansen expressed his view on the appointment at the time. 'Peter Kenyon's move was an unbelievable statement by Chelsea, a real coup over their rivals Manchester United. But it is only the start, not the end of what will be a very long battle to catch up with the Premiership champions. In football, like any other business, money talks and Chelsea have, it would appear, given him a lot to move. But the switch is not without its risks for him. He has left a job at a club that simply went from strength to strength and had its place in history firmly secured, in order to join one that is only just beginning to make a name for itself as a major force. Chelsea might have lots of money to spend on players, but what they are trying to do has never really been attempted before. There is no blueprint for success and the accumulation of so many players is not without risks. It is unthinkable now, but what would happen if Roman Abramovich were to pull the plug on all the money he has pumped in. As the new chief executive builds for the day that Chelsea become more self-sustaining and less reliant on Abramovich's money, he will know that what is really important is the level of performance on the pitch. If Claudio Ranieri keeps winning matches, there will be no need to hunt for a new manager. It will be for what this team wins that they will be judged, not the chief executive that they poached. Chelsea have accumulated the means to be successful, but they have not yet won the right to be described that way.'

The question of Bates's future arose again, but he said defiantly, 'Am I staying as chairman? There have been no discussions to the contrary.' Yet it was obvious that it would be difficult for Bates and Kenyon to forge a working relationship. After all, asked at a Manchester United shareholders' meeting about Chelsea's new owner, Kenyon laughed off Tony Banks's concerns that Abramovich wasn't a fit person to own the club. 'They're ironic comments when you consider the case of Ken Bates ...' Little wonder then that Bates was suspicious of Kenyon's appointment and role, and when, after a period of gardening leave, Kenyon finally arrived at the Bridge, it wasn't long before Bates was on his way out.

Kenyon began gardening leave while lawyers sorted out when he could join. Kenyon's appointee, Paul Smith, moved in. 'They have brought Kenyon in to try to surpass United as part of the "new Chelsea",' said former chief executive Colin Hutchinson at that time. 'He is a very good businessman. If you look globally at their financial situation – compared to Real, who have assembled a superb squad, but also piled up a load of debt – they are on a sound footing. And he will be a big loss to United. What he has done commercially has made them streets ahead in England as far as resources are concerned. It is a shock and it is out of the blue, when you consider the rivalry down the years between United and Chelsea.

'I think the interesting thing is, Chelsea, in recent times, has got its soul back and it is back to being a football club. There has been a feeling among supporters over the last couple of years that perhaps the priority was not football and there was a distraction from the Plc. I think obviously that Peter will be involved throughout, but it won't make that much difference on a day-to-day basis to Claudio Ranieri. The football side has got its own structures.' Hutchinson's reference to the club 'getting its soul back' had Bates spitting blood at his one-time confidant and chief executive whom he blames for the overgenerous player wages and inflated transfer fees.

Peter Ridsdale, the former Leeds United chairman, said, 'Peter spent a lot of money when he bought Rio Ferdinand from me at Leeds, so he is obviously used to writing big cheques and that is what probably attracted Roman Abramovich.'

Kenyon is a powerful figure in football politics, leading opinion at the G-14, the collective of Europe's biggest clubs.

Sir Alex's thoughts on Kenyon's appointment at the time reflected his fears of a potential shift in power both on and off the field. 'What we've seen so far is a clear indication of how committed they are to turning Chelsea around. It's a declaration of intent, to show they mean business. I'm sure they'll be interested in some of our players – but we are quite good at holding on to them when we want to.'

Paul Smith observed, 'It's a terrific time to be here. Clearly Chelsea is at the very centre of world football right now, and there are big plans for the club in the future. I've been involved in football for about twenty years now, mostly working for the major football federations, such as FIFA, working with them on the World Cup, in sponsorship terms and staging, and with UEFA with regard to the European Championships, and, more recently, advising some of the European clubs on how to maximise their commercial interests.'

Birch's world fell apart as the club hired Kenyon. 'It wasn't easy knowing that I wouldn't be part of that excitement any more. It's not something on which I want to elaborate and I have absolutely no hard feelings. When you make the kind of investment that Roman has, that gives you the absolute right to make any decisions you need to. It was felt the club needed Peter Kenyon and I respect that. Those are the rules and you obey them.' Birch was rewarded with a more-than-generous compensation package. 'Like most things in football, the speculation tends to be inflated. I made some good friends at the club. The spirit was first class and the people a pleasure to work with. There were a few tears at the end. I remember walking around the touchline on that final day when we played Tottenham and the reception the supporters gave me is something I will always treasure.'

Kenyon was instrumental in the appointment of Jose Mourinho, and made it clear at the end of Ranieri's first season that even finishing second in the title race and reaching the semi-finals of the Champions League was not good enough. He told an audience of Chelsea fans at the time, 'I'm on record on this and you should look at what John Terry said. He, as club captain, feels as though the players have failed. I've been around enough footballers who've thrown away their runners-up medals because they're not proud of them. Finishing second in the league and reaching the semi-finals of the Champions League is a good achievement and thanks to everyone involved in that, the players and the staff. We've had a good season, but we are not where everyone at Chelsea wants us to be. We want to do better than this next season and better than that the season after.'

A voice from the floor said, 'What about the manager? Don't ignore that.'

Kenyon replied, 'I didn't ignore it. We've had a good season, but we're not where anybody at Chelsea wants us to be and that's what we're all planning and working hard to achieve.'

Bates, in a Sky TV interview, said, 'The way Ranieri has been treated is quite shameful, and he doesn't deserve it. The job he's done this season ... could you do your job if you were being vilified every day in the press and media and not lose your temper, but smile and make a joke? He's a gentleman – the Russians don't deserve him. I speak to Claudio and he's a proud man and I think he's done a great job. I've sacked a few managers in my time but I've done it – bang, out. I haven't done it by death of a thousand cuts. If you want to change your manager, you change the manager, but there's a way of doing it and a way of not doing it. Some of the players signed this year are only highly paid mercenaries. They don't give a damn about Chelsea, they just give a damn about their wage packets and it's interesting that not many of the new players, the foreigners, have made it into the team successfully.

'Chelsea are losing the reputation that was built up over the last twenty years. I treated the staff well and got an extra 10 per cent out of them, but they're in danger of losing that, if it hasn't been lost already. It's a great pity, the staff and the fans are what makes the club.'

Asked if that was down to Abramovich, Bates replied, 'It's his henchmen. Remember, if you're aged under eighty, you've only ever lived under communism and the communist way of life is very different from the Western way of life. It's not the way of doing things in England and they are learning that the hard way. They will end up losing all the good people because they'll be headhunted elsewhere.

'Claudio's done a good job here: semi-finalists in the Champions League and runners-up in the Premier League. I would keep him. He would've done better [under me] as he would not have been under the pressure he has had for the past nine months.'

It was knockabout stuff, but there aren't many fans who are still hankering for the days of the Tinkerman.

The entire structure of the club was changed under Kenyon, and clearly Bates objected to the new order.

One key appointment by Kenyon was that of lifelong Spurs fan Simon Greenberg, who was appointed as director of communications. Greenberg, thirty-four, was assistant editor of the *Evening Standard* and was appointed to head up a new communications team to work closely with

Kenyon. Kenyon said, 'Chelsea will continue to be one of the most exciting stories over the next few years and Simon will play a key role in communicating our aims and ambitions both on and off the field both domestically and further afield.'

Greenberg said, 'I am incredibly excited about this new challenge. I am looking forward to working with the great team of people who are already at Stamford Bridge, on and off the pitch.'

The men in charge at the Bridge turned to Old Trafford again to recruit another key executive. Ron Gourlay, formerly the commercial director of Manchester United Merchandising Ltd, joined as managing director of Chelsea Merchandising.

Early on in Kenyon's reign, he gave an insight into Abramovich's thinking. 'Nobody wants a Leeds experience. That's not good for the club or the game. It's our job to make sure Chelsea are successful and healthy in the long term. Financially, Chelsea are already much more secure than before and that is a positive thing. Ultimately, he wants the club to be able to do without a sugar daddy. Roman is very committed to rebuilding Chelsea in the medium and long term. You don't do that unless you are: a) committed to the long term; and b) emotional about the product. What sets him apart is that most people spend their money acquiring a club; very few have then spent the same again improving it on the field. You don't do that unless you are committed long term and emotional about the product. Football clubs give you feedback very quickly and the experience is very positive for him. There is a really good feeling around Chelsea. You talk to supporters and they will tell you going there is a really exciting experience. He's added to that. He has a vision about the way he wants Chelsea to play. It is not just about Chelsea winning with more draws than anyone else or fewer goals, it is about winning with style and good, exciting football. He understands that from a fan's perspective we all want to romance about the fifth goal going in from thirty yards out. It is our job to build a long-term sustainable football club, but everybody is conscious that it takes time.'

Kenyon insisted his parting with Manchester United was 'amicable', despite an official complaint to the Premier League. 'I wasn't looking to move, but this job represents the single most exciting challenge in European football over the next five years.'

Kenyon spoke early on about his working relationship with Abramovich. 'He's involved in the business, but I am there to run it. He's passionate about it and we have to move away from this perception that Chelsea is his hobby or his plaything. This is a serious commitment by a very serious businessman. He wants Chelsea to achieve European status, to be number one, and while we are prepared to invest we also want, over a period of time, to get a return for that investment. I first met Roman Abramovich when he came to Old Trafford for the Champions League quarter-final against Real Madrid. There was nothing unusual in that, there were lots of guests there that night. We met again shortly after he took over at Chelsea. I was approached and nothing happened then because the summer is a particularly busy time, both with transfers and the end of the football year. I didn't want to consider anything until I had finished with the year-end business at Old Trafford. That was important because then we were out of any potential conflict areas in terms of transfers, which was critical because corporate governance is high on the agenda, particularly at United. The next time we got together was in August and that led to me resigning on 7 September.

'There are huge differences between the two clubs. I had the privilege of working for the best club in Europe and I've been fortunate to have been a big part of the United story over the last decade. The reason why I have joined Chelsea is because they represent the biggest opportunity and challenge, both professionally and personally, in English football. Chelsea as a club are based on history and that history suggests that, for their size and position, they have underachieved on the field. Now they have an owner whose investment of more than £200 million so far emphasises his commitment to make it the biggest and best. It can happen, but what we have to be realistic about is the timeframe. The expectation is there from fans and other people from within the industry, but these things don't happen overnight, it's a continual process.'

One of Kenyon's greatest achievements at United was to mastermind the brand marketing. 'That is the aim, but first things first. Manchester United and Liverpool are so far ahead in the marketing sense and why? Because Liverpool dominated English football in the 1980s and they were followed by United. The Premier League is the best in the world. More people watch it and more tune into it than any other league in the world. The stage is there and now Chelsea have to perform; we have to start winning trophies, that's the base from which we have to work. The rest will follow.

'There was the perception last summer that, if any high-profile player was available, then Chelsea were in for him. To continue to progress now, though, doesn't mean wholesale changes every season; it doesn't mean spending £100 million every year, because I'm afraid that doesn't guarantee you anything. Not long ago Chelsea didn't have one English-born player in their team, but now we have a realistic chance of having six in England's squad for Euro 2004. We have players like Frank Lampard and John Terry, who we want to be part of the team for years to come. We need to supplement that base with other world-class players, but always within a strategy. It's about finding the right mix, not changing that mix all the time.

'We have to invest in the club's facilities. Some of those have been neglected in the past. We can't have the best team in the country based at the worst training ground in the Premier League. That has to be a key objective, although planning and construction will take time. Another area of neglect is that we haven't had an academy and that's just not acceptable for a top-flight Premier League club. These are things we need to put right and which need investment to signal longevity and future benefit.

'We have a fantastic stadium holding 42,000 fans and it is now selling out regularly. I believe, however, that a 50,000 capacity is a good size for a high-performing London club and we have to look seriously at that idea. All sorts of issues are involved, but I think the success of Chelsea will warrant a stadium of bigger capacity than it is now. We won't be moving, though. Stamford Bridge is the heartbeat of the club and will remain so.

'Changes in academy structures have made it more difficult to sign talent outside its immediate area. We've also seen the influx of European players which has been generally good for the game. Talent today doesn't just come from this area of London. It's important to have the best scouting set-up and have the ability to work with other partner clubs. In that way, youngsters coming through the system can play in competitive football. We can also identify talent that we wouldn't otherwise have access to, so that they may grow up in France, but in their hearts they are already becoming Chelsea players.

'I've only been at the club for a few days, but I'm delighted with what I've seen. Like any organisation, it's the people who make the difference and there is a great loyalty, a great willingness, a great buzz.'

Kenyon insisted that there was no conflict of interest over Veron. 'We'll discuss next season's team requirements at the end of May, talking about contracts coming up for renewal and areas of the team we want to strengthen. That is exactly what we did last year at United which led to the decision that, if someone came in at the right value for Seba, then we'd seriously consider it. If not, Seba would have stayed part of the plans for the forthcoming season. As it happened, Chelsea came in, but the whole reason why we didn't enter into anything before that was that we didn't want anybody coming back and saying that we weren't doing things in the right way.'

While he was at Manchester United, Kenyon told the England captain David Beckham he was being sold. 'Any club would like to see David Beckham wearing their shirt. He's that type of player. But I don't think he has any aspirations or plans to come back here at the moment. David's move from Manchester United was a serious one for him and it has worked out very well. He and his advisers don't do anything on the hoof. Whatever he does is always well thought through and I genuinely think his move to Real Madrid was based on making a career out there and not on doing it for just a year or two. The end for David at United came following a lot of discussions.

'I wasn't nervous of delivering that news. It was my job, it had to be done. I wouldn't say he was shocked. There was a recognition that a long relationship at the club probably was not going to continue. That was the tone of the conversation, not that he had never heard such a thing was possible before. I didn't feel sorry for him. He's a professional, as were we. I like David a lot. He was a huge part of United's success. He contributed immensely to the image of Manchester United. I wished him very well and I think it was the right move for him. He has settled in so well and I think his football has moved on. I think he needed the change and we haven't fallen out at all. He appreciates why it happened.'

Kenyon made it clear that he didn't quit Old Trafford because he foresaw internal conflict, even a takeover. 'I am a United supporter and always have been. I haven't got that heritage with Chelsea, but I am committed to making Chelsea the best. It was a big decision to leave United, and I won't shy away from that, but it was balanced by the personal and professional opportunity that Chelsea represents today. There's a lot of excitement about what's happening here. From my first meeting with Mr Abramovich, it became clear that there was a vision here to make this one of the major European clubs. I'm pretty good at marketing and understand the value of football, but unless we perform on the field you are never ever going to capitalise on the business opportunities. It has to start there.'

Kenyon's remarks about the manager were seized upon. Ranieri's reaction was imminent. The routine press conference that afternoon was transformed into an even closer scrutiny of his future. Ranieri said, 'I know that when the owner and chief executive change it's also normal to change the manager. It's unusual for a club to keep the manager. It's the story of football and I'm trying to work against the story – and I knew that before I met Roman Abramovich and before he met Sven-Goran Eriksson.

'You ask if I'm scared about losing my job. I'm not, because all I can do is wait for what happens.' Pretending to hold a gun to his head, Ranieri added, 'I work and then, if somebody wants to kill me, I'm here. I am waiting for it. What can I change? Nothing. I can only work well for my conscience. That's my motivation, so that at the end of the day I can look everybody in the face. Black is black and white is white. This is nothing new to me. I am happy with myself.

'The new man has arrived, seen that Mr Abramovich has spent a lot of money and declared we must win. That's normal. I have a contract here to 2007, but I am not the owner and I am not Peter Kenyon. I am only Claudio Ranieri ... and it is not important what he thinks.

'I could be sacked even if I win something. It's part of the show. Everything is a show in football and I accept it.

'I have met Mr Kenyon and we agree on most things. But I can only do my work. We try to win games, that is my ambition. Everyone will be disappointed if we don't win things. Mr Abramovich, Mr Kenyon and myself. But I want to build here. I will continue to do it my way. I want to win, but I cannot buy victory. Mr Kenyon is a new man and says the things he believes. It is normal. Winning the championship for some people may be a success. For others it is not a success. For me every match is a success. Everyone can say what they want, but I continue to work. It is no problem. I come from Italy where clubs have three or four managers a year. It is crazy. I am in my fourth year here – and that is a very long time.

'I continue to say what I said to Mr Abramovich right at the start of season – for me success is to build a team. I don't want to see Chelsea win one thing and then go down. I want to put Chelsea on a new level and if I can win things that's my pleasure. If not, it will be the pleasure of the next man – I don't know who! My plan is to build a side based on English players and if I take the fruits at the end it will be good. My philosophy is to build a good side, with good spirit. To me that is victory.'

Kenyon explained his position. 'Changing the manager is a big, big decision for the directors of Chelsea. It would be a combined decision which is as it should be. Of course, the speculation would not have been as high if there had not been a picture of Sven walking into Roman's house. I know that. The picture is there, the picture is history. We aren't going to change the picture, are we? Will the manager be changed if you don't win something? We review all these positions. It's an ongoing process. It's like speculating in March who we are going to buy in the summer. We will sit down and have those discussions at the end of the season. The manager has a contract until 2007. We are third in the league, still in the FA Cup and probably further along in the Champions League than people expected. The conversations we've had are that this is now a critical part of our season. We want to concentrate on getting this season through and winning something.

'I am not going to give any guarantees as to where we start next season. I am a week into the job and have got a lot of work to do. We are trying to build for long-term success.'

Creating a European superpower doesn't happen overnight. 'There are financial disciplines, and we won't ignore those. Nobody should think that what we want, we get; that's not a culture I come from. Secondly, it is important how much we pay for the paper clips. It's too easy to say that because you can afford it, you have to pay it. Mr Abramovich is a very nice guy. He listens, he has his views, and I think I will enjoy a good working relationship with him. I think it would be really concerning had we been bought by someone for whom it was a pure financial play. He will be good for Chelsea. It's fantastic headlines that we bought in fourteen players and spent about £100 million. But I don't think you need to do that. Football is littered with people who have just spent money and won nothing. What will constitute Chelsea next year will be different to what it is this year. We are always looking at talent, but it's too early to talk about transfer funds. It's up to me to justify what we want to spend on new players, but for the right projects we are a well-funded business, and that's a nice position to be in.'

Ranieri out and Mourinho in was the biggest change, in addition to a turnover of players, and changes off the field would unfold as Kenyon orchestrated the biggest shift in footballing power: to start with the changes occurred on the field and, progressively, events started to take place off it.

L

Frank Lampard

Frank Lampard was the marathon man of English football, breaking Wayne Bridge's record of consecutive Premiership appearances.

Lampard was the player Jose Mourinho turned to first in his team, along with centre-half John Terry and goalkeeper Petr Cech.

And the personal honours started to roll in. Frank was voted the England Player of the Year in 2004, beating Wayne Rooney into second place. Lampard amassed around 35 per cent of the votes in a poll conducted on the FA's official website, with Rooney grabbing 25 per cent. A total of 10,000 fans voted, with polling closing on 20 January 2005.

Lampard was one of England's most consistent performers in Euro 2004 and scored six goals for his country, the same as Rooney, but in two more matches.

Lampard expressed how much the atmosphere had changed at Chelsea due to Mourinho's regime, and how much Chelsea had raised their expectancy levels and status. 'Fans and other players are always asking the same thing – "What's it like at Chelsea? What is the manager like? What's Roman Abramovich like?" Even on England duty, people like David Beckham, Gary Neville and Wayne Rooney all ask about it. They want to talk about Arjen Robben, Damien Duff and John Terry. It just shows the level that we have reached now at Chelsea, and it is terrific. There's an amazing buzz about the place. The buzz of a club that's going places, where something big is happening. And we have become such perfectionists about everything we don't feel it strange to look down and see Manchester United and Arsenal below us. Right now I think Chelsea are the most exciting club in the world. In the past you'd look at clubs like United, Real Madrid or AC Milan and wonder what it would be like to be there. Now, people look at Chelsea, and so much of that is down to Mourinho. I think people are beginning to realise that there's a lot more to our manager now. When he first arrived, a lot of people thought he was too arrogant, but now they are seeing he can do what he says he can and also that he has a wicked sense of humour. Suddenly he's not always as serious as they first thought. He has fostered a real team spirit based on the necessity of winning. Even in pre-season games that don't really mean anything apart from fitness, Mourinho came in and said we want to win this game; we want to win every game. He really has given us that belief, determination and direction. He has really pushed and we didn't have that last year, but he can blow his top, he can give you the hairdryer treatment like Fergie. Jose has had a real go at us at half-time during a couple of matches. He doesn't throw things around or smash things up, but he does tell you the truth in no uncertain terms. He'll be quick to tell you that you're playing s**t when you're not performing. He's had a bit of a go two or three times this season, but, by the same token, if things are going well he'll be the first to say so.'

Mourinho enjoys practical jokes, as Lampard reveals how he played one on masseur Billy McCulloch, who had just started with Walter Smith and Scotland. 'When he came back the boss asked him how it had gone. Billy said, "Brilliant, they love me, Walter loved me; the lads loved me." Mourinho got his secretary to type up a mock letter from Walter Smith saying he didn't want Billy's services any more, saying his massages were terrible and that his jokes awful. He gave it to Billy after training. It was hilarious and Billy wasn't sure whether it was for real or not.'

The atmosphere has changed, as Lampard added, 'The build-up is much more relaxed. We used to have no music, no television, no nothing. Now before a game we have it all. The night before a game is more relaxed; the pre-match meals are more relaxed.'

Mourinho is also clear in his admiration for Lampard. 'Frank is improving every day. He works hard, rarely has injuries and works for the team. Like Steven Gerrard, he is one of the best in the world. It's difficult to say who is the best because some midfield players are more defensive, some more offensive. I would say Frank Lampard and Steven Gerrard can both do things. They are great players.'

It had been such a succesful season that both Terry and Lampard were in line for individual honours. Lampard was the front-runner to be voted as Chelsea's Player of the Season, although he insists there are other candidates, such as Terry. 'It would be a great honour for me, but JT has had a great year and so have other players, including those who don't get as much credit, like Wayne Bridge. Obviously I want to win things, but coming second to Thierry Henry was like coming second to Gianfranco Zola in the Player of the Season awards at Chelsea last year.'

Initally, Lampard struggled to justify his £11 million price tag following his arrival from West Ham, and at the start of Claudio Ranieri's final year expressed his concerns when an influx of midfield stars were signed. 'I was a bit worried. I thought, 'Am I going to play.' His doubts seemed justified when, in Chelsea's first major match with all the new recruits available, Sparta Prague away in the Champions League, Lampard was left on the bench. The other four all played. Lampard, however, came on at the interval and helped win the tie. 'I have had to kick on to another level because of the pressure of new players.' The goals have helped ...

His father, Frank Lampard Sr, recently paid his son a rare compliment when he compared him to Bobby Moore, a former team-mate. 'Bobby knew how to meet the challenge of big circumstances and take command of them. I'm proud to say I can see a similar quality in Frank.'

Lampard's attitude impressed Ranieri. 'He never wants to come in from training. When I've finished the training session, Frank, Joe Cole and a few other players often want to stay out there. But I have to say no. I still think he can improve as a player and playing alongside Claude Makelele will help him.'

The day Abramovich bought Chelsea is one that anyone connected with the club will never forget. Frank Lampard recalls, 'I was in Vegas on holiday lying by a pool last summer and Rio (Ferdinand) rang and said that there was a Russian billionaire taking over Chelsea. He told me this geezer was really rich and was going to buy everyone and I was a goner, but I took no notice. A week later I came back and it was all true.'

That first encounter with Mourinho is etched on Lampard's mind. His new boss stared into his eyes and asked each of his new players, 'Are you a winner?'

Lampard recalls, 'It was a strange scene, but it felt right and walking out we all thought, 'We're going to win something this season.'

'In a way he asks us that question every day. There is never a moment when you are allowed to relax. He'll have a joke, but you know with him the only thing that matters is winning and that has rubbed off on everyone.'

Equally, Mourinho planned to turn Lampard into the best midfielder in Europe. The manager surprisingly missed UEFA's gala awards ceremony in Monaco to work with Lampard and his team-mates ahead of the home clash against Southampton. At that awards ceremony, Porto midfielder Deco was handed the Champions League Player of the Year. Mourinho arranged for his own award for winning the Champions League to be given to him at Chelsea's home European clash against his old club. He targeted the future player's award for Lampard. 'I want to change Frank Lampard as a player. I want to make him a better one. I want him to win the same trophy that Deco won on Thursday night. The best player in Europe. How can I achieve this? By winning, because Deco is the same player that he was two years ago. The only reason he won on Thursday was because he is a European champion. Frank will be the same player, but he will have adapted to a different philosophy.'

Lampard responded to Mourinho's boast that he would make him the best in Europe. He said, 'It's great to hear the manager saying things like that about me and I've been really impressed with him. We've already spoken about how he wants me to play. He wants me to carry on from last season, but to add a few bits to my game. I've already learned from the things he's said in training and during games. We're trying to build up through the midfield a lot and we're not playing 4–4–2 so much. We're trying out different formations and you have to be more intelligent to take different tactics on board. The manager wants intelligent players at Chelsea. Everything about him is so organised. We came back into training and every player knew his schedule from that day to the first time we kicked a ball in the new season. Psychologically, the manager was very clever. We probably did more running in pre-season than we've ever done but, because it was all with a ball, the players didn't realise. It just felt fresh and new and enjoyable.'

As a testament to his fantastic 2004/2005 season, Lampard was voted the Sports Writers' Player of the Year.

M

Jose Mourinho and Claude Makelele

When Bobby Robson arrived in Lisbon to join Sporting in 1992, an immaculately dressed young PE teacher stood waiting for him at the airport. The twenty-nine-year-old offered his hand and, in perfect English, introduced himself as Jose – the translator.

A decade on, Mourinho has progressed from being a translator to the continent's must-have coach. His father, Felix, revealed that he announced his intention to become the 'greatest coach in the world' at the age of fifteen.

Mourinho followed Robson from Lisbon to Porto, where they won two league titles and, in 1996, to Barcelona. Robson still insists that 'fundamentally his job was interpreter' but, astute, clever and a quick learner, Mourinho took on an increasingly active role, carrying out scouting missions, dealing with players such as Ronaldo and talking to the press.

Robson was constantly under attack from press, public and even other managers. When Robson moved on, Mourinho stayed on under Louis van Gaal, winning two league titles which legitimised a position many had judged an Englishman's indulgence. Offered the chance to go solo, he left for Benfica, only to fall out with the club's president Manuel Vilarinho, and then joined Uniao Leiria, leading them to their highest-ever finish, fifth, in 2000–01.

When he joined Porto in January 2002 they were languishing in mid-table, but still he told the press they would win the league the next season.

He announced that Porto would 'do things my way' and promised, 'If we do do it my way, we'll qualify for the UEFA Cup and next year we'll win the league.' He was right.

Mourinho's secret is that he pores over manuals and statistics. Roger Spry, a fitness expert who has known the Chelsea manager for almost twenty years, points out that Arsène Wenger and Carlos Queiroz, Sir Alex Ferguson's influential right-hand man at Manchester United, made no impression at all as footballers. 'The three of them are highly educated and you wonder how many languages they can speak in total,' said Spry. 'Jose has all the Brazilian and Argentiniean coaching literature available to him and it has never been translated into English.'

Mourinho says, 'It wasn't just when I was young and had no CV behind me, but even now. You have to try and study everyone who is involved in football.'

He considers himself, as he put it in Portuguese, a *grande cabeça* (big brain) in the modern school of football thought. 'Jose's training the mind and the body all at the same time,' said Spry. 'The drills they are given are never mindless. There will always be some element of decision-making in them.'

Craig Brown, the former Scotland manager who was to the fore when Mourinho came as an unknown figure to an SFA coaching course in Largs, gives a very basic example of this approach. 'In a shooting exercise the player who gets the ball doesn't have to shoot. He might decide to pass it right or left or even run with the ball.'

Spry, currently working with Panathinaikos, elaborates: 'You create match situations, but they are repetitive. You do something twenty times that might only happen once in a game.'

Spry argues that there is nothing unusual about his habit of keeping a 'Bible', a running record of every football experience. Similarly, the Chelsea manager is following standard practice in having an assistant, Andre Villas, prepare a report on each opponent.

Luis Lourenco, biographer of Mourinho, believes that the references to the manager's IQ are inadequate. 'I don't think it is a question of being more intelligent,' he said. 'The word is perception.'

He had no compunction about dispatching the most globally renowned players at Chelsea, Juan Sebastian Veron and Hernan Crespo, on loan deals. The restriction of the squad to twenty-three players enriched the manner in which people could deal with one another. 'I guarantee that he will treat every one of them with respect,' said Spry, who also worked with Wenger at Monaco and sees the similarity with Mourinho. 'He and Arsène have got their own personalities, but their approach is similar. They're both hyper-intelligent and they make every player feel special.'

Mourinho can also make an individual feel unwanted. At Benfica he dropped the most popular player, Sabry. When the Egyptian complained to journalists, the manager told them how often Sabry lost the ball, how rarely he recovered possession and referred to the eight minutes and three boot changes the sulking playmaker had needed before coming on as a substitute. 'It was courageous,' says Lourenco. 'You have to remember that it was this first time in his life that he had been the main coach and he had just arrived at the great Benfica. Another guy would have been scared to face Sabry. Mourinho – no.'

Joe Cole has not been guilty of misbehaviour, but he scored Chelsea's winner over Liverpool in October and all Mourinho wanted to talk about afterwards was how little Cole had done for the team subsequently.

Mourinho emphasises the group rather than the individual in his recruitment. He caused unrest at Porto by bringing in unheralded players he had used at Uniao Leiria. The fans were dismayed by the arrival of Derlei and Nuno Valente, but would eventually idolise them. 'His preference is for young players who are very ambitious,' Lourenco said. 'That's what he wanted to do at Chelsea. He has a clinical eye for these players. What makes Mourinho so special is his confidence. It is his message to his players.'

In the QWest Stadium, Seattle, the temperature hit 100 degrees, yet the Chelsea squad worked hard to impress Mourinho, who was standing in the centre circle watching the two groups. On the sidelines, Peter Kenyon said, 'You know what that reminds me of? Training sessions at United in pre-season where every player is almost scared to let the level drop because they know they might not get a second chance.' For Kenyon, Sir Alex and United were still the benchmark.

Kenyon perceived a rival to Ferguson. 'Meeting Jose was like turning the clock back to when I first met Alex. The thing that strikes you most of all is that they are both absolute winners. Jose's approach is single-minded, dedicated, detailed and thoughtful, and he won't be blown off course by anything.'

The instant impact was not lost on owner Roman Abramovich or Kenyon. Kenyon spent seven years working alongside Sir Alex. Ferguson has been in charge of United for eighteen years, while Arsenal's decision to give Arsène Wenger time to build his own squad has been rewarded with a seven-year spell of success. Chelsea believe they can only enjoy glory on a regular basis if they stick with someone in charge for as long as a decade – and, in Mourinho, they are confident that they have found their man.

Kenyon said, 'To achieve the size and scale of success which we want for the club, it is about building a structure for successful generations. It's no good winning the Premiership and then disappearing into the relegation zone. It is about getting success and then maintaining it. Only doing that gives you the status of being one of the best and biggest clubs in Europe, which is what our ambition is. It was that ambition which saw us get Jose Mourinho. That's what he was looking for. He was looking for that next level of challenge. He's got a fantastic CV in terms of what he had already achieved but, at forty-one, we have got a manager who could be with us for a long time.

'We are talking very much in terms of a ten-year vision. It wasn't by accident that we went for someone of Jose's age – you can quite obviously see a future. I also don't think it's an accident that England's two most successful football clubs in the last decade have had managers who have been there for significant periods of time. Continuity is a big factor once you have got the right guy.'

Kenyon added, 'It was obvious from the very first time I met Jose that this was a manager who was very different in terms of his approach, desire and belief and the way he goes about things. He completely does not shy away from his responsibilities at any level – he is involved in everything. He's got a regime that is team-orientated.

'There is a spirit within the squad now that reflects that Jose is clearly a very, very good man-manager, and the ability to manage a team that contained players of several different nationalities is part of the modern game. Clearly his language skills, his command of English and his experience of working in several clubs in several countries – all of that has come together here.'

Mourinho signed a four-year deal when he was chosen to succeed Claudio Ranieri in June 2004. But the man who led unfancied Porto to Champions League success has already grown to like the English game and has admitted that he would love to stay longer than his current deal. Talks have not yet been opened over a new contract – but, if Chelsea continue to show the kind of form which has taken them to the top, then Mourinho's future will be all but secure for the next decade.

Mourinho signed a four-year £4-million-a-year deal, but such has been his success that he was already in line for a pay rise. He harbours ambitions of working in Italy and coaching the Portuguese national team, but wants to dedicate the rest of his forties to Chelsea. In an interview with Portuguese newspaper *A Bola*, Mourinho said, 'I signed an extraterrestrial contract and the intention here is to extend it. It was much more than I was earning at FC Porto, it was much more than what someone could earn in Portugal, it was also a sum that only a handful of clubs can pay. I'm not saying it's not enough. I have a great four-year contract that I never thought I would ever have. The intention here is to sign a new one and ideally it would be from four to eight years. Improving the four-year one makes no sense, because I knew what I signed and I know that I'll abide it. I'm happy with my conditions and I'm completely committed to the growth of the club on many different levels. I like English football a lot, I like to live in England a lot, therefore I can't see myself anywhere else. I mentioned, it's true, that I'd like to coach in Italy and also the national squad, but I see this day as very far away. It's not winning the championship here and leaving. No way.'

Chelsea are growing quickly and Mourinho likes that. 'It was one of the reasons I wanted to join. Peter Kenyon ... is completely focused on the Chelsea brand and making them one of the best clubs in the world. That makes me want to be a part of that project. You can have top stars, the best stadium, the best facilities, the most beautiful project in terms of marketing, but, if you don't win, all the work is forgotten. You have to win. The new training centre will be fantastic; the work the club is doing in terms of merchandising is fantastic; the way Mr Abramovich is ready to help the team in all the areas where you need big financial investment is also fantastic. But our role, mine and the players, in terms of achieving football success, becomes the nucleus of that.'

As for Abramovich's hands-on influence, he said, 'He is not able to be here every day, but there was one thing I wanted him to know: he is always welcome. I always feel that with a president, an owner, the players like to see him. When he comes here, he is not coming to interfere with my work. He just comes to give his faith, to give his support, to communicate with people. The reason I was a little late for our meeting was that I spent an hour-and-a-half with him and Mr Kenyon in talks about the club. That's normal. He's always present. He's committed. He knows what Mr Kenyon is doing, he knows what I am doing and he doesn't need to be worried about training players or the club organisation. Abramovich is a top man.'

How does he react when he experiences difficulties? 'I know football very well. I was nine or ten years old and my father was sacked on Christmas Day. He was a manager. The results had not been good – he lost a game on 22 or 23 December. On Christmas Day, the telephone rang and he was sacked in the middle of our lunch. So I know all about the ups and downs of football. I know that one day I will be sacked. I know that one day the results will not be good. But I think it's more normal for my team to have no success than it is to win two consecutive European Cups.'

In press conferences, he often speaks out against other coaches. Is it a message more for his dressing room that they don't have to fear anyone? 'It depends. Facing the press is not easy, but you have to try to take positive things from these meetings. I try to have some messages I want to pass on. After the game [against Liverpool] I could guess how the questions would go. Joe Cole scored the goal, Joe Cole goes to the national team, Joe Cole is not playing for Chelsea. I could guess they wanted to put Joe Cole on the moon. So, because he got all the plaudits from the press, I had to kick him a little bit. When I face the media, I feel it as part of the game. I'm not there to be what you want me to be or say what people are waiting for me to say. It would be much easier if I go and say, "Of course, Joe Cole was amazing," and so on. But I need him to give me more, so I didn't go there to be a part of your movie. My movie is another one.'

Mourinho has been hailed as a 'young Brian Clough' – by the former Nottingham Forest manager himself. Clough, whose death led to fulsome tributes from across the game, won two European Cups with Forest despite their lack of spending power. In many ways it was a similar achievement to that of Porto. Just like 'Old Big 'Ed', Mourinho is not averse to making bold public statements. In an interview with the official Champions League magazine, Clough said, 'I like the look of Mourinho, there's a bit of the young Clough about him. For a start, he's good looking and, like me, he doesn't believe in the star system. He's consumed with team spirit and discipline. The players have to fit in with his vision and pattern of play, which is right. Don't confuse footballers – keep it simple. I was very encouraged by Porto and Monaco getting to last season's Champions League final. They had nowt to play with financially, compared to the big guns like Real Madrid and Manchester United, and they embarrassed the lot.'

Clough would have approved of the way Mourinho said he was 'special' and mentioned himself in the same breath as the Almighty.

Lifting the European Cup after only four seasons as a manager is a standard he expected to maintain at Stamford Bridge. Immediately after winning the Champions League, Mourinho said, 'It is a great feeling to win the European Cup at forty-one. When you look at the great managers in the world who worked for twenty years at the highest level, some have never had the chance to win the UEFA Cup or the Champions League. I've had great success in winning the UEFA Cup and the Champions League so quickly, but, although I know I'm going to have a bad year sometime, if you tell me that in ten years I will just have the same medals, I will be very sad. As a manager, I have got to do more. I want to continue to be ambitious, to become better and better. I believe a lot of things can grow in my performance. It is not my ambition in fifteen years not to have won anything else. I want to continue to be ambitious, to try and be better and better. I want to grow as a manager. When I say that, I know many good managers can go thirty or forty years without this kind of success. I'm aware of this and, because of it, I want to enjoy this night with my players before I discuss the future.'

He revealed the speech that helped to inspire Porto to their 3–0 victory over AS Monaco in Gelsenkirchen. 'My last words to the players were: "We will not forget this day, not even when we are very old, so you had better have a good memory. It is better to have a good memory than sadness for the rest of your life." You always play to your strengths, you look at your players and it doesn't matter what system you play, 4–3–3, 4–4–2, you have to be the same model, you always have to be true to your identity.'

The next task – win the same trophy for Chelsea. 'Basically, they have got to win the European Cup next year,' said Porto striker Benni McCarthy. 'He's got a really, really difficult job on his hands. People have got to give him time but, for me, he's the best coach in Europe.'

John Giles, Don Revie's on-field lieutenant in the great years of Leeds, was in the AufSchalke. Giles says, 'Mourinho is clearly his own man and, because of that, I imagine he has made some quite strong demands on Roman Abramovich in terms of his control of football matters. It always seemed to me that, if he is coming to England, Liverpool would have been the perfect club. He would have had the freedom, and the resources, to go his own way and he seems to be a man who relishes that. People are talking about his tactical triumph here. Well, I think the most important thing was the effect he had on his team at half-time. I could see that he was appalled at the way they were playing in the first half; they weren't anything like the team that beat Deportivo. That was the one that came out in the second half and made every tackle and covered every yard. Deco was voted Man of the Match and took his goal brilliantly, but it was a disappointing performance from him when you compare it to some of his work earlier in the tournament. He was far from as sharp as I've seen him, and it does happen occasionally that a player like him gets to a big match and finds that his legs are just not right. Mourinho dealt with that problem, and in the end he came through because he has developed a terrific attitude in the team. When the team weren't playing well in the first half, the defence still operated superbly. For me, the Man of the Match was central defender Ricardo Carvalho.'

Mourinho's arrival at the Bridge was guaranteed to spark more transfer activity, with several players leaving, but Joe Cole made it plain that he was hoping not to be one of the departures. 'I really want to make it work at Chelsea. They are a club who are really going places and I really want to be a part of that. There looks as though there could be a new manager in place and I want to be given a chance at both club and international level. My real wish is to play at the top of a diamond formation. All I've ever wanted is a manager to say, "Go and play there and show what you can do." I've never had that at club football. It's going to be my best position, I am sure, and I have to find a manager who will put his trust in me and give me a run there.'

The Chelsea players must have had an inclination that there was going to be a new manager with new ideas as Mourinho said before the Champions League final, 'I want happiness in my football club. I want players who I trust and who trust me. The greatest thing in my life is when, after I have lost, my children say, "You are the best daddy." But then I also like to win football matches.'

Mourinho's methods were endorsed by experienced Porto defender Secretario. 'Jose has an excellent relationship with all his players and his success is based on his human qualities. He doesn't try to control us. He gives us all the freedom in the world and the squad have responded to that responsibility.'

Porto 'keeper Vitor Baia, observed: 'Mourinho is very intelligent and his organisational skills are a real strength. He pays attention to every little detail. The way he transmits his message to the players is very clear and the whole squad loves to work with him. I am sure he is the best coach I have ever played for in my life. I have a lot of experience and I have played for many bosses.'

Again, on the eve of the Champions League final, Mourinho said, 'My reputation is very important to me. I want people to remember me as one of the all-time great managers. I want to leave my mark in football history and be remembered like Bill Shankly, Bob Paisley and Matt Busby. I loved the way Liverpool played in the seventies and eighties. I loved Kenny Dalglish, Graeme Souness, Phil Thompson, Ray Clemence and Ian Rush. Now I want the same success.'

He recalls how he 'wound up' Ferguson who called them cheats after Porto won the first leg of their last-sixteen match 2–1 in Portugal. 'When my team are involved I don't care about my image. Sometimes I make enemies because of my reaction, but when my players are under attack they are my family and I will protect them. I think Ferguson's comments were a strategy. He realised for the first time that United had lost their invincibility and I saw fear in his eyes. I think he was very disturbed. Afterwards, I told my players that he was surprised by our quality. He thought it was going to be easy for them to beat us, but we beat them. Now he is afraid of the second leg and this is a ploy to unsettle us, so I need you to be with me in this fight ... go to Old Trafford and play, don't be afraid, show your character.

'I had met Ferguson in the past and he was very polite, but at the end of that first leg he had an angry reaction when I went to shake his hand. He told me that my players were cheating, so I had to use his rage to fire up my team.'

When Mourinho tasted victory, the moment went to his head. 'When Francisco Costinha scored, I ran all the way to the corner flag. It was one of the best moments of my career and very emotional. It was like a golden goal. At that moment, I knew Manchester United were out of the competition. They are the biggest club I've knocked out in my two years at Porto, and that was the reason I ran along the touchline and jumped for joy.'

Striker Benni McCarthy explained, 'The manager has been world class and has inspired the whole team. He brings out the best in all the players and we all respond well to him. He's a great person and an excellent trainer with perfect manners and that's why he's working so well for Porto. He understands the way players think and works with us all individually. He knows what it takes to get players to work to the best of their ability and understands people very well, that's one of his strong points. Not a lot of coaches can put that on their CV. He's definitely the best coach that I've played for or worked with.'

Mourinho's methods are to treat all his players equally, taking time out to talk to each of them individually, and McCarthy says, 'There are a lot of good coaches around, but none of them can boast what Jose Mourinho has. Any players that come to him he talks to and brings them success. If a player is down in the dumps, he doesn't forget about them. Even the squad players are as important as those who play regularly. He treats everybody the same and that's why he's had so much success. He makes everyone feel important, not just the big players. He gives everyone equal attention, which is very important, as when the stars are injured you need the best players. If you don't treat them with respect, they won't give you their best.'

McCarthy was confident that his mentor would succeed at Stamford Bridge. 'It'll be very difficult for Porto to keep hold of Mourinho, because so many people are talking about him. There's a saying in Portugal: "When the river makes noise it's because water is coming," and that suggests he is going to Chelsea. He can do it at the very highest level. He's got a good mentality and, if the players give him the right co-operation at Chelsea, he can achieve anything he wants to. Mourinho can handle the big players. He worked with Ronaldo at Barcelona and gets on very well with the big players at Porto. He'll do very well at Chelsea and I wouldn't be surprised if they won the Premier League or the Champions League next season.'

And McCarthy speaks with first-hand experience of Mourinho's skills. After two desperate years on Celta Vigo's bench, the South African striker's confidence had vanished. Mourinho told him, 'If you were with me you'd be top scorer,' and told the press, 'I have three transfer options – the first is McCarthy, the second is McCarthy and the third is McCarthy.'

Ironically, he said at the time, 'We can do nice things in the Champions League but we can't win it – that's just for the sharks, clubs that pay 20 million euros (£13.5 million) for one player.' Could he have meant Chelsea? Surely not!

As a disciplinarian he has the full respect of his players. 'I've known him a long time, and he has this special way of organising his players and understanding how they want to play,' said Porto goalkeeper Vitor Baia, who first worked with Mourinho a decade ago.

'He stands out as the best in Portugal,' said the midfielder Costinha. 'He's young for a head coach, and that can be a good thing. He knows how players think.' 'An expert in developing a player's confidence,' said McCarthy.

Portugal, though, is officially the sixth-strongest league in Europe and Ranieri quickly questioned whether Mourinho could cut it in a 'big' league like England. No Portuguese club had reached a European Cup final since 1987, when Porto won it; no club from outside the four richest leagues – Spain, Italy, England, Germany – had won the European Cup since Ajax in 1995.

'After the Bosman ruling, Portuguese football lost some ground,' Mourinho said. 'We are up against clubs from bigger economies, who get three or four places in the Champions League every year. So this is a fantastic moment, not only for Porto, but for Portuguese football. These players are going to leave a mark.'

Mourinho's background as an interpreter meant that he would be able to converse with the broad spectrum of players inside the Chelsea dressing room. He owns up to finding German a little tough, but has mastered English, Spanish, French and Italian. 'I would find it completely impossible to work at a club in a country where I hadn't learned the language,' he says.

As Robson recounts, 'He told me what the players were saying when they thought I couldn't understand.'

On the bench and patrolling the technical area, Mourinho chews gum, takes notes and can get very excited: there was his jubilant leap and sprint down the line when Porto scored their late goal at Old Trafford to knock Manchester United out of the European Cup; or a notorious slanging match he became involved in with the Sporting player Rui Jorge in a league game.

Mourinho acknowledges his debt to Robson and Van Gaal. 'One of the most important things I learned from Bobby Robson is that, when you win, you shouldn't assume you are *the* team and, when you lose, you shouldn't think you are rubbish.' He speaks to Robson often 'about football, family. We'll talk about my Porto team, about his grandchildren, lots of things.'

After he left Barcelona in 2000, Mourinho was offered the job of Robson's No. 2 at Newcastle with a view, his old friend told him, to Robson moving upstairs after a season and Mourinho becoming head coach. Mourinho says, 'He had forgotten I worked with him for many years. Bobby Robson will only leave the pitch when he retires. It is unthinkable. I didn't accept.'

Porto players returning from their holidays in the summer of 2002, at the start of Mourinho's first full season in charge, all received a letter. It read, 'Welcome to Porto ... Hope you have recharged your motivation and ambition ... From here, each practice, each game, each minute of your social life must centre on the aim of being champions ... First-teamer will not be a correct word. I need all of you. You need each other. We are a TEAM.' Along the bottom margin of the page, there was an equation: 'Motivation + Ambition + Team + Spirit = SUCCESS.'

JOSE MARIO SANTOS MOURINHO FELIX

BORN: 26 January 1963 in Setubal, Portugal.

MANAGERIAL CAREER: Benfica (2000–01), Uniao de Leiria (2001–02), FC Porto (2002–04), Chelsea (2 June 2004–)

HONOURS: Portuguese League (2003, '04). Portuguese Cup (2003). European Cup (2004). UEFA Cup (2003). All Porto.

BACKGROUND: Never a professional player. Father Felix was Portugal goalkeeper. Low-profile positions at Estrela Amadora and Vitoria Setubal before working under Bobby Robson at Sporting Lisbon. Moved with Robson to Porto in 1993. Both went to Barcelona in 1996. Robson left Barça and Mourinho worked under Louis Van Gaal. Appointed to his first full-time manager's post at Benfica in 2000.

Claudio Ranieri bought Claude Makelele and the biggest shock was that Chelsea had the purchasing power to go to the best club in Europe for their shopping, Real Madrid. Ranieri, at the time, explained the rationale behind the move for Makelele: 'Last season we did not buy any players. This season we buy ten or eleven players and change everything. Now we are working to build a good team. I know that Roman Abramovich wants to put Chelsea at a high level like AC Milan or Real Madrid. I said to Mr Abramovich that Real Madrid are one of the best teams in the world and they have a great player and everything goes around him, and this man is Claude Makelele. I would like to buy him. For me Real Madrid *was* Claude Makelele. With him in the team Zidane played well, Figo played well – everyone played well. Now in England everybody is slowly understanding that maybe you don't notice him, but he is everywhere. He always stays in the middle and is such an intelligent player who can link with the attacking players and has good balance in his play. He is one of the greatest players in the world.' So Chelsea bought him.

Makelele's move brought Abramovich's spending to £111.25 million on ten star recruits in sixty-two days – £1.79 million a day. World football, let alone the English game, has never seen anything like it. The purchase of Makelele attracted worldwide attention. Overvalued, most definitely, but a key signing as Wenger observed at the time, 'Makelele's signing shows that Chelsea are now on a different planet. Real Madrid didn't want to sell, but Chelsea can buy when they want and that makes them a world force. None of us can compete financially with Chelsea at this moment.'

Deschamps concurred with Wenger's assessment. 'To have a winning side you must always have a balance. Of course, you need players with fantasy and flair, but you also require ones with a strong spirit and a willingness to work for the team. Makelele is just that sort of player.'

Vieira was also impressed by the capture of Makelele. 'It is very good for Makelele. They are one of the contenders for the title; we will see that on the pitch. If Makelele settles in well, then they are a team capable of winning the title. They have signed several top-notch players like Juan Sebastian Veron, Hernan Crespo and Claude Makelele and they look like one of the big sides in Europe. But so far, it's just on paper. They will have a big problem keeping everyone happy. They have got great players with strong characters, and they will want to play all the time.'

Makelele waltzed into Stamford Bridge fifteen minutes late for a 3pm press call. Ranieri said, 'I have a fantastic watch and every good watch needs a good battery – Claude is the battery for my watch. He will play just in front of the defence and is one of the best, if not the best, players in the world in that position. He was one of the top names on the list of players that I wanted to buy. All the players I have chosen are very special. You have to pick the best players for their positions. And it is also very important to have that link between the left flank, right flank and the middle of the field.'

Makelele admitted, 'The players are the ones who should have to deal with the pressure, not the manager. We have to do our jobs on the pitch. It is the players who are there to support Mr Ranieri and, if it goes wrong, it should be us and not him, who are punished. I have only trained once with the squad since I arrived in London, but I have already seen what a gifted squad this is. I want to help make Chelsea one of the biggest clubs in the world.

'It was a big decision for me to leave Real Madrid and I thought about it for a long time. Before making the decision, I spoke to my France team-mates Marcel Desailly and William Gallas. They spoke very highly of Chelsea's plans and ambitions and that convinced me to come.

'Chelsea have always been a club that has had big names and star players. Only now are they trying to boost this image even more. If things go well, there is no reason why we can't win the Premiership and European titles. Real Madrid is in the past. Now I must focus on building up a good atmosphere within Chelsea and making sure I am in the right shape and frame of mind to help the team. I wouldn't have left Madrid for just any other club. Chelsea were looking to the future and building a team. I can help Chelsea. There are players with different characteristics, but we are capable of great things.'

Makelele stands at 5ft 7in, weighing in at just over 10st, though his footballing stature is considerably greater. He was known as 'Three Legs' at the Bernabeu, a nickname which, like Vieira's, carries more than a hint of innuendo, though the official line is that it refers to his awesome ability to get around the pitch. Makelele said, 'Patrick and I are players of different characteristics. You can't compare the two of us. I train to play well and will always do my best to help the team. I am an ambitious player and will do everything I can to ensure that Chelsea are successful. I will do everything for the players, the club and the fans.'

Makelele featured in UEFA's Team of the Year in both 2002 and 2003 and was named the Champions League's best player in 2004.

Makelele's influence was most obvious in his absence when Real were beaten in the semi-finals by Juventus last season.

The first impressions have been positive. Makelele said, 'Chelsea are a side full of quality international players. The most important thing for me is to help build a good atmosphere in the team. I want to be in the right shape for the team and the trainer. I want to make the team very competitive. The players have to deal with the pressure and have to get results on the pitch. The players have to support Ranieri in his job. If they do not do that then they should be punished. We can help Ranieri do his job.'

Florentino Perez, the Real Madrid president, has lived to regret selling Makekele, but Real's loss has unquestionably been Chelsea's significant gain.

His first season at the Bridge was far from convincing – perhaps he was still sulking following his Bernabeu exile – but his second season under Jose Mourinho has been a revelation. Makelele's explanation is far more simple than merely the change in manager. It took him some time to get going, as his pre-season work was hampered while he was in limbo between Madrid and Chelsea. 'Success in football is not given to you. Success in football is working every day. What we reap is what we sow.'

Makelele was born in Kinshasa. Although his family left for the Paris suburbs when he was three, his Zairean roots remain. 'Every year I return to Africa, where my parents have a little business and a holiday home. I love the ambience. It's a force of energy.'

As a youngster he began his football education at Nantes, famed for its highly technical and tactical football school. 'At the time we had the No. 1 team in France, with an exceptional academy, great results, and everything was on the up. We won the league in 1995 and the following year reached the semi-finals of the Champions League. For a young team from a small club like Nantes to play a semi-final against Juventus was incredible. We lost 4–3, it was a beautiful adventure, and it made me even more ambitious. I saw myself going to a big club and winning big trophies.'

Makelele had outgrown Nantes by the time he was twenty-four and, with the World Cup in France a year away, it was time to push on. Although clubs in Spain and Italy expressed an interest, he decided to stay in his adopted homeland. 'I felt I was too young to go abroad, and also with the World Cup coming I didn't want to jeopardise anything.' That is precisely what he did by joining a shambolic Olympique Marseille side. It was an awful season. 'The pressure was enormous and the team was hardly superb,' he reflects. 'It was a season of sufferance.'

Makelele missed the World Cup victory, as a reborn Emmanuel Petit and a youthful Patrick Vieira seized their chance to grab the midfield spots alongside Didier Deschamps.

He moved to Celta Vigo and came back stronger in Spain. 'After Marseille, I came to appreciate football again in Vigo. I arrived at a club I didn't know anything about, so it was a bit of an adventure. And I was pleasantly surprised at what I found. There were some very good players – Valery Karpin, Alexandr Mostovoi and Michel Salgado, who went to Madrid with me. In Vigo I regained the taste for playing football.'

Real Madrid noticed him, while France forgot him. 'It's difficult to introduce a player into a close-knit group because it makes the group more fragile.' Makelele was on the periphery when France were at their all-conquering best, and only established himself as a regular when the burden of expectation became overpowering and results dropped.

He chose to retire from les Bleus early, earning only thirty-three caps. 'Yeah, it's a shame. But in a way it's a good thing France forgot about me, as it means that everything I achieved in my career I did by myself. I didn't need the help of the French team. That gives me great personal satisfaction. I am sitting here at Chelsea today and I only owe that to myself.'

Makelele was a late developer at the highest level. The early years were modest. It took him nine years to develop steadily at Nantes, Marseille and Vigo before he was catapulted into the most famous club side in the world.

Although not the most glamorous player in the Bernabeu's dressing room, he became a pivotal player who was greatly appreciated. He played in the role that Eric Cantona famously called the 'water carrier' to perfection and he was perfectly happy. 'Every player had his responsibility on the pitch – the wingers, the creators, the ball winners. That was our strength,' he reflects. 'We knew each other by heart, and there was a perfect balance. We knew when the moment was there, like telepathy. On top of that, we had a team with geniuses on the pitch. We were practically unbeatable.'

Was it difficult to feel part of the team when others clearly commanded both a higher status and salary? 'Not for me. In general, you can't ask for the same salary as another player because his career is his career and yours is yours. In my eyes, everyone has the opportunity to get what they deserve. My complaint was that I didn't feel I was getting what I deserved. It was nothing to do with any comparison to anyone else.'

Roman Abramovich and £16.9 million of the Russian's fortune secured his transfer in August 2003. His departure left a large chunk out of Real's team and neither David Beckham nor Guti, and now Gravesen, can stylistically fill the hole.

Makelele has never been under the impression that pure ability is everything in football. This theme comes across in his appraisal of his all-time favourite player, Pele. 'I loved him not only for his skill as a player, but for his awesome charisma. Just having him on the pitch must have given you the impression of having a lion out there. I reckon that's why people were scared of him, because he possessed such aura.'

Makelele is only 5ft 7in, but his physique is well developed. With Frank Lampard on one side of him and either Tiago or Smertin on the other, Chelsea's midfield is a formidable force. 'We have great solidarity and you can see that on the pitch. When one tackles, another supports him, and that is what makes us move forward. The system suits us very well because we have a strong defensive base, and on top of that we can score at any moment.'

He is, however, less likely to score. He has a career ratio of 0.01 goals per game. 'At Madrid I scored once! It was a great goal, one that qualified us for the European Cup. I hope to manage at least one goal for Chelsea. But it's OK. I know what my work is.'

He is serious about winning. So much so that he will go to extremes, such as when a Monaco player was unfairly sent off in last season's Champions League semi-final. He demonstrates a more agreeable example of his winner's mentality when asked who would win should Madrid and Chelsea meet. He replies, 'The one that I play for!'

Makelele said, 'Abramovich is an incredible man and you can see his passion and his commitment to the club at every level. You can feel it all round the club and the players realise what an effort he has put in. He has such a positive energy, and it is important to create harmony at Chelsea, given the transformation the club has gone through. When you see Abramovich during the game in the stadium suffering and living for his team it is very moving. That is why we try to do the same on the pitch. We all want to win something for him, because we all know we have a debt of gratitude to him for what he has done at this club. The Champions League would be perfect, as would the title, but teams like Arsenal and Manchester United did not just appear in one day. We need time, even if we give the impression that we are ready. I won titles and medals and had three years at Real that you cannot forget, but now Real is in the past. What's more important is the future and that is Chelsea. I asked Desailly a huge number of questions. When I knew I wanted to leave Real, I had offers. But Marcel told me Chelsea are the club of the future in England with big ambitions.'

N

Pat Nevin and John Neal

Pat Nevin is a Chelsea folk hero, a sheer entertainer who shed so much light during the dark days of so much frustration and limited success. But Pat is a player apart, one who is miles away from the usual stereotype; he is a lover of classical literature and fine art.

Signed from Scottish club Clyde in 1983, Pat played 242 games from 1983 to 1988 scoring forty-five goals in his five years with the club before being sold to Everton, eventually moving on to Tranmere and finally back to Scotland with Kilmarnock and Motherwell. He became director of football at Motherwell. He is now living in Scotland and working in the media, notably for Channel Five's football programme hosted by John Barnes.

It is no surprise that he selects Franco Zola as his 'favourite player of all time'. Among his other all time 'best' list are current players Damien Duff, another winger, John Terry and Frank Lampard. Of Lampard he says, 'I love watching him. If you look at British football at the moment, at the people who can run games, there's very few: Roy Keane, Vieira, Gerrard and Frank. He's up there with the best players of the last thirty years, and I like attacking players.'

There is also a special place for Ruud Gullit. 'We're talking about someone who was the best player in the world here. I loved the non-English way that he ran out on to the pitch; he was so cool and had total belief in his ability. I played against him a couple of times and he was totally unstoppable. How many players could be picked at centre-half, central midfield or centre-forward and it wouldn't make a difference to them?'

From his own era he most admired defenders Tony Dorigo, Colin Pates and Steve Clark, but he holds John Terry in high regard. 'A legend already, not just for his playing but because he's the heart and soul of the team at the moment and hopefully for many years to come.'

When selecting his best team he would pair Gullit up front with Kerry Dixon. Of his former team-mate, he says, 'He was the most natural goalscorer I ever worked with. When Kerry faced the goal, he had a magnificent touch, one that was never truly recognised. He made life easy for me. He just knew where to go. He had pace and power and he must have been a dream for a manager.'

⚽ ⚽ ⚽

John Neal became the seventh Chelsea manager in seven years in 1981 and was in situ when Ken Bates took over the club. 'It wasn't a football club; it was a social club with a bit of football played on Saturdays ... occasionally.' It is a remark which sets the tone for the unique Bates era.

Chelsea just avoided relegation to the Third Division in the first season of the Bates–Neal regime, finishing two places and three points from the drop. That was the lowest point in the club's history.

Brought up in the lower reaches of the league at Wrexham and Middlesbrough, Neal was a shift in character from his predecessors Danny Blanchflower and World Cup-winner Geoff Hurst, but the arrival of Bates was to herald the start of a brutal overhaul of the entire club.

Neal and his assistant Ian McNeill used the close season after their traumatic near demise into the Third Division to search through the lower divisions for a new set of players. He revolutionised the team with seven new signings.

In came Scotland's Pat Nevin from Clyde for £95,000 and Joe McLaughlin from Motherwell at £80,000. Bournemouth's Nigel Spackman cost £35,000, Eddie Niedzwiecki from Wrexham cost £45,000 and Reading's prolific scorer Kerry Dixon joined for £175,000. John Hollins rejoined his former club as player-coach along with David Speedie for £80,000 from Darlington and Joey Jones, who had signed the year before. The bargain-basement signings were supplemented by youth-team products John

Bumstead and Colin Pates. Mickey Thomas also arrived and Chelsea pipped Sheffield Wednesday to win the Second Division championship for the first time. Chelsea had beaten Leeds 5–0 to clinch promotion and then won away at Grimsby to take the title. Against Leeds, Bates was out in front of the West Stand at half-time with a megaphone in his hands imploring the fans to stay in their seats. But, when Paul Cannoville scored with a minute to go, and the ref wisely blew early, the fans rejoiced in the return to First Division football after a five-year wait.

Live television came to the Bridge for the first time for the third match of the new season back in the big time against FA Cup holders Everton.

The sceptre of hooliganism was looming over the club. Bates had tried electric fences, but soon had to pull them down, and the club were in deep trouble with the FA after a 3–2 defeat by Sunderland in the Milk Cup prompted crowd unrest at the Bridge.

Neal's brief reign came to an end after 1984 because of ill health and he was forced to take a position on the Board.

With player-coach Hollins coveted by QPR, who were losing Terry Venables to Barcelona, it was decided to move fast and promote Hollins to manager at the Bridge.

Under Hollins the club won the Full Members Cup, defeating Manchester City 5–4 in the Wembley final with a hat-trick from Speedie, but the competition failed to attract the participation of the major clubs in the First Division.

By Christmas 1986, Chelsea were on top of the league, but they crashed in the second half of the season and the slump continued into the next.

There were traumas in the dressing room and crises in the boardroom. David Mears sold his shares to SB Property, a company who were involved in a struggle for control of the ground. The shares sale put the pitch in danger of being redeveloped and finally ended the Mears connection with the club: a connection that had been in place since its formation in 1905.

Hollins had been an outstanding player for the club in a team that came so close to the championship in 1986 but, as a manager, there was never quite the same sparkle. Spackman and Speedie were banned from joining first-team training or games by Hollins because of the disruptive influence he felt they had on the team. By the time Chelsea had hit the relegation play-offs, Hollins had been sacked. The play-off system involved third-, fourth- and fifth-placed teams from the Second Division plus the fourth-from-bottom team in the First Division, a concept that was only ever employed twice. When Chelsea lost to Middlesbrough in the final of the play-off, they became the only First Division team ever to have been relegated after finishing fourth from bottom.

The new man at the helm, Bobby Campbell, arrived too late to halt the inevitable fall into the relegation play-offs after Chelsea failed to beat Charlton on the final day of the season at the Bridge. A comfortable two-legged win over Blackburn put them into the play-off final, but then came the game against Middlesbrough. Chelsea were down – after just four years at the top. The hooligans got to work and Chelsea suffered a heavy FA fine and had to close the terraces for the first six games of the following season.

Campbell added steel with the signings of Graham Roberts and Peter Nicholas, but the team managed just three points from their first six games, with the home matches played in front of tiny all-seated support as a punishment for crowd trouble during the Middlesbrough play-off. Then, they launched into a record twenty-seven-game unbeaten run and the biggest points haul and record margins for promotion. Again, it was clinched against Leeds with Bumstead scoring the winner, and, with Manchester City losing on the same day, Chelsea were also declared champions.

In 1990 and 1991, Chelsea finished fifth and eleventh: the latter year saw them win the Zenith Data Systems Cup against Middlesbrough, thanks to a stunning Tony Dorigo free-kick, and they also reached another Milk Cup semi-final. Despite expensive signings – Dennis Wise and Andy Townsend were brought to the club – the second season back in the top flight was disappointing. One of the casualties was Campbell, who followed the Neal path upstairs' and in came former coach Ian Porterfield, who brought ex-goalkeeping favourite Niedzwiecki with him from Reading. Spurs offered £2.2 million for Gordon Durie and £1 million for Dixon and the Board told Porterfield that he had to agree to one of the deals: he chose to let the injury-prone Durie go. FA Cup disappointment in the quarter-final replay at Sunderland led to the transfer-day departures of Jason Cundy and Clive Allen. It had been the club's first quarter-final for ten years. There was also a first Anfield win in sixty years, but precious little else.

The following season, Don Howe had to stop work because of illness and Porterfield's side faced relegation. Bates acted swiftly: Porterfield was sacked in February 1993 and David Webb was brought in on a short-term contract. Bates did not make the position permanent after his three months' work, however. He had grander plans ... the recruitment of Glenn Hoddle from Swindon Town. Hoddle had the task of leading his club into the Division One play-offs before he could formally commit to Chelsea; in the meantime, Alan Sugar made an approach but it was too late. Hoddle told me at the time that he did not feel it was a good idea to replace Terry Venables after all the internal turmoil at his old club.

Hoddle began as player-manager at the Bridge and completely revolutionised the playing side of the club.

There was stability, at long last, off the field at the Bridge. Several years earlier, SB Property chief executive David Bulstrode had died of a heart attack. Marler Estates had bought SB Property and, after a long-running battle with the new owners, the Royal Bank of Scotland finally bought the stadium in December 1993 and agreed a lease with Chelsea. Bates could now go ahead with his Chelsea Village dream.

Hoddle's sweeper system didn't hit if off, and there was friction developing in the dressing room which came to a head by Christmas, but a defeat at Southampton was the turning point. Dennis Wise and Steve Clarke had been openly questioning the manager's tactics and there was a stormy debate in the dressing room at the Dell. Mark Stein, a £1.5 million signing, suddenly burst into goalscoring form with five consecutive league goals, a record for the Premiership. Despite a deplorable display in the FA Cup third round against Barnet, and then a draw against Sheffield Wednesday at the Bridge, it all came together in the replay with John Spencer and Stein up front together for the first time. Hoddle guided the club to the FA Cup final and things could have been so different if Gavin Peacock's lob which beat Peter Schmeichel had gone in. It didn't: it bounced off the bar and Chelsea then collapsed in the second half to suffer a Wembley mauling. There was an upside, however. United had won the Double and Chelsea had qualified for the Cup-Winners' Cup. There was also a downside: the 4–0 defeat was the biggest in Wembley history.

1

Peter Osgood and the King's Road Boys of the 1970s

Dave Webb headed home Chelsea's winner in the 1970 FA Cup final against Leeds, although he probably bundled it into the net off his cheek. However it really happened, the ball ended up in the back of the net to hand the Blues their first FA Cup – and put one over their bitter rivals.

When the two teams met at Wembley, they already had a fierce dislike for each other; Chelsea were the class act from the King's Road, while Leeds were a ruthless, but efficient, side marshalled by skipper Billy Bremner and managed by 'The Don', Don Revie.

After kicking each other for ninety minutes all over the hallowed turf of England's national stadium, eventual hero Webb and his Chelsea teammates were happy to hear the final whistle. The defender had been turned inside out all game by Eddie Gray as Dave Sexton's side grabbed a 2–2 draw to earn a replay at Old Trafford. Many believed that Chelsea had got away lightly after taking a real battering. 'Keeper Peter Bonetti was crocked early on by Mick Jones, but this was in the days when there was no replacement sitting on the bench to take his place.

The Cat struggled on, without taking goal-kicks, and still managed to pull off a string of fine saves. Leeds took the lead through Jack Charlton after twenty-one minutes, but the Blues levelled matters four minutes before the break, courtesy of Gary Sprake's howler. Peter Houseman, never a favourite with the Chelsea faithful, drove in a long-range effort which Sprake allowed to creep under his body. Chances came and went at both ends in the second half as the usually immaculate Wembley pitch took its toll on the players.

The Horse of the Year show had been held at the stadium shortly before the final and the heavily sanded turf did neither side any favours. But, with six minutes remaining, Leeds thought they had finally killed the game off when Jones beat Bonetti. Chelsea, however, had other ideas. They threw players forward and Hutchinson struck just two minutes later to earn the Londoners another crack at the Cup.

Come the replay, Sexton moved Ron Harris to right-back in place of Webb, who filled in at centre-half. Harris, known as 'Chopper', wasted little time in putting Gray in the stand time and time again – as a result, the winger, unsurprisingly, struggled to have the impact he had had at Wembley. It may be hard to picture in today's age of bookings and red cards, but Chelsea and Leeds literally kicked – and punched – lumps out of each other. It was a battle, pure and simple. Peter Osgood and Charlton squared up to each other, while Bremner and Harris played a tough, hard game.

Jones was on target again to hand Leeds a first-half lead after thirty-five minutes, but Chelsea refused to lie down and, although it was a long time coming, they equalised in the seventy-eighth minute. Osgood had scored in every round of the FA Cup and he kept the record going with a fine diving header.

Apart from the odd bruise, nothing separated the sides come full-time. And it appeared as though extra-time would fail to settle the occasion – until Hutchinson wound up one of his trademark long throws. Webb arrived at the far post and bundled his way towards the ball, forcing it in off his cheek to stun Leeds after 104 minutes of pulsating action. The Blues dug in to hold on to the first of what would later become three FA Cup final victories. Leeds, on the other hand, were left with a bruised ego as Chelsea paraded the Cup.

Peter Osgood

Osgood, Hudson and Cooke rolls off the tongue like Best, Law and Charlton or Greaves and Gilzean. The King's Road set of the 1970s was synonymous with Peter Osgood, Charlie Cooke and Alan Hudson. 'Blue is the Colour' was released before the 1972 League Cup final against Stoke after the club first rose to prominence with their FA Cup win followed by their night of European glory in the Cup-Winners' Cup.

Osgood was Chelsea's answer to George Best. The Manchester United wizard of the wing had come through the ranks, but Chelsea also had a reputation for developing young talent: Brabrook, Greaves, Tambling, Bridges, Shellito, Bonetti, and then Osgood.

Osgood was 6ft 2in, thin and outrageously skilful. Still only eighteen, he equalised in the third round of the FA Cup at Anfield in 1966 against the FA Cup holders and Chelsea scored again to come away with a 2–1 victory. But then Ossie broke his leg in a tackle with a young 'Crazy Horse' Emlyn Hughes in a League Cup tie at Blackpool. Tony Hateley was bought for £100,000 to fill in the gap, and Osgood eventually returned as a heavier character, but still with sufficient brilliance as a goalscorer. Nine months later and two stone heavier, he scored on his comeback with two goals in the 6–2 home defeat by Southampton: one of the goals was a run past half of the opposition.

Although he never actually ever lived in London, he became as much a part of the nightclubbing set as a part of the success that was occurring on the pitch.

A mere four England caps was a poor return for someone of his outrageous talents. Yet, he scored in every round of the 1970 FA Cup, he scored in both the European Cup-Winners' Cup final and replay and got his only Wembley goal in the 1972 League Cup final.

I chatted with Ossie over a convivial lunch at Cafe Blu in Virginia Water, a logical meeting point as his family connections remained in nearby Windsor.

He told me, 'Tommy Docherty called us in before the Cup final in 1967 and told us that we were only going to get ten tickets each. Everybody went berserk. But when he was spotted opening up the boot of his car, there must have been 500 tickets stashed in there! The Doc wasn't everyone's cup of tea and I know George Best very well and they just didn't get on, but he gave me my chance and I idolised the fellow. He knows my family, he would ring them up, and he had a certain way about him, he was most definitely a character and he was "top man" for me.'

The disappointment of losing that Cup final under the Doc was replaced with a remarkable year for Ossie and the boys of 1970. Ossie recalls, 'There is no doubt that, of the great memories I still cherish of my days playing for Chelsea, the best would have to be winning the FA Cup in 1970. That was a great year for me, third in the league, called up for England to go to Mexico in the World Cup squad with great players such as Alan Ball, Bobby Charlton and Nobby Stiles – who had won the World Cup in 1966 – and to win the FA

Cup. The only pity was that we had to win it at Old Trafford in a replay instead of at Wembley, but yes, that was the icing on the cake. It was simply fantastic and the memories will live with me forever.

'It's every kid's dream to win at Wembley, to run out for an FA Cup final. As a kid, I would watch the Wembley final and then I'd go out to kick a ball around, pretending to be one of the players. I always seemed to be Jimmy Greaves.

'Scoring in every round of the FA Cup was something special and then scoring against Real Madrid in the final the next year. We played the final on a Wednesday, it went to extra-time and then went on to a replay two days later. Dave Sexton told the players that there was no point training, just have a swim and a sauna. It was traditional after a match to have a night out followed by a day off and so we carried on that tradition out there! Charlie Cooke, Tommy Baldwin and myself, the usual pack, went down to the Hilton Hotel had a right old session and spent the next day lying around the pool sobering up. I had missed the semi-final against Manchester City with an injury, but I played in the final with the aid of cortisone injections. I was in absolute agony when they wore off though, so I sat around the pool dangling my foot in the water. Alan Hudson strolled past and took a look at us lot and wondered what was going on. He was a fresh-faced lad at that time and was concerned about the state we were in for the replay. We told him not to worry. "Make sure you do your job and we'll do ours." In the replay, Charlie was the Man of the Match. Of course, it didn't take Huddie long to see our way of thinking!

'I noticed that Jose Mourinho likes his players in for training at 9am sharp. Well, that would have suited Huddy and the rest of us. We were always getting into trouble for being late, and that was in the days when training was much later. But 9am would have been fine as we would just be coming back from a night out – we would all have been early for a change!'

The high point of Osgood's Chelsea career was simple enough to pinpoint: winning the FA Cup and then following it up with the European-Cup Winners' Cup. The low point was equally glaringly obvious. 'Breaking my leg at Blackpool in a tackle with old Crazy Horse. It was just after we had beaten Manchester City 4–1 at Maine Road and we were flying. But I was out for quite a while.'

Osgood was still good enough to continue scoring spectacular goals and he revelled in his lap of honour when he collected his 100th league goal, blowing kisses to the crowd. But he fell out with manager Dave Sexton and was transferred to Southampton at the age of twenty-seven. He managed to appear in another FA Cup final when the Saints won their only major trophy. Nearly five years later he returned: he was sold for a record £275,000, but came back for just £25,000. Ten months later, in September 1979, he retired.

He was delighted to return to the Bridge in his capacity as a host for sponsors, until he fell out with chairman Ken Bates. Most people did fall out with chairman Ken from time to time.

By coincidence he found himself sharing the same restaurant as Bates, the famous celebrity eatery Langans in Stratton Street opposite The Ritz. Ossie says, 'I know Ken's dining companion told him to go and shake my hand and make it up, but he said it wasn't the right time or place. You know, I still don't know why we fell out! I was employed at the Bridge for eight years and Bates even invited my wife and son to the club, I couldn't have wished for better. He said that I didn't get on with the girls at Stamford Bridge, it was some sort of insinuation about what I did, but he was never specific and it hurt. I thought about suing him, because he was so wrong: I never had a bad relationship with the girls who worked at the club.

'I received a letter from Ken, out of the blue, you know the usual one: "Dear Peter ..." The letter thanked me for all my efforts on behalf of Chelsea FC, but informed me that a "number of first-team players" would now be getting involved in the hospitality.

'No mention of the fact, of course, that I had been promised a testimonial, and I have got that in writing. One of the stipulations was that 25 per cent of the takings would go to one of the leading charities and, of course, I said yes to that. I had a testimonial when I finished playing, but at that stage I had done twenty years' service with the club. I did everything the right way: I asked Bates if I could go to see Claudio Ranieri, which he said I could. Claudio expressed his appreciation that I went to see him face to face and he said that he would do all he could to help me organise a game, but, when it came to setting a date and then seeking the release of the players, the manager said that I could only have three because the rest were on international duty. That was a waste of time. The date had been set aside; I had contacted Peter Taylor at Leicester and he agreed to send down a couple of his players, such as Frank Sinclair, and I spoke to David O'Leary and he would have done the same.'

The fall-out with Bates occurred when Bates made reference to the King's

Road Boys of 1970 after the death of Ian Hutchison. Ossie says, 'Bates had said that Hutchison, Osgood, Hudson had done nothing for Chelsea since 1970 and just lived on the past. I couldn't let that go and responded in the papers. I think the headline was something like "You are a Prat, Bates!"'

Well, now we know why Ossie was banned!

Ossie is now back at the Bridge. 'Now that Ken has gone, I am back at the Bridge and I thoroughly enjoy it. I work there on match days, and I do the same sort of work at Southampton as well. I am also involved with Radio Saints on Monday nights.'

Charlie Cooke

Twice voted Chelsea's Player of the Year, the fans would sing 'Cooke's better than Eusabio', and only the brilliance of Gianfranco Zola eclipsed Cooke as perhaps the greatest, most entertaining and naturally gifted player in the club's history. Cooke became Chelsea's second Player of the Year after the establishment of the award in 1967.

Charlie destroyed England at Hampden Park in 1968 with his dribbling prowess, although the game finished 1–1. 'When Charlie Cooke sold you a dummy, you had to pay at the turnstiles to get back into the stadium' was the tribute paid to Cooke by the legendary Jim Baxter. Osgood chipped in, 'A great dribbler, a great runner, a terrific player and a great character.'

Charlie was bought from Dundee by Tommy Docherty to replace Terry Venables. 'If you remember,' says Charlie, his Greenock accent altered by years in the States, 'the Busby Babes had come and gone, and, in the years before I joined, Docherty's Diamonds came along, and Chelsea were known as the up-and-comers. I thought to myself, If there was any team I would have liked to go to, it would have been that one. So when Tommy Doc came in I was delighted. I didn't really need any selling on it. I wanted to go to England and would have chosen Chelsea over any other team. I was very happy to sign. People said to me about taking Terry's place, it hadn't occurred to me. That's how naive I was. I was excited to be joining a big club. I had no idea about the cliques or the politics within the club. Back then, you didn't have Internet access, you didn't know nearly as much about what was going on. Afterwards, people talked about the break-up of the team as something that was instigated solely by Tommy Doc. I would say it was probably a fifty–fifty thing. Once the players had dug their heels in about their beef with Tommy, it seemed to me as though it was as much their doing as Tommy's. If there was guilt involved, everyone was guilty.'

Out went Venables, George Graham and Barry Bridges; in came Cookie, Hudson and Baldwin. Cookie was at the epicentre of the swinging sixties in London. 'My move was all about soccer, joining Chelsea and playing European football, it wasn't about London. Once you got to London, you realised it was a big change.'

Tommy Baldwin, who signed from Arsenal, was a soul-mate and a drinking partner. 'You meet so many people in the game. You live in different parts of the city. You're travelling, practising and playing together. Sometimes I think you saw enough of people. I wasn't one for having a great group of friends, people I kept in touch with for the rest of my life. But Tommy was a real close friend. We used to go all over the place. I'd always been a drinker, but I think at that time it was probably standard within the game. It was fun and craziness from start to finish. The country was doing well economically, the music and the film businesses were on the up, and a load of things were happening in London. It didn't feel very glamorous, though people outside might have thought it was. That was always a subject of great mirth.'

Cookie was cool, brilliant and the fans' favourite. 'Although it was true I became a big fan favourite, I never thought of being so. I was always focused on how I was playing, whether I was playing well or poorly. It was great to have that adulation, if you want to call it that, but I felt as though it was shared by everybody.'

But, unlike Venables, he wasn't a midfield playmaker; he ended up on the wing, but he is best described as a genius of the dribble, a creator, a provider for Osgood and the other forwards.

In Charlie's first season, Chelsea finally broke their jinx and reached their first FA Cup final in fifty-two years, only to lose to Venables and Spurs. But it was the start of the new Chelsea. His first two managers were poles apart. 'Tommy Docherty was full of bounce, full of fun, always looking for a joke, real fun to be around. Dave Sexton was fun to be around in a different way: he was a much more serious personality, much more reserved. But, when he started talking, he was obviously a deep thinker about the game.'

The Doc's swansong was the FA Cup final defeat by Spurs in 1967. Charlie says, 'That was a real disappointment, just a non-event for us. We played awfully.'

The new manager, Dave Sexton, tried Osgood in midfield, but it didn't work out and he eventually brought in Hudson. Sexton moved him to the flank with enormous success.

In 1970, though, Cooke was unstoppable as Chelsea finished third in the league and won the FA Cup. With Hudson injured for the final, Peter Houseman filled in, but in extra-time and in the subsequent replay Cooke switched to midfield. It was from Cooke's superb chip that Osgood headed the equaliser in the replay. 'I remember feeling that the game was kind of drifting, we were going nowhere. "We need to crack something open." That was on my mind, and, when I picked up the ball, it was pretty far out, and I was just trying to force something to happen.' Cooke ran with the ball, created a crossing opportunity and steered a superb diagonal ball for Ossie to convert. 'It was a beautiful cross. Ossie always makes the most of those things.'

Although players like Osgood insist that they would have preferred to have won the FA Cup at Wembley rather than at Old Trafford, Cookie recalls, 'I liked the Old Trafford replay. It was tough, exciting and there was a lot at stake, too. They were our archrivals for quite a few years. It was cut-throat. This constant whining at referees they did, the referee baiting. That gamesmanship used to ruffle our feathers.'

The following year, Cooke was the star of the European Cup-Winners' Cup final replay. Again he played in the centre of midfield with Hollins injured and Keith Weller on the flank. Spanish international and Real Madrid striker Amancio said before the European Cup-Winners' Cup final of 1971, 'If we stop Cooke, we will win.' They didn't.

Cooke recalls, 'You didn't read the newspapers, especially foreign ones, except the headlines, but I'm proud if that's what he actually said.' Charlie was the provider for Dempsey's opener in a 2–1 triumph: 'I remember the game itself. It was mostly even, but we deserved to win. I think we wore them out.'

Twelve months later, he was one of the few to show top form in the League Cup final.

Although the team thrived on the field, with pure entertainment value, off it, Cooke, along with his close pal Tommy Baldwin, became hooked on the social scene, and their form was sometimes inconsistent. There were numerous excuses put forward for the quick demise of a potentially wonderfully gifted team, from their wayward behaviour and Sexton's man-

ove: Russian billionaire, Roman Abramovich, has fallen in love with Chelsea since he ıght the club. Peter Kenyon was brought to the club by Abramovich from Manchester ıited. The club Chief Executive is the highest paid executive in the modern game.

low: Abramovich's wife Irina and their son watch Chelsea play. The couple have e children.

Roman Abramovich salutes the faithful fans at Stamford Bridge.

ıudio Ranieri called himself 'the Tinkerman' because of his constant changes to the ɜ-up of his team. After Abramovich bought the club, Ranieri faced a difficult final ıson when he was under mounting pressure – his days were numbered. After much dia speculation, Ranieri was replaced by Jose Mourinho.

low: An emotional Ranieri bids a tearful farewell to his fans.

Jose Mourinho took over the manager's position in 2004. In just a single season, Mourinho has guided his team to Premiership and Carling Cup success.

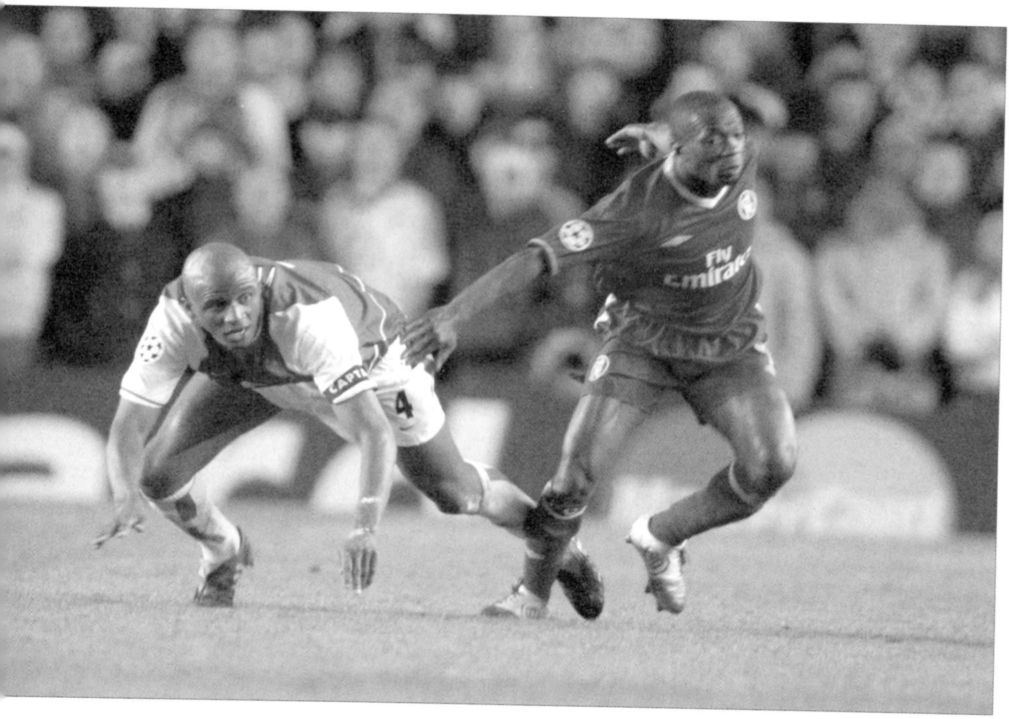

ve: Mourinho has forged an unlikely friendship with rival manager, Alex Ferguson of
ichester United. Both men have spoken openly of their respect for one another.

w: Claude Makelele was one of ten players bought by Abramovich in a shopping spree
h stunned the world of football. Makelele's move was particularly sensational as
sea bought the player from Real Madrid even though Real seemed reluctant to sell.

Glen Johnson became the first player to be bought with Abramovich's millions. At th
time he was a little-known England Under-21 player.

ch winger, Arjen Robben joined Chelsea in 2004. Although his season was disrupted njury, he still managed to impress with his pace and goal-scoring ability.

Mateja Kezman and Arjen Robben are nicknamed 'Batman and Robin'. The nicknan comes from their days at PSV Eindhoven but was quickly adopted at Stamford Bridg following the practical jokes they play on their teammates.

management to the lack of funds released by the Board. Cooke says, 'It's a blame game. I think we were all a bit churlish, immature about it. I think these days we would have been a bit better informed about what was going on. The ground was getting rebuilt, the team was being changed and results were pretty crappy. It was a pretty depressing time.'

Then a boozy book launch was the cut-off point for Sexton, and Cooke knows it should have been handled differently. 'No question, no question. That was just total stupidity. I've seen Dave many times since. We never discuss it. It's a non-event. A lot of the guys, if we're really honest, have to say the same. We were just a little out of control.'

But there were many ups as well as downs, regrets and bad decisions. Charlie recalls, 'We did have a lot of fun, but when we were training, when we were at work, we put everything into it. If I have one regret, it's that I didn't score more goals. I had a great strike in both feet. I scored goals in Scotland, but people said I was a "creator" and I liked that and believed it. That was one of the biggest regrets of my career. One of the reasons, and it'll sound bulls**t to some, was that I was a young boy in the game, away from home, and you read the newspapers and they say you're the guy who makes the goals for other people, and that's what I prided myself on. Scoring goals meant didlysquat to me in comparison. I always liked highly skilled players. The kinds of players who play upfront and couldn't beat a tram ... I didn't have a lot of respect for them. Being a goalscorer was a much, much more important thing than I'd ever given credit for. And it could have changed my career if I'd put a bit more focus and energy into it. It was a terrible weakness.'

He scored thirty goals in 373 matches and became categorised as a 'roamer', a latter-day schemer, rather than as a goalscorer. 'Nothing excites me more than to see midfield players scoring goals. I think the young lad today, Frank Lampard, can do all the hard work in midfield, he has good, quick skills, he can do all the things you would want from a ball-playing footballer and he's still got some finish in his game. That's fantastic. There are similarities with Alan Hudson, though Lampard's nowhere near as smooth. Alan was a lovely mover, very elegant, with two or three yards of pace that got him out of all sorts of jams, and you always got the feeling he was thinking two or three moves ahead.'

He recalls one of the 'tricks' he and his pals would get up to in their heyday. 'We were in treatment on a Friday at the Bridge, me Tommy, Ossie and I think Alan Hudson. Harry Medhurst, the trainer, had finished with us and told us to be back at 1.30pm. We went to a small restaurant round the corner which isn't there now and had a fun lunch. It got really fun, and we didn't go back. All of a sudden, Dave Sexton turns up and wants to know what we're doing. He orders us back, but we're so far gone all we can do is laugh. We go back, he's furious, and there was a bar we had to step over and I just fell over it. I was lying on my back, looking up at all the others, and, because we'd been having a fun time, just laughed. It's so embarrassing to think of it. I think we were all dropped next day and we deserved it. In my day, whether the rules were written or not, everybody realised we were out of order if we were out doing things. With the huge rewards in the game nowadays, players have to get in shape and stay in shape. There are so many new facilities for training and preparation that help a player these days that we didn't have. I can remember doing weight training in a very haphazard manner through most of my career. It didn't make a lot of sense, there was no consistency. With the rewards on offer now, I would think it might be in the players' interest to become "gym-rats". But managers are charged with getting results for the first team. At the end of the day, if he puts the club right off the field, but first-team results are not good, would everything still be hunky-dory?'

With his drinking problems mounting, however, Sexton sold him off to Crystal Palace. It was such an unpopular decision that Sexton brought him back within two years. He won the Player of the Year award again and even got back into the Scotland team. It took sixteen months at Palace for Cooke to rediscover his desire, and, when he returned to the Bridge, it was to a young team. 'I was always ever so impressed by "Butch" Wilkins's performances. I always loved his skills, technique and his finishing ability, too. He set a great standard to all the guys around him. Sadly, it coincided with a time when it was very difficult to shine. The club was a wounded giant and it had a long way to go to get better.'

He left Chelsea for America, where he played for Los Angeles Aztecs, Memphis Rogues and California Surf. Charlie quit in 1978. On his retirement he gave up alcohol, and decided to stay in the States, where he first coached the Wichita Wings in the MSL and then ran successful soccer schools. Now, at the age of sixty-two, he says, 'I've been out in America for twenty-four years and I've been off the alcohol for a long, long time. I do feel great. Things are going well. I have got schools in thirty-eight states now.'

Alan Hudson

When Alan Hudson played against Derby in 1969, he was just four months past his eighteenth birthday and had played four games. He replaced Peter Osgood, who had been switched to midfield after a barren period in attack, but then Osgood dropped down to substitute. When he came off the bench to play in attack, the side suddenly clicked. Hudson went on to play every game for the remainder of the season until that dreadful day on 30 March when ankle-ligament damage at West Brom forced him to miss the FA Cup final.

Hudson was truly a 'local' boy made good. He grew up in a wartime-built prefab at the World's End. He was one of the most naturally gifted talents to emerge.

Sir Alf Ramsey once said, 'There is no limit to what this boy can achieve.'

However, he failed to fulfil all those promises and, having missed the Cup final, he was never quite the same player.

He won a European Cup-Winners' Cup medal when he was still only nineteen, to make up for the heartache of missing the FA Cup final, but he went AWOL when he was supposed to join the England Under-23s tour. As a result, he was suspended from international football for two years.

He observed, 'George Best wanted to come to Chelsea at that time and if there had been an Abramovich around at that time we would definitely have got him, even if we'd had to have mashed the transfer record.'

But he became part of the King's Road set that manager Dave Sexton could not control and both he and Osgood were sold off. Hudson played 189 times for Chelsea scoring fourteen goals before joining Stoke for £240,000 in January 1974. Hudson took unfashionable Stoke to the top of the table while Chelsea were relegated, won a couple of England caps and moved on to Arsenal, where he reached a Cup final only to lose surprisingly to Ipswich.

Typically, he had an argument with Terry Neill, and walked out on the Gunners to play in America with Seattle Sounders. He returned to the Bridge nine years after leaving, but didn't play for the club again and left after another argument to return to Stoke. He finally retired through injury at the age of thirty-four.

He returned to Chelsea on match days in a hosting role, but that role also ended after a row.

The biggest battles were still to come: a life-threatening road accident in

1997 and a downward spiral that included a divorce and an attempt to refinance himself by media work and writing books.

'He should have been at Chelsea longer and achieved much more than he did for them,' says Charlie Cooke.

Hudson has selected his all-time best Chelsea side, which includes himself and Ruud Gullit in central midfield. He explains, 'Every team I ever pick, I always pick myself. I can't be left out!' As for Gullit, he suggests, 'For Chelsea Football Club to get Ruud Gullit as a player after what he'd done in his life was fantastic. He had made the heights that Chelsea are trying to reach now. He played at the back, in midfield and up front. I'm glad I never played against him man-for-man, he was just awesome. He changed so much just by coming here.'

Up front he went for Greaves and Osgood. On Ossie he said, 'Do I need to tell you about him? He was the king. Everyone who saw Peter Osgood play knows all his strengths, and the bigger the game the better he played.' And on Greaves: 'Probably the greatest player Chelsea ever had for quality, scoring goals, and probably the best player Tottenham ever had. I was fortunate enough to play against him in my second match. He had so much consistency in scoring goals, and if he was being kicked you didn't see him on the floor. Anyway, he didn't get kicked, he just went past everyone.'

Charlie Cooke, inevitably, makes his selection, too. 'Ah, a million memories. One of the greatest players of all time. He had a terrible mental problem, a terrible drinking problem, but if Scotland had got to the World Cup stage in those days he would have been seen as a truly world-class player. Super skills. Training with him when he was sober, you had to work so hard to keep up with his quality.'

John Hollins

John Hollins was the player who moved into the manager's office. While Osgood and Hudson were the heavy drinkers and late-night party-goers of the era, John was happy at home in Surrey. He played once for England and 592 times for the club. He was voted the club's Player of the Year in both the FA Cup final and Cup-Winners' Cup final years. He won one England cap against Spain, and also played in the 1967 FA Cup final. He played right-back, midfield, and even scored the BBC's Goal of the Season against Bob Wilson. He moved on to QPR and Arsenal, but returned in 1983 as player-coach to help win the Second Division championship. He later became manager, but left in acrimonious circumstances.

Hollins is not envious of the kind of budget now afforded to Chelsea managers in comparison to the days on the poverty line when he was in control of the dressing room.

Now fifty-eight and still hoping for a revival in the management stakes, he remains a regular visitor to the Bridge. He can see some similarities in the youthful Chelsea side in which he excelled. 'We were a team in the real sense. We had the right attitude and so do Mourinho's team. The first Chelsea team I played in as a seventeen-year-old, the 1964 side, had Terry Venables, Eddie McCreadie, Barry Bridges and George Graham. We were young and confident and could outrun anyone else in the First Division. Isn't that an outstanding quality of the present team, too, to run and work for each other, to want to play, no, to *desire* to play for Chelsea.'

Hollins is overjoyed at the prospect of Chelsea fulfilling their destiny which they failed to do in his era. 'Abramovich has the money he needs to buy the very best. I remember how difficult things were when I was manager. Once I couldn't believe how long the grass was getting. I asked why it hadn't been cut and was told that they owed money on the mower and weren't allowed to use it! I gave the groundsman £50 of my own money and told him to go out and buy anything that would solve the problem. But it's not only the money; Mourinho also has scientific knowledge that was not available to us. For example, as players we used to have a big steak and rice puddings before every match: we know now that it takes five hours to digest that sort of meal, but we weren't aware of that then and, in a couple of hours, we'd be out there running like hares. It helps when you know. Jean Tigana, for example, when he was coach at Fulham, insisted on regular hand, feet and teeth examinations. You can discover a lot from the condition of teeth. If we had a toothache, we'd just ask for a touch of whisky, but it wouldn't stop us playing. Now, if you have so much as a sniffle, you are left out, although I noticed John Terry, who has been outstanding, coughing hard in the warm-up before the Middlesbrough game. I thought then that he was taking a big chance if he had failed to tell them he wasn't 100 per cent.'

Hollins has coached for six months in China, and in Scotland, helping Nicolas Anelka's brother Claude at Raith Rovers, 'I have never lost the enthusiasm to coach, to work with players, to make them better if you are in China or with Chelsea, that's the point to it all. I live every day, fresh, bright and sharp.'

Peter Bonetti

Voted Chelsea's Greatest Ever Player in the club programme in 1969, halfway through his Stamford Bridge career, he was affectionately known as 'The Cat'. Despite his slight 5ft 10in frame, he dominated his area with his ability to catch crosses.

He also had a sense of style, with green shorts and socks to co-ordinate with his jersey. He was an all-round distinctive star and was the first player to wave to the fans when they chanted his name before games. He missed just two games in the year that Chelsea won the FA Cup in 1970, when the team also finished third in the league; crucially the games he missed out on were against the two sides who finished above Chelsea, champions Everton and runners-up Leeds. Both games were lost 5–2. Bonetti played on past his thirty-fifth birthday before he retired in 1979, having played 729 games. From 1960 to 1979, thirteen other 'keepers started a game, but Bonetti was always the first choice.

He was two years younger than Gordon Banks and, as a result, was restricted to just seven England caps. The low point of his career came when he deputised for Banks in the 1970 World Cup finals; he was blamed for West Germany's comeback to knock holders England out.

Alan Hudson said of him, 'Bonetti was somebody who shouldn't have been a goalkeeper, there was nothing of him. I call him a Biafran runner, he'd run for miles. I was stood right behind Bobby Charlton one day and he whacked it and the whole ground stood up and shouted goal, and "Catty" didn't just save it, he caught it. I played against Gordon Banks and with Peter Shilton and Pat Jennings, but he was the best.'

P

Pioneers

The inspiration for the formation of Chelsea FC came from brothers Henry Augustus and J.T. Mears, sons of one of the captial's wealthiest building contractors. Stamford Bridge stadium, which had been home to the London Athletic Club since 1877, provided the perfect setting for their vision. Augustus Mears first approached the stadium owner, Mr Stunt, in 1896, but it wasn't until Stunt's death, six years later, that Augustus obtained the deeds to the stadium. The Athletic Club remained leaseholders for a further two years, as the Mears brothers prepared for entrance into the Football League.

One version of how and why Cheslea were formed was provided in Gus Mears's obituary in the *Fulham Chronicle*: 'How and when the idea of starting a football club first suggested itself to him is not defintely known. But it was generally agreed that the directors of Fulham FC first mooted the idea of football at Stamford Bridge. They were at the time desirous of leaving Craven Cottage and approached Mr Mears with a view to securing a lease on his newly aquired land. Mr Mears considered the suggestion, but came to the conclusion that he would do better to start a football club himself.'

Mears, it was rumoured, offered Fulham a lease for £1,500 per annum, and when it was rejected, opted to start his own club. Fulham chairman Henry Norris was irritated that he had given Mears the idea of starting his own club! Fulham blocked Cheslea's entry to the Southern League, so Mears took them into the Football League, which, eager to move into the South-East, expanded by four clubs.

Mears and Fred Parker, an old friend and a former steward at the London Athletic Club, visited Glasgow to inspect great stadia such as Hampden, Ibrox and Parkhead and met architects Archibald Leitch, who agreed to design the East Stand as the centrepeice of a ground which had three enormous open terraces. Mears wanted a ground to hold 100,000 'that would stagger humanity'.

Augustus Mears, although never chairman, continued to be the driving force behind Chelsea, until he died in 1912. The *Chelsea Chroncicle* paid this tribute: 'He has left behind him a monument that is more eloquent than any carved epitaph. In the Chelsea Football Club and the Stamford Bridge Sports ground which he gave to the sport-loving masses of London, his memory will remain green so long as the Chelsea ground shall exist.'

Chairman Claude Kirby, an old friend of the Mears family, was determined to carry on the Mears traditions, but he did not have quite the same financial muscle.

Q

Quickest Goal in FA Cup Final History

Bob Chatt scored the quickest FA Cup final goal in 1895 when he gave Aston Villa the lead against West Bromwich Albion after just forty seconds – but that final was held at Crystal Palace.

Roberto Di Matteo scored the fastest FA Cup fnal goal at Wembley in 42.4 seconds on Saturday, 17 May 1997. The goal helped end a run of twenty-six years without a trophy for Chelsea.

Roberto Di Matteo's blind sister, Concetta, was at Wembley for the big occasion. Roberto didn't even know that he had made Wembley history until an hour after the final whistle. As he groomed himself in front of the dressing-room mirror, he laughed, 'Yes, my hair is OK. Was it the fastest goal ever, surely not? I didn't know I am in the record books. But it's not too bad, is it? When I scored, it did my head in. I didn't know where I was for two minutes afterwards. I was surprised that they let me run so far. Maybe they didn't expect me to shoot. But I just shot and I was lucky because it dipped. I've been very lucky. I think my sister Concetta will have heard the crowd when I scored and she will have been celebreating. My father was giving her a running commentary.'

Not only is Roberto famous for the record fastest goal, but also for becoming the first Italian to win a trophy in English football. Fitting, then, that he should celebrate with a Roman pose. 'It was so quick. I was so excited, I couldn't calm down. It was an unbelievable feeling, so great in emotion, the first time I had experienced anything like this.'

As for the Cup final atmosphere itself: 'It was better than I could ever have thought.'

Di Matteo finished the season playing in more games than anyone else, starting forty-three times and scoring eight goals, a season's best, but: 'This one was my best goal.'

The capacity crowd of 79,160 for the match with Middlesbrough, once again witnessed a below-par final, but for the Blues it was one of the most wonderful days for their fans, who had waited since 29 April 1970, when the club won their replay against the might of Leeds United at Old Trafford and then won the Cup-Winners' Cup a year later, but had won nothing of any consequence since.

Ruud Gullit devoloped the team and they continued the progress that had been made under Glenn Hoddle. Under the dreadlocked Dutchman, Chelsea played off the cuff – epiomised by their comeback against Liverpool at the Bridge – and with a swagger that became labelled 'sexy football'.

Before the team left the dressing room, Steve Clarke turned to captain Dennis Wise and uttered the best motivational speech: 'This is it, this is the day we lay to rest the ghost of the 1970s. It's about time people started talking about this team, instead.'

Franco Zola, voted the Football Writers' Footballer of the Year on the fiftieth anniversary of that prestigious award, had been wisely rested by Gullit for the final two league games, as he struggled to shake off a niggling hamstring injury, while Wise had missed the final league game against Everton with a stomach muscle injury and required painkilling injections in the few days leading up to the final and on the day of the final itself.

Seconds after referee Steven Lodge started the contest, Di Matteo collected a short pass from Wise. Clarke was the only other Chelsea player to touch the ball. Di Matteo drove forward fully expecting to be tackled. With Mark Hughes creating space ahead of him, he eventually let fly from thirty yards: his right-foot shot dipped over 'keeper Ben Roberts and rapped the underside of the bar before going into the net.

Finally, the irrepressible Zola helped create Chelsea's second goal eight minutes from the end; Newton began the move and Petrescu's delicate chip to the far post seemed beyond Zola, but his delightful backflick was finished off from close range by Newton.

Bitter memories of the 4–0 FA Cup final hammering by Manchester United under Hoddle were vanquished. Regrettably, Di Matteo's career was cut short through injury.

R

Claudio Ranieri

The Sayings of Claudio Ranieri

On growing pressures: 'I want us to be one of the best teams in the world, but everyone wants to crucify me like Jesus Christ.'

To the Press before the Champions League semi-final second-leg with Monaco: 'Hello my sharks, welcome to the funeral.'

On why Chelsea are not ready for trophies: 'It is my baby. Maybe soon it will be ready to get out of the pram.'

On the pressure from owner Roman Abramovich: 'Look, I already have his sword embedded in me.'

On too many players: 'If you need just a first XI and three or four more, then why did Christopher Columbus sail to India to discover America?'

Claudio Ranieri simply couldn't resist tinkering. He called himself 'the Tinkerman', and the description fitted perfectly.

He couldn't resist change, sometimes changing things just for the sake of change. He hardly ever fielded the same side twice, and his policy of using the full range of his extensive squad for rotation meant that he sacrificed continuity. From the very start of his final season in charge, with all the money available from new owner Roman Abramovich, he argued that the object was to ensure that his players were fresh come March and April, and he was proved right: results picked up in the latter stages of the season, but by then it was far too late to catch Arsenal in the league.

Ranieri called himself a gladiator, Christopher Columbus, Rudyard Kipling, Michelangelo, and once suggested that he was the Thinkerman as much as the Tinkerman. The argument is that perhaps he thought about his tactics and deployment of his players far too much.

He took Chelsea on a voyage of discovery like Columbus, won Champions League glory in Rome with his gladiators, quoted Kipling as he responded to endless questions about his future, or lack of it, and painted marvellous pictures with his tactics. He insisted that he wanted an English backbone to his team, but he was never a Churchill-type figure in the dressing room. He failed to galvanise his players into winning a trophy.

So Ranieri became accustomed to being dubbed the 'Dead Man Walking' and started to refer to himself in the same manner.

But first, an analysis on why Ranieri was labelled 'not good enough for us' by the Abramovich regime.

He had his moments in his final season: twice 1–0 up against Arsenal in both Premier League games, had his team run out winners on both occasions they might have won the title. Even with Chelsea's total of points, in most seasons, it would have been good enough to land the club's first title since 1955. And, of course, Chelsea went further on their Columbus expedition in the Champions League, reaching the last four, beating Arsenal in an epic quarter-final along the way.

However, the downside was pretty spectacular.

A complete mess of the second-half substitutions in Monaco cost Chelsea a place in the final in what would have been a winnable contest. Wasted opportunities in a variety of Premiership games that saw bizarre tactical changes ferreted away vital points. Ranieri's tinkering moved in such mysterious ways that fans even started to place bets on the line-ups. He often deployed players in unusual positions. For example, £17 million was invested in left-winger Damien Duff, and he often played on the right or behind the front strikers. It's a credit to Duff that, despite his long absence with a dislocated shoulder, he had a successful season.

The reality for Ranieri was that he was actually a Dead Man Walking from the moment the man who appointed him, Ken Bates, sold up to Abramovich. Abramovich has an inner circle of advisers, around five to six who he trusts and consults. It was unanimous from the start that Ranieri was not the calibre of coach required for the new Chelsea, the one that would invest £250 million in the best players available and £140 million in the first season alone. Having also spent £60 million buying up 100 per cent of the shares and taking on the £90 million worth of debts – the final bill amounts to £400 million – you would be right to to believe that you are entitled to some tangible return.

Sven-Goran Eriksson went to tea with Abramovich in his London pad, but the England coach was not ready to leave his Soho Square posting. However, Eriksson clearly had some input into the 'committee' deciding on how to spend Abramovich's millions in the transfer market.

Yet Ranieri began well, and Abramovich warmed to the coach who was turning media and public scrutiny in his favour with some impressive results. He has been reinvented by the media who had ridiculed him as a clown for his broken English – to the point where he refused to conduct post-match press conferences – into the media darling, because he was the underdog who said he would like to be the dog for a change.

He was charming in the face of adversity and polite and self-effacing under a barrage of questioning about how long he thought he would survive. He affectionately called his inquisitors 'sharks'.

But a dip in the team's performances over Christmas and the New Year, coupled with rows with players like Jimmy-Floyd Hasselbaink behind the scenes, permeated the dressing room. Word reached Abramovich's men that the players had become baffled by the tactics, unsettled by the rotation system and mystified by the positional experiments.

While Liverpool were plotting Gerard Houllier's demise with discreet soundings of potential successors, the newly installed chief executive, Peter Kenyon, was followed by photographers ready to snap him in action talking to the England coach or accompanying Abramovich to Vigo for talks with Jose Mourinho.

Sympathy abounded for Ranieri: his tears when he finally beat Arsenal provoked backing from everyone in the country and he was named Man of the Year by the Variety Club of Great Britain, but in the cut-throat world of football, Liverpool were doing exactly the same thing, but without the kind of media hordes that wanted to know every move of the mysterious new Russian owner and his plans to revolutionise the Bridge.

The sterile home draw with Stuttgart in the Champions League, coupled with the inability to beat Arsenal until they eventually performed the miracle in the Champions League at the seventeenth attempt under Ranieri, convinced the Abramovich courtiers that it was time to put a new man in charge. Kenyon started work on 1 February, and instantly made it clear that, given the huge investment in players, the inability to win a trophy would be deemed a failure. With that as the benchmark, Ranieri failed to deliver, irrespective of how close he might have come.

Eriksson initially said 'yes', only to change his mind when his trusted allies, such as Tord Grip, warned him of the consequences of trying to work and live in this country after being branded a traitor for deserting England. Having eventually signed a new agreement with the FA, he burned his bridges at the Bridge, so Mourinho became the target.

The sniping began early. When Ranieri became aware that he was being replaced by Mourinho, he pointed out that his successor was a novice in the big leagues of Europe – even though he had won the UEFA Cup and reached the Champions League final.

Ranieri finished second in the Premier League and reached the Champions League semi-final, but Kenyon and Abramovich did not regard him as a coach who could fulfil their ambitions.

The reaction to Ranieri's demise was predictably mixed. Lampard broke off from his preparations for the England friendly with Japan in Manchester to say, 'In the three years I've been at Chelsea, Claudio has done loads for me. He gave me a chance and, without that, who knows where I would be? I cannot say enough about him. The way I'm playing and how I've developed in character, that's got to be down to him. He is a very honourable and dignified man. I respect everything he's done and I will be talking to him and thanking him. There is some sadness. It's a difficult situation, but the club is the be-all and end-all. Managers and players move on. What's made it difficult is that it has lingered over a whole season. We've done very well this year, without winning anything, but the core of the team is already there. There will be changes, we all anticipate that, but I don't think there should be too many wholesale changes because we have got to know each other this year. New players have come in and the majority have fitted in very well. Hopefully, we can add to that core and come back even stronger than we were.'

Peter Osgood believed Ranieri had 'gone with dignity' but questioned his

'Tinkerman' approach. 'He has brought this upon himself and I am not surprised he has gone. He tinkered too much. We beat Lazio 4–0 and then we beat Newcastle 5–0 to go top of the league. It was the best football I had seen, but the following week he changed his team. Ranieri said the players were tired, but players don't get tired when they win. Against Monaco the game was at 1–1 and he brought on Veron who had played thirty minutes' football in five months. That can't be right. Roman Abramovich has put a lot of money into the club and he can do what he likes. I don't feel sorry for Claudio. He'll get another job.'

Former assistant boss Graham Rix, who worked under Ruud Gullit and Gianluca Vialli, said, 'For the amount of money he has spent, Abramovich can expect a trophy or two.'

Newspaper columnist David Mellor, the former MP and Chelsea fan, agreed that Ranieri had to go. 'Chelsea spent massively last summer and they have two internationals for every position. He should have done better. If Roman Abramovich had been looking for a manager when he came in, nobody would have suggested Ranieri. I would love to say, "What a lovely fellow, he should have been kept on", but you cannot watch Chelsea without thinking there is something eccentric and unusual about how they manage their resources. It could have been handled better, but I believe he had to go.'

Another legend, Ron Harris, said, 'He spent a lot of money and won nothing. Gianluca Vialli won five trophies in two years and got the sack. It seems to be part and parcel of football these days – if people don't win anything, they're on the way.'

John Hollins reacted: 'I'm surprised Ranieri has gone, he seemed to have weathered the storm. He has done a good job. There are some good young players who have come in, but what really confused him was bringing in ten or eleven players – he was just spoiled for choice.'

Ranieri's book *Proud Man Walking* does not reveal the full extent of his problems during the Champions League semi-final first leg in Monaco. He made irrational substitutions which led to Chelsea throwing away a winning position.

In Ranieri's account he describes his emotions as 'anger' at discovering that his Chelsea bosses had been talking to Jose Mourinho just twenty-four hours before the match in Monte Carlo.

Ranieri confesses that he was 'troubled' when 'it came to my knowledge that, while we had been preparing for the match, Chelsea had had a meeting with representatives of Mourinho. I had put up with a lot in these last few months, but this was really hard to take. It showed a lack of respect, not just for me but also for the players and for all the effort we were putting in to try and achieve something historic for Chelsea.'

However, the truth is that the players were not the slightest bit distracted, but Ranieri was deeply affected. After a series of bizarre substitutions, Chelsea surrendered a 1–0 lead to lose 3–1 to a team that had been reduced to ten men.

Ranieri, in his book, now confesses, 'I wanted so badly to win this game, but instead we lost, and I was the main culprit. I had let myself be affected by anger over the meeting between the club and Mourinho's agent, and wanted the win as a way of retaliating, proving a point. But it was a mistake. Utmost respect for the opposition, the chance to take advantage of their misfortune and the events of the night before had combined to influence my judgement, and I made the wrong choices.'

However Ranieri might have been far more profoundly affected by more than mere anger. Jon Smith, of First Artist Management, was orchestrating his UK affairs and co-ordinating talks inside Chelsea on his client's future, his contract and potential pay-off.

Smith tells me, 'Claudio was very emotional when he found out the day before the game, perhaps more emotional than I have ever seen. Word had got out in Spain and Italy and he had been told. He said he would try to remain focused on the game, on the football, and despite what occurred in the match he had no intention of using those talks as an excuse. Of course it affected him, how could it not?'

At the entrance to a genteel London hotel restaurant Memories, a sombre string quartet strike up a plaintive melody on cue. 'This is my first lunch in London since I left Chelsea,' he laughs, 'and they send us to a place called Memories! They start playing this sad, but beautiful, music when I walk through the door. What are they telling me? I am a sensitive man. I understand. I am not bitter – but I will tell you when I was most disappointed. The day before the first leg of the Champions League semi-final against Monaco, I hear that Roman Abramovich and Peter Kenyon are about to meet Mourinho's agent in Monte Carlo. It was a little ...' He continues, 'I knew they wanted Mourinho, but the timing was very wrong. In that moment I said to myself, "I'm going to try even more to win this game." So I go too strong. The emotion takes over. But this is my fault. It is my responsibility.'

In his desire for 'retaliation', for 'proving a point' to Abramovich, the club's owner, and Kenyon, the chief executive, Ranieri seemed to lose all his tactical composure. When Monaco were reduced to ten men, he 'wanted to kill the tie there and then'. Some already dubious selections were exacerbated when, with his choice of substitutes, he left Chelsea vulnerable and exposed. They conceded three goals on a night which still haunts him. 'Before the second leg at home I also think we can do something fantastic. The guys were very strong. We go 2–0 up and then Monaco score with a handball in the last second of the first half. This is pain! If they start the second half two goals down then they have to attack. The game is completely changed. But that is not how the story worked out.'

He shrugs when asked if even winning the competition could have saved him. He suggests that, at his first meeting with Abramovich, 'calmly and with the greatest sincerity, I had presented him with an opening, a perfect assist, to end my contract painlessly. No answer. Instead, he began to ask for my opinions on the team ...'

Ranieri reveals more: 'I did not say this in the book, but something happened before that meeting. When Roman arrived for the first time during pre-season, I was in Trevor Birch's office. Suddenly I see four or five men walk past. Trevor says Roman was one of them. I tell Trevor that if Roman doesn't meet me today then I have no chance. And of course he did not ask to see me. We only met about a week later. I took this as a very clear signal.'

Though Ranieri describes Abramovich as 'a very loyal man', he is aware that the Russian had initially planned to replace him with Sven-Goran Eriksson. 'Oh yes. This was clear. I can either say "bye" or try for a miracle. When he cannot get Eriksson, I am looking for the big bingo number. I say, "Come on, Claudio – try!" For a long time I could almost see the winning numbers in front of me.'

He goes on to say that Abramovich is 'very mysterious. He is hard to know, but he was very generous to me. Abramovich asks simple questions. "Who is the best manager in England?" They tell him Eriksson. He says, "I want Eriksson." He then asks, "Who is the best in marketing?" Someone says, "Peter Kenyon." So Roman says, "I want Kenyon."' Ranieri adds, 'I think Roman is a strong man. Kenyon is different. He is not a fantastic person. Oh Peter Kenyon! He gave me fantastic emotion! When he came, the atmosphere outside the dressing room changed. Kenyon did this with one interview. Roman never said, "Claudio, you must win to survive." Kenyon said that as soon as he arrived. He was not speaking for Roman. This was just a reflection of Kenyon. So people say, "Who do we like? Ranieri or Kenyon?" This is great for me. It is no contest. Suddenly everyone is with me. The whole nation is with me. Thank you, Peter Kenyon!'

After Chelsea beat Arsenal in an emotional Champions League quarter-final, Ranieri and Abramovich hugged in delight. 'I was happy to share this with Roman, but I could not embrace Kenyon. A handshake is all I gave him. I made a point of that. You see, I wanted to finish my job at Chelsea. I start with the foundation and then the first floor and second floor before we reach the roof garden.'

Ranieri sidesteps comparisons between his tinkering with Chelsea and the pragmatism of Mourinho. 'I only saw ten minutes of their first match against Manchester United. I'm living in a hotel in Valencia and they don't trust me to watch football. I switch on my television and there is no football. There is golf! There is a Japanese channel! But no football. Unbelievable! I must move out soon. But his story at Porto tells you that Mourinho always has a strong defence. My friends who have seen Chelsea this season say it is sometimes painful to watch. It is difficult for them to see a player like Frank Lampard, who was special to me, play this way. I don't know. I would think for the players his system is easy to understand. And his sides usually win. Porto won the league, the UEFA Cup and the Champions League. The players he has at Chelsea are even better than the ones he had at Porto.'

Ranieri snorts at the suggestion that there is something Italian in Chelsea's new mastery of the dour 1–0 win. 'No! Mourinho is typically Portuguese. His teams keep possession of the ball very well to slow down the tempo. We do something else at Valencia. But I think Chelsea and Valencia are two of the favourites for the Champions League. If we both reach the final, no one can say they will be surprised.

'I did not win the Champions League last season, but something special happened in England. I understood it when we played our last away match – at Manchester United. Both at the beginning, when I was walking to the bench, and then again at the end, the Manchester fans applauded me with real emotion. This is amazing. How the English people link with me is incredible. It was even more powerful in my last game at Chelsea. I could feel it so strongly.

'I don't think Peter Kenyon will ever know that feeling.'

Ranieri would like to think his contribution will be recognised. 'They know I brought on Eidur Gudjohnsen, John Terry and Frank Lampard, and I bought Claude Makelele, Petr Cech, Arjen Robben and Damien Duff,' he said. According to his book, he also sought to buy Jose Antonio Reyes (as an alternative to Robben), Adriano and Roberto Ayala, with whom he was reunited at Valencia.

Among those he signed were Hernan Crespo and Adrian Mutu, both of whom he criticises. Mutu's attitude did not impress Ranieri, who writes, 'He had all the skills and flair, but to win championships things have to be right.' Of Crespo he notes, 'A player cannot use every slightest setback as an excuse ... I wanted to see a little more character.'

Later, he details an extraordinary exchange when he called the squad together to tell them that he was omitting Crespo because the team were not passing to him and telling them to look for his runs. As for Robert Huth, after he trod on Alan Shearer at Newcastle, Ranieri told Kenyon, 'If I should still be here next year, a player like that I can do without.'

Terry and Lampard come across as favourites, primarily for their willing attitude that reflects Ranieri's observation that 'a country's football is linked to their culture. In Italy we think we are very clever, we want to break the opponent [tactically]. Then we try and score. We have strong defenders. In England all the team must be strong. It is a battle, face to face.' Punching his hand for emphasis, he adds, 'We are strong: come on.' Ranieri continues, 'In Spain they enjoy *la vida*: food, women, the sun. They want to enjoy. There is a lot of possession of the ball and defenders have to be able to play.'

Ranieri's observations were made at the outset of Mourinho's reign, but, as the season progressed, the fans who had suffered along with him during his torturous demise were soon singing the name of Jose Mourinho, and Ranieri was consigned to history.

In his four years in charge, Ranieri failed to win a single trophy. His popularity derived from being downtrodden, and so close to glory. Ranieri received supportive letters from fans from all over the country. 'I am amazed. It seems I am very popular with supporters – people from everywhere, like Newcastle, have written to me. But I want to say thank you to everyone who has sent me messages and written to me from Manchester, Liverpool and Newcastle. They have given me a lot of strength. It makes me feel proud. It really has helped and I am very grateful. I am very focused on the job I have to do and that is winning.' But he failed to win, and he was replaced, just as all the speculation had predicted. Ironically, he was not replaced by the England coach.

At the beginning of August 2003, Ranieri unveiled his first five signings – Duff, Geremi, Johnson, Bridge and Ambrosio – and vowed to build a championship-winning side. 'The owner said you can buy the players but not the wins. It is important to work hard. I think we all want to win – the owner, me, the players – we all want to win. I said, Manchester United, Arsenal, Liverpool? They are better than us because they have a bigger squad. But now we are building. The first step is to build a squad. This is very important. I have confidence in myself, in my players and, of course, in my new owner. We are building a good team, a team like Real Madrid, AC Milan, Manchester United.'

Fed up with suggestions that the new owner dictated the spending spree, insulted by insinuations that it was Eriksson who identified transfer targets and asked if all the players sitting alongside him were his choice, the Italian snapped momentarily, but tellingly, 'Maybe Eriksson's.'

He later dismissed the remark as a joke for the media. Ranieri snapped, 'Who do you think bought these players? Eriksson? That is ridiculous, a joke. That sort of speculation is not good for him and disrespectful to me and to the players. I was the man who recommended all these signings to the new owner. It is my team, my responsibility and, if it does not work out, it will be my downfall. Fortunately, all these players know they were my choice. The new owner gave me the opportunity to look for good signings and I have wanted to buy Geremi, Duff and the others for a long time.'

He confronted Abramovich about his future the minute he was introduced. Ranieri insisted, 'I was very calm when the new owner came in. My first question to him was "OK, do you want me or not?" I wanted to know straight away. Not because of his meeting with Eriksson and all the other rumours, but because I have a lot of experience in this game and know how things can work. When a new owner comes in, he can change everything. When any new boss comes in, he can say, "I don't want you." There is nothing you can do about that. So I said to Mr Abramovich, "If you believe in me, that's OK. If you don't, why wait? Get rid of me now." Fortunately, he said I am working very well and told me to continue in this way.

'I never asked him about the meeting with Eriksson. It was not important for me. He can do anything he likes. I understand that. For me, the only problem will be if my team does not win matches. The meeting lasted for one hour during which I told him straight I saw no reason for him to get rid of me. I simply told him the truth; that last season people called us no-hopers, but we made it to the Champions League ... But I also told the new owner that it was already in my plans that we should do much better this season. He told me and the players that he wants to be the top club in Europe. My eventual aim is to create a team as good as Real Madrid, Manchester United, Juventus, AC Milan and Inter. But we will need a lot of good champions [his synonym for world-class players] to achieve that. I have been building for the last three years and now I have the chance to put in some new champions. I am very happy with the five signings I have made so far, but we are not finished yet. This is just the beginning. I'm not going to say how many more I want to sign or tell you their names, because I am tired of all the bullshit.'

After the pre-season match in Rome against Lazio, Ranieri quipped, 'I know the bookies have stopped taking bets on me.' When asked by a media inquisitor if he found that situation funny, Ranieri quickly retorted, 'Of course I do. Very funny.' He added, 'The owner is working very hard to give me the best team possible. Now it is my job to fit together the old team with the new. I'm confident I will get it right, but I need some more months. I've been waiting all my life to get this opportunity. I've been working very hard for the last fifteen years and, finally, I have this chance. It's a great opportunity and I'm confident I'm not going to waste it. This is the biggest challenge of my career. It's the first time in my career that I can look for the greatest players and I can choose which ones I want. I am interested in everybody. We are looking in every nation. For now, for us, it is important to listen to everybody and then we'll pick up what we need. We're asking clubs to see which players are available and then we will close the deals. I feel excited about the whole prospect. Our philosophy is to try to put together a squad of young, good players and some champions – the same plan as last season.'

But later, Ranieri warned, 'Rome wasn't built in a day. I think Alex Ferguson took seven years to win his first title and, for me now, it is important to build a team and secondly a group. I want to build a spirit for the group because you can have all the best players in the world, but if you do not have a group you cannot win. They must be a group, then maybe you can win. This is my target and then I want to see if we can close the gap between us and Manchester United, Arsenal and Liverpool.'

Ranieri relished the possibilities that had opened up before him in his search for new players. 'I am the luckiest manager in the world ... I have waited a long time for this moment to arrive.' He said, 'I cannot believe how things have changed at Chelsea. It is beyond my dreams and I feel very privileged. I think back to last summer when I had nothing to spend and it shows that life is very strange. Before Mr Abramovich came, I could say, "I like this player and this player," but I knew it was very difficult to buy them. Now with Mr Abramovich, I can put more players on my list and we are buying some of them. There is pressure, but I do not worry about losing my job. Everyone knows they will die sooner or later, but do you think every day, I might die? No, you live your life. A real problem is what I had fifteen years ago, when I started my second season as manager at Campania Puteolana. I had only ten or eleven players and no one for the bench. The bookmakers have closed the book on me being the first manager to get the sack. They should open it again because, if they do, they will make money. I do not know how long my chance at Chelsea will be. No coach can put a time limit on his job. But how can I not enjoy what is happening here?'

But when he was asked which managers in Italy had made the most impact on his career, he said, 'Capello, Sacchi, Trapattoni ... and Eriksson ... ha, ha, ha.'

Eriksson denied any interest in taking over when the issue first hit the headlines. 'I can confirm that I met with Pini Zahavi and the new owner of Chelsea Football Club, Roman Abramovich. The meeting took place at Mr Abramovich's property in London. Due to the intense media profile given to Mr Abramovich's involvement with Chelsea, I accept that this meeting may create unfortunate speculation. Therefore, I would like once again to categorically reaffirm my total commitment to my role as England head coach. I am thoroughly enjoying the current European Championship-qualifying campaign and I am looking forward to leading England to success in the future.'

He explained that he had been friends with both Abramovich and Zahavi for some time. 'Pini Zahavi and I have been good friends for twenty years, since I was coaching Benfica. As Pini spends a lot of time in London, we regularly meet socially. Additionally, I have known Roman Abramovich for several months and, during that time, have also enjoyed socialising with him when he is in London.'

Chelsea officially distanced themselves from the speculation. The chief executive of the time, Trevor Birch, leaped to the defence of Ranieri. 'There is no truth in the rumour that we are trying to bring Sven-Goran Eriksson to Chelsea. Claudio Ranieri is the coach, has four years remaining on his contract, has just got us into the Champions League and has already had a very positive meeting with Roman Abramovich. Together, we have charted the Chelsea path forward.'

Ranieri criticised Eriksson's 'naivety' at being caught by a photographer when meeting Abramovich. 'In my opinion, if it is true that Sven doesn't have his mind set on this job at Chelsea as he has claimed, then I am willing to believe him. However, that means he was very naive to let himself be photographed so obviously going into Mr Abramovich's house in London.'

Ken Bates fought his corner. Bates told me at the time. 'If I didn't think highly of Claudio, I wouldn't have given him a four-year contract. He didn't have a penny to spend last season because *we* didn't have a penny to spend, and yet he took us up from sixth to fourth and we reached the quarter-finals of both cups. Don't forget, Claudio took us to sixth in his first season and to fourth last season with only free-transfer players. He's now obviously getting better players – and the players he's bought so far are the ones he wanted last summer. All this thing about money. Did you know we've actually spent less money than Manchester United spent two summers ago? How much more money are we willing to spend? It's not a question of money, it's a question of getting the right team – you can't buy success. Mr Abramovich isn't a multi-millionaire because he's a fool with his money.'

Ranieri said in early September 2003, 'Last June, if a genie had come out of a bottle and told me what would happen at Chelsea in the next few months, I would not have believed him. Never in a million years. At the time, I was mainly concerned with finding a way to keep Gianfranco Zola at Stamford Bridge and worrying about how to strengthen the squad for the Champions League with so little money available. The last thing I imagined is that someone like Mr Abramovich would materialise out of thin air. And when he arrived and invested so heavily in the team, I quickly realised that I was in a unique position. Very few managers have been in this situation, with an owner who can and will buy them just about any player they request. Arrigo Sacchi at AC Milan in the late 1980s was one, and Vicente Del Bosque at Real Madrid over the past few seasons was another. Plus, of course, Sven-Goran Eriksson at Lazio in the late 1990s. He was able to go out and get whomever he desired.

'Mr Abramovich asked me questions about certain players. I would reply that, if I could get this particular player, he would be especially useful to the team because he could do this or that or something extra besides. For example, I explained to Mr Abramovich that we needed a new striker with a particular set of characteristics, as we didn't have that type of striker before. He is interested in this type of thing and seemed very happy with my explanations. He never once tried to change my mind about any of the players we have brought in. Never. The only thing he wanted to know above all was whether I was convinced in my own mind that this would be the right man to buy. He would say, "Are you sure?" and I would say, "Yes." And that was it.'

Before Abramovich arrived, Ranieri was not afraid to spend big, when Bates allowed him to! He splashed out £11 million on Lampard. 'I signed him to replace Gus Poyet, to be that goal-scoring midfield player. He has the innate ability to time his runs into the box perfectly, a rare quality he shares with players such as Paul Scholes and Michael Ballack. But he's also a fighter, a man who will run for ninety minutes. In fact, sometimes I need to tell him to slow down. As a footballer, you must learn to budget your energy to ensure that you are still fresh late in the game. Of course, being an Italian manager, I'm also going to be concerned with the defensive side of things and I will confess there are times when I worry when he comes forward. But Lampard is continually improving in that department and, with his tremendous work ethic, I'm sure he will do well.'

Chelsea fans chanted, 'We don't need Eriksson' after the 5–0 win at Wolves as the team briefly topped the Premier League. When asked about the chant, Ranieri said, 'They were singing that because they are very intelligent.' He added, 'Ah, thank you, thank you, I will buy you a coffee, an Italian coffee [laughs]! I am an honest man and, when it comes to my job, I try to do everything with all my passion, with all my soul and with all my heart. I enjoy the pressure. Managers in Italy are used to pressure – not every week, but every day. But I also put myself under pressure and that's the worst pressure in the world. I think I have an opportunity to improve my career, but Chelsea comes first. When I first arrived to take over from Vialli it was not easy, but I am used to working with pressure. I am an ambitious man and I want to build something great. In the first year, I want to build the foundation.'

Ranieri had his problems with Mutu, Crespo and Veron, but at the outset it didn't look that way. Crespo got off the mark against Wolves, and said, 'That was a good way to finally get going, but I was always convinced that I would score goals here in England. I want to emulate Gary Lineker. He was a great player, who scored so many goals and whose movement in the box was superb. I never thought that I was going to struggle. I was always going to need a little time to adjust, but now I think I'm there and I believe we can do great things at Chelsea.' Like winning the Champions League? 'Yes, why not? Juventus and Manchester United are favourites, because they have experience in this competition. We do not fear any opponent in Europe, but we have to prove ourselves. The key is to get to the last sixteen, and then anything can happen. People say that Chelsea are undergoing a revolution. Well, that suits me fine, because I am a true revolutionary. I like to push myself to the limit of my abilities. I like tough, unpredictable challenges like this one. Knowing I was going to have the opportunity to help write new chapters in Chelsea's history was all the incentive I needed. I have always liked to be part of revolutions. I strongly believe that, if you can survive for seven years in Italian football, you can make it anywhere else. So when I got the call from Chelsea, I just thought to myself, 'Look, Hernan, you've never settled for the easy option and you've never shirked a challenge, so why start now?'

Ranieri described himself as Michelangelo, carving impressive footballing figures from promising blocks of marble, chiselling Lampard into a strong midfielder. 'I feel like Michelangelo. If the marble is good, then fantastic, then I can improve the player. Lampard is a fantastic player. He was always a potential champion, but I had to chip away at the marble and improve him so that all the little things would work and make him an even better player. Now you see what I was doing. It has been a fantastic experience for Frank and the other young players like him.'

In mid-October 2003, Ranieri dubbed himself Christopher Columbus on the day he picked up the Best Performing Manager award for the first quarter of this season from watchmakers Tissot, and the Barclaycard Manager of the Month awards, but still believed Arsenal were the stronger team. 'If the Tinkerman doesn't change all the time maybe we'll get better – I'm only joking. I have been changing teams around since I was a manager in Italy. It's like Christopher Columbus; he set out to discover India and discovered America. He could have stayed at home. Sometimes the first thing that I think [of] is good condition ... whether I prefer this player, or that player. Of course it's very important to link the team very well. You have to rotate the squad with so many games in a season. You have to be aware when players are tired and when they are not playing their best. Other big clubs do exactly the same, but because it's Chelsea we get more attention. But I don't need to motivate any of my stars. Everyone at Chelsea wants to win every possible title. It would be a dream to win the Champions League this season – and it's not impossible.'

His struggle with the language continued. 'I'm at the same level of English now as I was in Spanish after four months in Spain. How is it possible that after three years I don't speak English well? I don't understand. Maybe English is more difficult. I took lessons three days a week for two years, but with the work it was very hard. Sometimes I take a book or listen to the television, but by the end of the day I am always very tired.'

Ranieri compared himself to Gordon Ramsey, but considered himself to be a chef without as many Michelin stars as Sir Alex. 'Without good players what can you do? It is like a chef. With good ingredients you can cook anything, a fantastic dinner. I hope I can become the Gordon Ramsey of football. At the moment, Sir Alex is Gordon. I have only one Michelin star and he has three. Having so many great players at my disposal is bringing out the best in me. When I chose these players I had in my mind: "OK, I can do this or that with them depending on what I need to do in a game."'

As 2003 came to an end, the Christmas party at the training ground was a low-key affair with Abramovich making an appearance with his wife Irina to join players and staff. Ranieri said, 'Mr Abramovich didn't say anything to me in particular. He is a very nice person. He showed his support and that is everything. He knows and understands that teams cannot always win and they go through good and bad spells. At a time when the club are having a bad moment, he wanted to show he was close to them. I know some will say there are no excuses for us not doing well because of the quality and quantity of players here, but I don't want there to be excuses either from myself or my players. I don't believe in that way of thinking. I said at the beginning of the season that it was important to put down foundations this season and build on them. If we exceeded that, then so much the better. But I never promised the supporters anything. The team has already exceeded my expectations. I didn't think we would be in this position, second in the Premier League and with a good chance in the Champions League by now. I expected it to take a long time to gel. It's not easy linking eleven players who have not worked together before. I hope it's not a crisis. I don't think it is. But, when I said that I want to see my team in the bad moments and how they react, this is their chance and time to do that. We've had the good times against Manchester United, Lazio and Besiktas. They were good steps, but now we have another difficult exam and this is the time when we discover how good the team is.'

Fickle fans began calling for the head of Ranieri, demanding that he be replaced by Eriksson. Supporters bombarded radio station TalkSport. Fans criticised the controversial back three and slammed the rotation policy. After he was hailed as a genius for beating Manchester United to reach the top spot in the league, subsequent dropped points against Leeds and Bolton changed the supporters' perception of Ranieri. One fan rang a radio phone-in to threaten to return his season ticket. Ranieri responded, 'Our fans are not impatient. Maybe some fans want to win always, but that is not possible. I've always said that this season is about building a foundation. Of course we can't have the consistency of Arsenal and Manchester United. We've started well and have confidence, but we must continue to work hard. We will see at Fulham whether the team wakes up,'

Osgood defended supporters' rights to criticise, but Di Matteo defended Ranieri when he said, 'It's natural that when the team loses people want to criticise you. It's nothing new, is it? But it is almost Christmas and we are two points off the top of the league. That's a great position to be in. Claudio knows how fickle this business can be. He knows he is under pressure and that it will always be like that. People like Vicente Del Bosque at Real Madrid won the title and reached the Champions League semi-finals and still got the sack. But I just think Claudio needs time. People need to be balanced in their judgements. Gianluca Vialli before him was lucky in that, although he won five trophies, he had inherited a side that had been built. Claudio has come to the club and brought about a revolution. He has changed the team from front to back and made it gel in six months.'

Osgood was less charitable. 'Claudio had done a great job up until three games ago, but the last three games have been very disappointing. Leeds, Bolton and Aston Villa are the sort of sides that we should be beating. Leeds are struggling, Villa are fighting for their lives and, with all due respect to Bolton, Chelsea have the squad to be able to take all three points. Mr Ranieri should just stick to the side which took us to the top of the league, the quarter-finals of the Carling Cup and the last sixteen of the Champions

League. He has this thing where he keeps chopping and changing the side when he does not need to. Everyone jokes about it and he calls himself the Tinkerman, but it is costing us vital points and now it has cost us a trophy. He should just stick to a settled side and play them until they need a rest. He should also get rid of this formation with three at the back. I like the 4–4–2 or the 4–2–4 formation. Mr Ranieri has four of the best forwards in the league in Hasselbaink, Crespo, Mutu and Gudjohnsen. But he keeps chopping and changing. And I think the fans are right to be critical. They go and support the team week-in, week-out and they are perfectly entitled to have a go. Chelsea still have a great chance of winning the title. But Mr Ranieri has to keep it simple because the New Year is when Arsenal and Manchester United hit their best form.'

The torture reached new heights when the England coach was caught pictured with chief executive Peter Kenyon. Ranieri's *Times* column recalled a conversation he had with Birch back in July when they first heard of the takeover, 'I turned to him and said, "Trevor, I think we're both going to be out of a job pretty soon." A few months later Trevor was out, I do not have a crystal ball, but it's pretty normal that, when a team changes ownership, the new bosses want to bring in their people. There is nothing wrong with that. It's their club, their money, their resources.'

Birch called him and told Ranieri that his wife was upset, but Ranieri said, 'Didn't you warn her when I told you?'

Ranieri took great pleasure in developing the young players he signed even though he accepted that he wouldn't be around to see his labours fulfilled. 'I can be proud it was I who took them to Chelsea. Maybe Mr Abramovich will remember that.'

He concludes, 'I sleep well at night because I know I have done what I was asked to do. If I am no longer manager next August, I will walk away with my head held high. I was touched when I heard the fans sing my name on Wednesday night. I get so engrossed in the game that I don't really hear what the fans say, I'm just aware of their noise and enthusiasm.

'Equally, I saw the *London Evening Standard*'s "Save Ranieri" campaign with the little cut-out picture of me. It was very flattering.' He complained that the picture had him in specs and he couldn't be a gladiator with glasses! Even so, he stuck the picture on the door of his fridge.

'Look, I'd like to explain my philosophy, my strength,' added Ranieri during a press conference as he leaned forward, scattering the tape recorders before him and then hastily arranging them in a straight line. 'The best way from here –' pointing in front of him '– to here –' gesturing to the end of the table '– is the straight way. But you cannot win every time three points, three points ... only Arsenal. F**king Arsenal.' He waited for the laughter to die down. 'Sometimes you have to go around here,' he continued, swinging his arm in a circle. 'Sometimes you have to go around here,' swinging his other arm in and out. 'And then turn. I try to take ... the best route he can. Everything else I don't worry.'

Unfortunately, Arsenal were 'The Unbeatables' in the Premier League, and Ranieri's fate was sealed with defeat by Monaco in the Champions League.

Ranieri knew deep down that the Leeds match would be his last and that he would be replaced by Mourinho. So what would he say to his players after the final game? 'See you soon ... or maybe it will be see you in a different stadium!' Ranieri laughed as he said it. He planned to join his players on the traditional lap of honour around the pitch at the final whistle. He wanted to thank supporters who have backed him.

In his *Times* column, Ranieri said, 'I'd like to finish the job I started. It's like building a house. I've laid the foundations and the ground floor, now I would like to continue building higher and higher. If that doesn't happen, however, I will leave knowing that I have built something good. We may not have won any trophies during my stay at Stamford Bridge but, as a club, we have improved every year. The first season we gained sixty-one points, the second we improved to sixty-four, last year we went up to sixty-seven. This season we already have seventy-six points and, if we win, we will be up to seventy-nine – enough to win the Premier League in some years. To me, league performance, more than cup success, is the mark of progress. You play everybody twice, the effects of luck and injuries are diluted over nine months and you have a clear assessment of whether you are progressing or not.'

Ranieri insisted that he owed a big thank-you to the players. 'If there's one thing that surprised me this season, it's the way everybody stuck together and continued to perform, despite all the rumours regarding my future and possible new signings circulating around the club. In Italy, a team having to perform in those circumstances week-in, week-out would have probably finished in mid-table. I also need to take this opportunity to thank Chelsea's supporters for the way they stood by me and the team all season long. The support in England is not just passionate, it's the way supporters should be.

'I'm very proud of Frank Lampard and John Terry and the way they've developed into great players. But I want to emphasise that they are the first ones who should be credited for their development. A manager can only point a player in the right direction. It's up to the player to put in the hours of hard work, to be intelligent, to improve himself. Terry and Lampard have done that and the credit should go to them.

'I would love to say *au revoir*, but, given what is happening, it may well be farewell. Anything can happen in football but, if I go, I would like to think I left good memories at Chelsea.

'I was honest all along. I accepted responsibility when things went wrong, I never shifted the blame to others. If you can do this, you will leave behind friends and respect wherever you go.'

Ranieri left the field following his side's last game of the 2003–04 season draped in a Chelsea scarf with his palms together in thanks to the fans. The players formed a guard of honour. The fans chanted his name throughout the second half and the lap of honour. 'One Ranieri, there's only one Ranieri,' they chorused. Even Abramovich and Kenyon applauded politely. Up stepped the Italian to acknowledge the generous applause from every corner of the ground, including the away section. The banners portrayed the fans' views: 'Claudio, you may lose your job but you've kept your dignity', 'Don't tinker with the Tinkerman', 'We love you, Tinkerman', 'Claudio, thank you, together with all our hearts.'

As you'd expect, even Eriksson was there to witness it, his final player-spotting mission prior to naming his Euro squad. Would Abramovich and Kenyon have been embarrassed? 'No, they would not be embarrassed,' Ranieri replied. The Shed End made their feelings known: 'Stand up if you hate Kenyon,' they shouted.

Ranieri says, 'It was fantastic because all the fans shouted my name. The scenes will stay in my memory for all my life. There were no tears this time. I was very brave! But it was very emotional, especially when my players clapped me off the pitch. And I was moved when the fans shouted my name. I am a professional man, but I am a Latin man, too; a Latin lover. I enjoyed my best season, I had the chance to prove what I could do; maybe it is not enough. I want to thank them for their support during the season. They think it is my last match and they want to say to me, "Bye, bye." I don't know what is happening or what my destiny will be. I have a contract until 2007, but I said goodbye just in case. I don't know whether I'll be back and that's very sad for me. It's important for me to stay calm and see what happens. If Roman wants me I'll stay, but I think he is waiting for the Champions League final. I'm a little disappointed with the situation, but I can only thank Roman for giving me my job. I really don't know if it's open.

'I wanted to see the Chelsea Board before the game so I could tell the players what was happening. But that wasn't possible.

'I would like to finish my job at Chelsea. The foundations are laid, but the house is not finished. I'm a little sad and frustrated. I don't know when I'll hear from him.'

Ranieri insisted that he had not considered his options should he be given the push. 'I'm a very loyal man. My focus is only on Chelsea. I'll look elsewhere when someone tells me I'm no longer the manager of Chelsea. I'm now off abroad for the summer and will enjoy myself. But I hope to be back.

'The best aspect of the season was that the players followed me. I told them this was an important new era for Chelsea, so it was important to pull in the same direction. We've built the foundations. It was a good season for us.

'I would like to know my future as soon as possible, but I respect my owner. I shall be a little frustrated if I am not allowed to continue here.'

They paraded silverware at half-time. Chelsea Ladies won a couple of trophies. After Ranieri's 199th game in charge, the Asia Cup in the summer of 2003 remained the only trophy he had won in his three-and-a-half years as manager. 'When I spoke with Roman at the beginning we didn't speak about a trophy, we just talked about building a team. If you think of the money that has been spent and think of the players at this club then you think Chelsea should win everything, but football is not like that. Of course I wanted to win a title, but we only spoke about building and I think I have done that. The owner didn't tell me anything, but I knew I only had one year. Each season I want to add a piece of the jigsaw.'

Regrets? 'Yes, the Monaco semi-final in the Champions League.'

Job prospects? 'I told my adviser two months ago that I do not want to listen to offers. I don't do that. I only play at one table. I'm a loyal man and wanted to stay focused on Chelsea.'

As a tannoy announcement bellowed out around the press room, Ranieri immediately joked, 'Oh, perhaps it is my mother asking me why I did not play Damien Duff.'

Now for a holiday, 'Now for me is the moment to slow down, take time and look at what happens. My friends, I don't know how long my summer will be.

'I will miss you lot [the media]. You attack me like sharks and now you clap me. Only in England.'

Ranieri could not resist one last juggling of his pack in his last game in charge. He opted to play a lone striker in Gudjohnsen and handed Cole a rare opportunity in central midfield. They achieved their thirtieth clean sheet, but once again they failed to provide the flourish football that Abramovich craves.

Ranieri would collect a pay-off, but no amount of cash can make amends for his anger and frustration at being denied the opportunity to reap the rewards of his hard work. 'It's not important to be rich or not rich, it doesn't change your life. It will change my life if I leave Chelsea. I knew very well I only had one chance and feel I have achieved what I set out to do at the start of the season. I said I need these players to do this, this and this and I think I have done what I promised. I understand his point of view, because, if you consider the money we have spent and the players we have bought, maybe he thinks this team has to win everything. But you know as well as me that is not how football works. The correct way is to build, look at what is wrong and find ways to improve every year.'

Ranieri also hinted it was Abramovich and his associates who were responsible for many of the superstar signings who failed to deliver. 'At the beginning, people were saying it was Sven-Goran Eriksson who chose the players. But me and the owner know everything.'

He climbed into his car with his wife and dog and headed for the airport, to head for a shopping spree in Rome and wonder how to spend his multi-million-pound pay-off.

S

Dave Sexton and Stamford Bridge

Dave Sexton brought the FA Cup and European Cup-Winners' Cup to the Bridge in the early 1970s.

Sexton had been given a book by June Mears, the wife of chairman Brian, called *The Green Bay Packers*, in which coach Vince Lombardi led an underachieving team to Super Bowl triumphs three years running. Sexton read it avidly and the comparisons with the underachieving Chelsea were amazing.

Sexton was the players' choice to succeed Tommy Docherty having worked as a coach under the Doc from 1962–1965. He returned from a spell at Arsenal to take up his position in the little manager's viewing room, high above the old East Stand.

Fourteen years separated Ted Drake's league championship from Sexton's FA Cup triumph.

Peter Osgood once said, 'His knowledge is exceptional. I have never come across anyone with so much coaching ability. He made football an added pleasure. His ideas, assessments and tactical knoweldge were far in advance of anything I have ever encountered. He saw the minor details that can often be overlooked and brought in the best of the continental arts to add to the strengths of our side. At the time, it was because of him that I decided my future was with Chelsea.'

They may have been the King's Road set, mingling with actors such as

Michael Crawford, and movie stars like Jane Seymour and Judy Geeson, but the players still had a rapport with the supporters. Sexton, in fact, would walk from the Bridge to Victoria Station after every home game before catching the train to his Brighton home!

The 1970 FA Cup campaign began on 3 January at home to a Birmingham City side including former Chelsea players Bert Murray and Tony Hateley. After a 3–0 win, Chelsea were handed another home tie against Burnley, then a mid-table First Division side. Chelsea were two up, but let their lead slip and ended up with a 3–1 extra-time victory in the replay at Turf Moor – the only time that Chelsea travelled outside London on their route to the final.

The fifth round took Chelsea only as far as Crystal Palace. Having already won 5–1 at Selhurst Park in ther last league match of 1969, with four Osgood goals and a display of genuis by Cooke, it was another 4–1 triumph that took them into the last eight for the sixth season in a row. Osgood maintained his record of scoring in every round, while Ian Hutchinson and Peter Houseman each collected their third goals of the campaign. Dempsey completed the rout with his only FA Cup goal of that season.

In the sixth round it was an even shorter trip to Loftus Road to face former players Terry Venables and Barry Bridges. Chelsea won 4–2 in the mud with an Osgood hat-trick and a superb display from the emerging Hudson, who was still only eighteen.

For the fourth time in six seasons and the tenth time in their history, Chelsea were in the semi-fnals. While Leeds and Manchester United were paired in one semi-final, Chelsea were handed a tie against Second Division Watford. The sandy White Hart Lane pitch was again not conducive to Cheslea's style, but goals from Osgood, Hutchinson, Webb and a Houseman double sent them to Wembley, while Leeds won through after their three-game semi.

The final was an intriguing contest of contrasts ... and feuds. Chelsea were still stinging from a 5–2 drubbing at the Bridge and Leeds were still resentful of a last-minute Peter Lorimer equaliser that had been dubiously disallowed in the 1967 semi-final. But at the heart of the contest was the anitpathy between the Revie side of the North and the King's Road set from the soft South.

Yet, if Leeds had a reputation for toughness, then so did Chelsea: there was a mean streak about their defence that contained Chopper Harris, a centre-back who resembled Desperate Dan, David Webb, alongside Dempsey who arrived from Fulham the year before. The back line was completed by a rugged Scot, Eddie McCreadie.

The absence of Hudson with a leg injury was a cruel blow for both the club and the individual. He was replaced by Tommy Baldwin, affectionately known as 'The Sponge' because he soaked up so much work. Alongside him was the equally hard-working John Hollins. In attack there was Cooke, Houseman, Hutchinson and Osgood. Osgood was as uncompromising as any of the Leeds stars of that era, and Hutchinson could also mix it with the best. Signed from Cambridge United for an initial fee of just £2,500, he had one of the longest throws in the game and an eye for a goal.

The final was held on 11 April, a month early to allow England a lengthy preparation for the defence of the World Cup in Mexico.

Wembley hosted a show-jumping event that had left the pitch, well, similar to most of those Chelsea had been forced to play on on their way to the final.

Webb suffered a torrid time up against the skills of Eddie Gray, with the Scottish winger pulling the Chelsea left-back all over the place. Yet, Webb symbolised Chelsea's attitude: they had a steely determination to win through.

Leeds went ahead when a Charlton header bounced under the foot of McCreadie on the goal-line but, four minutes before the break, Houseman dispatched a hopeful twenty-five-yard shot that squirmed through Gary Sprake at the far post.

Leeds appeared to have claimed the Cup with a Jones drive six mintues from the end, but Chelsea won a free-kick following a seemingly innocuous tangle between Charlton and Osgood. Harris tapped the ball to Hollins who lofted the ball into the box where Hutchinson headed the equaliser. With no more goals in extra-time it was off to a replay at Old Trafford eighteen days later. Chelsea tuned up with their final league game of the season: an impressive 2–1 win over Liverpool, with Osgood rediscovering his goalscoring form, while Leeds lost a European Cup semi-final with Celtic, a result which left the FA Cup as their only chance of silverware. It certainly added intensity to the replay.

In two hours of gripping cup football played out in front of a 61,000 crowd and the millions watching on television, Chelsea came through in the two clubs' sixth meeting of the season, having twice met in the League Cup.

Sexton made one positional change, switching Harris back to right-back and Webb to the centre of defence. Paul Madeley hoisted a long ball into Chelsea's box and Jones crashed into Bonetti. Harris seized his chance for retribution, and simultaneously made it plain with his first challenge on Gray that Sexton had pinpointed the winger as the danger man! But the Jones challenge on Bonetti had taken its toll; the 'keeper took several minutes to recover and was left hobbling. Having softened him, Jones carved his way through the defence and his shot beat Bonetti. However, at last Chelsea had found a surface that suited their passing game, and they came alive in the second half. Osgood and Hutchinson combined in midfield, Cooke floated a tantalising cross and Osgood hurled himself full-length to head in the equaliser.

Chelsea took the lead for the first time deep into extra-time. After nearly four hours of this final, Hutchinson unfurled one of his trademark long throws. Charlton could only head it back across his own goal and Webb leaped above team-mate Tommy Baldwin and full-back Terry Cooper to force the ball across the line.

In the final minutes, McCreadie challenged for the ball in his own area and caught Billy Bremner on the side of the head, but the ref waved play on.

For the first time since they had entered the FA Cup sixty-five years earlier, Chelsea had actually won it. They marched on to beat Real Madrid in the final of the Cup-Winners' Cup the following year. When they reached the League Cup final the year after, it was their third showpiece final in three seasons, but they lost to Stoke. It was a defeat that marked the slide.
Chelsea had to wait fourteen years for their next Wembley appearance, in the ill-conceived Full Members Cup!

Sexton, having dismantled the side, jumped before he was pushed and was replaced by Ron Suart, with former left-back McCreadie named as coach, but they failed to keep Chelsea up and, by the 1975–76 season, McCreadie had succeeded Suart. McCreadie opted for youth: Ray Wilkins emerged from the ranks and, after finishing eleventh in his first season, Chelsea were promoted the following year.

A row over expenses and a company car led to McCreadie's exit, and Ken Shellito's appointment. Chelsea stayed up in 1977–78 but, by the following December, Shellito had been repalced by Danny Blanchflower: it was the former Tottenham star's first job as manager and he had inherited a difficult task. The club were close to bankruptcy after an economic downturn left them with massive debts. The players took a voluntary wage cut, but with little to no money for investment in new players, they were relegated having amassed a record-low points' haul. Relegation prompted a new management team – World Cup hat-trick hero Geoff Hurst and Bobby Gould – but Chelsea scored only three times in their last twenty-two league games in 1980–81.

There were spasmodic moments of glory. The 1982 FA Cup run, which began with five matches to overcome Hull City and Wrexham, brought a stunning 4–2 triumph over the European Cup holders Liverpool, with a crowd of 41,412 enjoying the goals from Peter Rhodes-Brown and Colin Lee. Yet, goals from Glenn Hoddle and Mickey Hazard, players who were later to shine for Chelsea, knocked them out in the next round. That season they were dumped out of the League Cup by Wigan.

Could it possibly get worse? It did. The following season only a goalless draw at home to Middlesbrough in the final game of the season prevented the drop into the Third Division. Cue jubilant celebrations.

Stamford Bridge: The Beginning

Stamford Bridge officially opened on 28 April 1877. For the first twenty-eight years of its existence, it was used almost exclusively by the London Athletic Club as an arena for athletics meetings and not for football at all. In 1904, the ownership of the ground changed hands when Mr H.A. (Gus) Mears and his brother, Mr J.T. Mears, obtained the deeds, having previously acquired additional land (formerly a large market garden) with the aim of establishing a football team.

The stadium was initially offered to Fulham FC, but they turned down the chance. Instead, a new side, Chelsea FC, were born in 1905 and they were the ones who moved into the new Stamford Bridge stadium.

Stamford Bridge was designed by Archibald Leitch and initially included a 120-yard-long stand on the east side which could hold 5,000 spectators. The other sides were all open in a vast bowl with thousands of tons of material excavated from the building of the underground railway providing high terracing on the west side. The capacity was originally planned to be 100,000 and was the second largest in the country behind Crystal Palace – the FA Cup final venue.

The name Stamford Bridge comes from even further back in history than the stadium itself and it almost arrived by chance. An eighteenth-century map shows a stream called 'Stanford Creek' which runs along the route of the present-day railway line behind the East Stand. The point where the stream crosses the Fulham Road is marked 'Little Chelsea Bridge' which was originally called Sanford Bridge (from sand ford). While a bridge over the creek on the King's Road was called Stanbridge (from stone bridge). It seems that these two names together gave rise to Stanford Bridge which later evolved into Stamford Bridge as the adopted name of the stadium.

The Shed – 1930

The stadium remained largely unchanged for the next twenty-five years until, in 1930, the Shed End terraced area was erected. A vast bank of terracing behind the southern goal, it was to become the Mecca for Chelsea's most diehard supporters and would forever be associated with Stamford Bridge. As the stadium developed, the Shed End really came into its own in the 1960s, '70s and '80s and was the focal point of the hardcore Chelsea fans and the origin of most of the singing and atmosphere. Adorned with a rather unique 'roofed' area (which barely covered a fifth of the whole terrace) there is debate over how and when it developed the name 'Shed', as it wasn't given a name when it was built.

The Shed was demolished in 1994 following new laws that compelled grounds to be all-seater and was replaced with the new Shed End seated stand in 1997. The final match with the old Shed was Sheffield United at home on 7 May 1994, although, sadly, no one knew at the time that it would be the last game so the Shed was never given the send-off it deserved.

The North Stand was built in 1939. A curious stand in the north-east corner, it was an extension to the East Stand and stuck out because it was a completely different design to the rest of the stadium. It did, however, provide extra seating. It survived until 1975 when it was demolished and the north end was then open terracing until 1993, when it too was demolished at the start of the modern redevelopment of the entire stadium.

In 1964–65, during one of Chelsea's best periods on the pitch, the vast western terrace was replaced by a seated stand. The stand was three-quarters seating and one-quarter concrete slabs and was affectionately known as the 'Benches'. The West Stand existed for twenty-five years until it was the last of the old stadium to be demolished in 1998 and, despite the fact that it was only a rickety, crumbling stand by that stage, it too was a sad day for many when it went: like the Shed, is was a source of nostalgia.

Its replacement is one of the finest stadium stands in the country costing an estimated £30 million to build, and housing 13,500 people in luxury surroundings with superb views.

The East Stand and the Financial Crisis

In the 1970s, Stamford Bridge became synonymous with the National Front. The Shed was a recrutiment area, and hooliganism reached such an extent that the Bridge had the dubious 'first' of being the first club in English football to put up fences, behind each goal, in October 1972.

The East Stand was built in 1973: a marvel of engineering of the time and still one of the most striking stands in the country, there's little doubt it was ahead of its time. The only part of the current stadium that survived the mass rebuilding of the 1990s, it has undergone extensive refurbishment and refitting.

The East Stand, for all its magnificence also has a controversial past. When Chelsea were at their peak in the late sixties and early seventies, the Board, led by chairman Brian Mears, decided that the all-star team on the pitch deserved to be playing in the best stadium in the country. Their plan to redevelop Stamford Bridge into a 50,000 all-seater circular stadium was hugely ambitious. Carlisle United were the visitors for the opening of the 1974 season and, although the visitors lasted for only one season in the top flight, they caused a shock by winning: the season ended with Chelsea following them out of the top flight. The team's demise was a catastrophe with regards to the huge investment in the stand. It was the archetypal chicken-and-egg scenario: do you build a successful team and then the stadium to go with it, or do you invest heavily in the ground and then build a great team to encourage the fans to fill the stadium?

Well, Chelsea had a great team in the early seventies and the plan had been to build a ground that was fitting for such an entertaining side, but the team crashed and the new ground was half empty for some Second Division matches. The mounting debts from schedule overruns and inflation were crippling. There was a £1.3 million underestimate of costs. The East Stand proved too ambitious and brought the club to its knees: they were forced to sell their star players and relegation nearly forced the club into complete ruin by the start of the 1980s. Martin Spencer was appointed by the creditors to manage the club's huge debts. Managers were coming and going through the Bridge's revolving doors and with ailing attendances and lack of success on the field, the debts mounted to £3.5 million. Brian Mears, the great-nephew of Chelsea founder Henry Augustus 'Gus' Mear, had been loyal to the club and was heartbroken about the demise of its stability, but he could no longer stand the pressures and so stepped aside to allow David Mears and Viscount Chelsea to take over the running of the club. They too were to be soon replaced. Spencer, a near neighbour of Bates in Beaconsfield, informed him that an estimate cash deficiency of £300,000 would be reached by the end of March and that the club were in danger of going under. Bates was asked for a £4 million buy-out package which was beyond his means. Instead, he bought the football club for £1 and the £1 million debts were moved, along with the valuable property site, into a separate company, SB Property. In a prickly meeting, Bates concluded negotiations with the sole remaining members of the Mears family on the Board – David, plus Viscount Chelsea and Spencer.

Battles with the potental developers, Bates's infamous electric fences and a growing hooligan problem dragged the club's reputation to an all-time low.

It took another twenty years to rebuild not only the stadium and team but also the entire club, yet, for all that, the East Stand itself remains as impressive today as it always did.

The Bridge in Peril

With the club virtually bankrupt in the late seventies the then owners made the drastic decision to sell the Stamford Bridge site to property developers to pay off some of the debts. It was a decision that very nearly saw Chelsea lose its ground.

With Chelsea no longer owning their own ground, they were unable to do any more rebuilding and the ground lagged behind those of other clubs in that respect. A bitter, expensive and close-run ten-year fight by chairman Ken Bates to fight the property developers and win back ownership of Stamford Bridge finally succeeded in 1992. With an ironic twist, it was the property developers who were forced into bankruptcy and Chelsea FC got its ground back.

It was a close-run thing at times, but Stamford Bridge had survived its biggest ever challenge and, in 1994, the process of the most extensive redevelopment of any stadium in the country began. Turning a dilapidated and crumbling ground with views miles from the pitch into one of the most impressive in the country was the Bates vision of Chelsea Village.

The rebuilding of Stamford Bridge began with the redevelopment of the North Stand area. The old banked terrace that, in recent times, had housed the away fans was demolished and the new stand began to rise. Renamed as the Matthew Harding Stand, in memory of the Chelsea director killed in a helicopter accident, it has now established itself as the home of the most vocal and diehard Chelsea fans.

Next in the redevelopment was the new Shed End Stand. The old Shed terrace was replaced with temporary seating for a couple of years before work began on the new Shed End. At the same time, the Chelsea Village Hotel, which would be the centrepiece of the massive Chelsea Village development, was built at the same time.

Like all new stands, as well as being modern, smart and comfortable, they were also much closer to the pitch – many feel the old stands had hindered Chelsea's atmosphere for some time.

The final piece of the new Stamford Bridge story proved to have one more hurdle to overcome. The lower tier of the new West Stand was built on schedule, but then problems with the local council over planning permission meant a two-year delay before the rest of the stand could be built.

Finally, that last battle was won and work began on completing the biggest and best part of the stadium: the huge 13,500-seater West Stand. It opened for the first time on 19 August 2001 and marked, at last, the completion of Stamford Bridge – a process which had begun way back in 1973 with the East Stand.

The Present and Future Bridge

The current capacity stands at 42,522 and the ground has gone from being a huge oval shape to four sides close to the pitch. There is almost no part of the current stadium that hasn't changed markedly in the past ten years. Stamford Bridge is currently the largest football stadium in London and one of the best stadiums in the country and Europe. As well as all the work on the stadium itself, the whole 12.5-acre site has seen the building of Chelsea

Village, a leisure and entertainment complex housing two four-star hotels, five restaurants, conference and banqueting facilities, a nightclub, an underground car park, a health club and a business centre. It has come a long, long way since the original athletics venue was first built in 1876!

But there are future plans to move the Bridge on to perhaps its final stage: a ground with a capacity of 60,000.

T

Bobby Tambling to John Terry

Bobby Tambling was the goalscoring star of the 1960s, whose career epitomised the majority of Chelsea's history: flamboyant, sparkling at time, but trophyless.

In all, Bobby Dazzler's record comprised 202 goals in 370 games. In Jimmy Greaves's first season, Tambling played both on the left wing or at inside-left, but he was the natural successor to Greaves when he left and he struck up a wonderful understanding with Barry Bridges.

But there was a relegation season rather than glory to go with his goals, and a year afterwards he was made club captain. In 1963, he became the youngest skipper to win promotion at the tender age of twenty-one. When Portsmouth needed to be beaten on the final evening of the season, he slammed in four to clinch promotion. But he was not a natural leader and, when he went through a barren spell, he handed over the captaincy to Terry Venables.

When Chelsea challenged for the championship and the FA Cup in 1965, Tambling finished the season as top scorer once again.

Even when he moved out to the left flank to accommodate George Graham, he still managed plenty of goals, including five against Villa in 1966, the season Chelsea reached a Wembley Cup final for the first time. Tambling excelled in the FA Cup: he is the club's top scorer in the competition with twenty-five goals. He scored Chelsea's first Wembley Cup final goal but, naturally, it all ended in defeat to Spurs.

Oddly, he played only three times for England, scoring once. And, as Chelsea finally neared the point of ending all those frustrating years without silverware, injuries robbed him of that vital yard of pace and, the January before the 1970 Cup final victory over Leeds, he moved on to Crystal Palace.

He was still only twenty-seven when he scored his last goal. 'Mr Tambling Man', as the fans sang in his honour; his finest goalscoring feat was hitting four against Arsenal in a 4–2 win at Highbury.

But the end of his football career brought misery in retirement. He temporarily became a Jehovah's Witness, moved to Ireland, then moved back to the south coast of England where he later declared himself bankrupt, before returning to Ireland.

⚽ ⚽ ⚽

While Tambling was a quiet, unassuming footballer, the opposite can be said of Chelsea's current captain John Terry, who has become the archetypal reformed wild boy.

Terry's status as Chelsea's lynchpin was underlined when the Blues captain, a product of the Stamford Bridge youth ranks, was handed a new five-year contract early in November 2004. The twenty-three-year-old is currently the only home-bred player in the Chelsea side.

His commanding displays are becoming the foundation on which the new Chelsea are building their success. Chelsea already had Terry tied down until the summer of 2007, after he penned a new four-year deal in July 2003 – but the Board moved to secure his future until the summer of 2009. Terry hailed the impact of new coach Jose Mourinho during the former Porto manager's first five months at the club as a significant factor in the negotiations. 'He's been a key figure in it really. He's come in and he's made me the club captain this year – so on the pitch things are going well and off the pitch things are going really well.'

Better than Rio at Manchester United, Alessandro Nesta at AC Milan or Sol Campbell at Arsenal? Mourinho said, 'For me, John Terry is the best central defender in the world. I know Sir Alex would say Rio Ferdinand, I know Ancelotti will say Nesta. For me it's John Terry. Since the first minute I arrived here, he's played at the same level. Not up and down, no mistakes. Not more committed against Manchester United and less concentration against West Bromwich Albion. It's not like he prefers to play against tall and strong strikers and has it difficult against fast ones. For him every game is the same, every opponent is the same, the level of his performance is the same. He leads the team. He is an important voice on the pitch, where I'm not. He's absolutely amazing.'

Terry is a key influence within the team, both on the field and in the dressing room, where he often gives fiery speeches ahead of games. Mourinho added, 'In some clubs the captain is the captain of the manager. In other clubs he's the captain of the players. In another club he's the captain of the club because he's been at the club for ten years. John Terry is everything here. He's the choice of the players, who respect him and feel he's the best guy to be the captain. He's my man. I trust him completely and I think he has the same feelings for me. He's the captain of the club because he is the boy who came from youth football so, in one person, we have this kind of captain and it's very difficult for a team to be successful without a big voice inside. He's a player with good passing quality, he can find people. He can play short and has good vision and a good long ball. He's the perfect player.'

Terry can make the same impact on world football as legendary Italian defender Paolo Maldini, according to former Chelsea captain Desailly. Lavish praise, indeed. The French star, who played alongside both, predicts that Terry will give Chelsea the sort of long and distinguished service that Tony Adams supplied to London rivals Arsenal. Desailly said, 'John can really be the image of the club – he is the one that stands out.'

Although it might have cost the better part of £200 million to build the current squad, Terry cost nothing – and he is thrilled to be captaining the club through their purple patch.

He explained, 'It was a mutual decision. I only signed last year, but I had a chat with Peter Kenyon at the end of last season and people who have been in since. It has been ongoing. But finally it's all done and all sorted, and I'm very happy.'

He has been keen to stress that his future, even beyond 2009, belongs to Chelsea. 'I have been here since I was fourteen and I would love to stay at Chelsea for the rest of my career. I hope I'll do that because I love playing for the club. I am just very, very pleased that it's another five years that I'm going to be here.'

Mourinho had nothing but praise for his skipper who marshalled a defence which has become the meanest in the Premiership. Mourinho explained, 'We said what we thought of John when we gave him his incredible new contract. He deserves every coin.'

During Claudio Ranieri's fourth and final season as manager, the Italian coach dubbed Terry the 'man of iron' whom he would not swap for Rio Ferdinand. 'It is difficult to say who I would rather have because they are both great players, so who do you choose? I am Chelsea manager so I choose John. I know Ferdinand is the most expensive defender in the world, but the money is not important. From the beginning John has had my confidence. I could see his attitude: that if you give me responsibility I can cut it. Both John and Frank represent now what Roy Keane represents at Manchester United. John is a big man, a champion, and in the future John – and Frank – could take that role. They are big men, strong-hearted and fantastic players. At this moment John is the captain when Marcel Desailly is not around, and for me it was an easy decision, even though he is so young. He is a leader – a leader inside. This is a quality of character that is only present in some players. Some men just have this ability to deal with the responsibility – and in my opinion John is one of them. Franco Baresi in Italy was another who became captain when he was young. But wearing the armband is not important in itself; the key thing is that they are just leaders. Baresi never went round saying, "I am the captain." He just led. And John is the same. He is the iron man – and I've said before that he can be for Chelsea what Tony Adams was for Arsenal. For Chelsea and for their national team both can be strong men, good for others, fantastic players. They are both intelligent men and have learned a lot from the example of players like Desailly and Gianfranco Zola. Now I see them out there pulling the group together. That is important. They looked at Franco and Marcel and saw what they had achieved in their careers and thought, 'Why not me?'

Gudjohnsen says even the internationals go to Terry when they have a problem. 'It shows both on and off the pitch how much John Terry has matured in the last year. He's a great leader and hopefully he can keep on progressing as he has done. He's obviously been given a lot of confidence and responsibility. John and Marcel are the two club captains. Whenever there is an issue among the players about anything that needs to be done or anything that needs to be talked about, we go to John or Marcel – or both of them together. In that sense, John is a big leader for us and he is also a big player for us – you can see that on the pitch. For me, John is one of the best defenders around and I do hope he can continue to progress as he has been doing. He's a young man with an old head – let's hope that his body can stay young.'

Michael Duberry left Stamford Bridge for Leeds for £4.5 million four years ago. Terry said, 'Michael has had a massive influence on my career. When I was an apprentice at Chelsea, Michael was there alongside Frank Leboeuf and Marcel Desailly. They spoke little English then, so Dubes would help me out all the time. At the time, there was a little group of senior pros who could make your day hell. Every so often they would call one of the youngsters into the dressing room. You were given three minutes to make them laugh or they would dish out a punishment. Usually, it was a bit of a slap, or, even worse, they would rub Deep Heat on your balls! It would make you red raw all day. So many times I would peer through the window and see one of the kids desperately trying to make them all laugh. They would do a sexy dance, put a bin on their head or just run headfirst into a wall to try to get them to laugh and escape without the punishment. Often you'd spy through the door and see one of the YTS kids with his pants round his ankles getting the Deep Heat rubbed in. It was agony. Luckily, for me, Wisey and Michael seemed to like me. So they made sure I never once got called in.

'I also had to clean Wisey's boots and, at Christmas, he really looked after me. Michael and him would come up and give you £100, though some other players weren't so generous. When the draw was made at the start of the season for whose boots you cleaned, you always hoped for Wisey or Dubes.'

Although he came through the Chelsea ranks, if Terry had followed his initial instincts he could have been a team-mate of Ruud van Nistelrooy. A massive United fan, Terry was regularly ferried to Manchester for training by club scout Malcolm Fidgeon. Alongside him in the back seat was David Beckham – four years older – and United thought highly of then midfielder Terry. 'When I had the chance to go up there it was a dream come true. I was about fourteen years old and Malcolm used to drive me and David up for training. United made an effort to sign me and that was a great experience. They were playing at West Ham one day and invited me and my family to the pre-match meal with them at the Swallow Hotel. I was sitting at the same table as Paul Ince and Eric Cantona, who were my idols. I had my photograph taken with them. They gave me beans on toast, but I was too scared to eat it. But when I came here I loved it so much that I decided to sign for the club. Chelsea looked after me and my family, giving me boots and training kit to play in. They might seem like silly things, but they made all the difference to me.'

The beginning of his career was tough, and at one stage he thought his first-team place looked under threat. His attitude off the field was suspect in those early days. Terry has come through the dark days of a court case that could have finished his career, and just a few years ago he remarked, 'I owe a lot to Gianfranco Zola who helped me through that. He used to take me out to play golf and I would open up to him. He made me realise that I had to concentrate on my football and I've grown up a lot in the last two years. I'm going out, doing the right things with friends and family. Claudio Ranieri has been great for me as well. He's a great character and I will never forget what he's done for me.'

Terry has made the effort to clean up his act off the field. 'I don't want it to be a big "I've Changed My Life" headline. It's just a case of concentrating on my football now. But the court case was the turning point for me. I was playing a big part in the England Under-21s and, because of the case, the FA told me I wasn't allowed to play for them. I was captain of the side and we had got to the finals of a big tournament, which I wasn't allowed to play in. Anything football-related like that definitely hits home and it did that with me. That's what made me look at my life. I was only young when I went through it and I should never have had to go through it, because it was rubbish in the first place. People who know me know that anyway and it's all in the past now. I never had a problem going out too much or anything like that, but I'm very happy at home. I've got a wonderful girlfriend who looks after me, I've just signed a new contract at Chelsea and things are going really well. It helps being skipper, not just because of the responsibility on the pitch but off it as well. With the young lads, I try and help them as much as possible. I do all different things, like helping pay for their driving lessons, because I know what it's like to be on their wages. I feel that if they need to come to me they should be able to talk to me. And I've got a good relationship with the fans. I've come from nothing and they can relate to that. I love it at Chelsea and want to stay here for the rest of my career.'

In November 2003, in the build-up to the European Championships, Graeme Le Saux said, 'I am not surprised that both Frank and John are in because both of them are hungry for responsibility. Frank, for example, certainly seems to have gone on to a new level this season. Everyone is replaceable in football and, with players like Dennis Wise and myself no longer there, Frank has taken on the role of the strong-minded English player in the team. Professional footballers feed off their achievements in the game and Frank has really relished the challenge of playing alongside the big names that have joined the club. He's scoring goals, which always helps keep your name up there, and he thoroughly deserves his place in the England team. I know that competition is hot in the England midfield, but I would say that one criticism of the present management is that players don't always get in on merit. I do think it's slightly unfair that, on occasions, people who are in poor form and not even playing regularly for their clubs are picked ahead of players who are performing consistently. Likewise, Terry deserves this opportunity to cement a place in the England team. When I was at Chelsea, John was never afraid to ask for help or seek advice. He was comfortable showing his own vulnerability and learned a lot that way. It's a refreshing trait and a little rare these days where youngsters are encouraged.'

More recently, Terry was one of three England footballers at the Bridge splashed over the front pages, spending £2 million between them on a year-long betting spree. Terry, Bridge and Parker bet thousands of pounds a day on horse and dog races. The three Chelsea stars spent their time at a betting shop in Cobham, Surrey, with team-mate Gudjohnsen. Terry and Bridge made bets of £13,000 in three hours. It is estimated that the four players risk £40,000 a week between them. Terry and Bridge were often seen in the Coral betting shop clutching rolls of £50 notes. Staff offered them credit facilities, but they said they preferred the 'buzz' from cash, although they used cards when that ran out. A fellow regular at the branch said, 'No one really notices when the Chelsea boys come in any more because they are here so often. They always get excited when they have a big win and don't seem to mind losing too much. On balance, they must be losing or the bookies would have gone out of business.'

Terry, Bridge and Parker live in Oxshott, three miles from Cobham – where Chelsea's new training ground will be built. Gudjohnsen, twenty-four, is a self-confessed gambling addict who last year admitted to losing £400,000 on roulette and blackjack. Coral said, 'It is not our policy to comment on the betting patterns of our clients.'

But Terry has come through the worst and has established himself as both the Chelsea skipper and an England player. Everybody in the crowd at Stamford Bridge now refers to Terry by his nickname. JT is what his friends call him and that familiarity has extended to thousands of punters. Terry is the one they identify with. Terry stands alone, the sole homegrown player in the ranks of lavishly assembled imports. He remembers well the joys of cleaning Dennis Wise's boots as a YTS trainee, a job that yielded a £25 bonus when Wise scored. Terry came through when there was, briefly, a notion that Chelsea were producing a batch of quality young players to supplement the foreign forays into the transfer market. Jody Morris and Michael Duberry had made inroads by the time a lanky centre-half from Barking in Essex stepped in from first-team fringes. Boxing Day 1998: a routine victory over Southampton at The Dell for Chelsea became a milestone for Terry as he sprinted on to the pitch, replacing Gustavo Poyet, for his first taste of Premiership action. Raw, hungry and just eighteen years of age. The Chelsea starting XI that day comprised: Ed de Goey (Holland), Albert Ferrer (Spain), Duberry, Frank Leboeuf (France), Bjarne Goldbaek (Denmark), Dan Petrescu (Romania), Morris, Poyet (Uruguay), Celestine Babayaro (Nigeria), Tore-Andre Flo (Norway) and Gianfranco Zola (Italy).

In the years since his Premiership debut, Terry has seen countless players come and go.

As a twelve-year-old, a career as a top-class centre-half for Terry was not glaringly obvious to the Chelsea staff at the time. 'I hope he doesn't mind me saying this,' says Graham Rix, the club's former youth-team manager, 'but I remember watching him when he was a short, tubby midfielder and he wasn't the most mobile. But he knew what he was doing, saw passes early and embodied the same determination that he has now. I remember one match: he injured himself and carried on playing with a pulled hamstring for twenty minutes. That hurts like hell, but he's as hard as nails. We took him on and he shot up over the next two years. Everybody was chasing him then, all the clubs, including Manchester United, but thankfully he was happy where he was.'

Terry had a choice to make when Manchester United came calling. 'It was a tough decision,' he said. 'Manchester United were my club and my dad's. We were mad-keen fans and it upset my dad, but he could see that Chelsea were going places.'

He was also confronted with his first taste of celebrity when a group of girls started hanging around the training ground and started to make eyes at him.

'It was great because I didn't feel as if I was anyone, but they always wanted my autograph,' he said.

The experience in court, however, had terrified him. 'When my solicitor told me that the charges carried penalties up to life imprisonment I was in total shock,' he says. 'I knew I was innocent, but it was still worrying that my future was in the hands of twelve people on a jury. If they had any preconceived ideas about me, or if the prosecution had done a really good job, I knew my career could be over.'

Bad lad? 'No way,' says Rix. 'I always found him to be quite shy and a sweet, innocent kid. He is spot-on.'

On the field, Terry went from strength to strength. Having been promoted to the first team under Vialli's stewardship, he pushed on under Ranieri. 'I first noticed him in my first week at Chelsea,' Ranieri recalls. 'I watched him playing for the reserves and he was unbelievable. He won all the high balls. He had the attitude of a born leader and played as if he had Chelsea in his blood. I said to myself, "This is a fine young player and when I have the chance I will put him into the first team." He has improved every day since.'

Terry ended up outshining Desailly and Leboeuf – two central defenders who had won the World Cup in their prime. Terry studied their technique. Although he may not be as elegant, his distribution and drive with the ball at his feet are as vital to his game as the traditional defensive virtues of tracking and tackling, clearing decks and crashing headers – not to mention his ruthlessness at set-pieces.

George Graham, who has a specialist's appreciation of defending, is a big fan. 'Some people doubt that defenders can play, but that's a load of crap,' he says. 'Terry can play and he's a born leader. He doesn't have to be beautiful on the ball, he's got qualities that the artistic players don't have. I can see him getting better and better.'

'I always knew what I wanted to do with my life and career, but I was helped along the way by a few people,' Terry said. 'I didn't need telling, but when people like Franco, Wisey and Marcel take the time out to say, "You've got the world at your feet if you do things right," then you think there must be something to it.'

Now he is at the heart of a club threatening to become the game's dominant force. They have the money to buy the best players and, just as significantly, a manager who can be trusted to spend it well.

'His knowledge is unbelievable,' Terry said of Mourinho. 'You can tell that from team meetings. You look forward to them because you know you are going to learn something. You see the players hanging off every word. When other managers come down the coach, you think, "Oh s**t, the boss is coming back." With Jose, you want to talk.'

Dressing-room fun and games sum up the camaraderie in Mourinho's squad. Terry and Lampard are gunning for dressing-room pranksters Kezman and Robben after they keep on being left exposed. Kezman and the Dutch winger were nicknamed 'Batman and Robben' during their days at PSV Eindhoven, but the pair has combined to play the Joker with Terry and Lampard, in a series of stunts that have the rest of the Chelsea squad in stitches – and which have often left Terry and Lampard without a stitch to wear.

Terry confessed, 'There are plenty of wind-ups at the training ground. Kezza and Robbie keep cutting up mine and Lamps's pants. But when it happens four days on the spin, you're like "Lads, leave it out".'

Terry said, 'The team spirit we have here is great. There are PlayStation competitions; we go go-karting and paintballing together. Going into the games we all want to fight and die for each other. We also have the pre-match talks now, when everyone has their turn to say something. I had to do it in the first game under Jose, against Celtic. Mine was all effing and blinding, but other lads will read out a quote. It always gets us pumped up. Jose's so thorough. He always wants to win. Even in training he doesn't like players conceding goals. We know what the opposition are about before we go into the game. And we always know what the boss wants you to do.'

Terry is a changed man when he walks out on to the pitch nowadays. 'I'm so focused on the game when I play against mates they go, "What's ****ing wrong with you?!" But I remember once David Dunn coming up to me in a game and saying, "JT, I'm gonna nutmeg you – and the fans are going to go mad!" I tried to block it out, but I had to giggle at that.'

Terry is determined to oust Rio Ferdinand or Sol Campbell from the England side. Terry believes that Sven-Goran Eriksson would pick Campbell and Ferdinand ahead of him. After all, when Eriksson last had to choose between his three leading centre-backs, following Ferdinand's return from international suspension in October 2004, Terry was on the bench for the qualifiers against Wales and Azerbaijan. Terry's club form since then has been superb. He declared, 'Chelsea are my bread and butter. If I can play well for Chelsea, week-in, week-out, and be consistent, then that's my target.

'Hopefully Mr Eriksson will be watching and will choose me ahead of the other two. They're good players, but it's down to me to prove him wrong. I was a bit gutted that I missed out on the friendly against Holland. I picked up a knee injury in training the day before the Manchester City game and I was struggling before the game with a bruised bone in my knee. It's all about opinions. I'm not Sven-Goran Eriksson's first choice. If Mr Mourinho had the chance to buy Sol Campbell or Rio Ferdinand, would he? I don't know, you'd have to ask him that.'

The 2004/2005 season cemented Terry's success as Captain, when he was voted PFA Footballer of the Year by his colleagues.

U

UEFA Cup Controversy

Six players refused to travel to a UEFA Cup tie against Hapoel Tel Aviv in the aftermath of the 11 September atrocities.

Thursday, 18 October 2001 was one of the most notorious days in Chelsea's history, as well as European football history. Marcel Desailly, Emmanuel Petit, Eidur Gudjohnsen, Graeme Le Saux, William Gallas and Albert Ferrer all chose not to travel to Israel in the wake of the previous month's terrorist attacks on the United States.

FIFA President Sepp Blatter criticised the Chelsea players saying the 'god of football' was watching as they lost to Hapoel Tel Aviv. 'I can understand if players are afraid, but they are in a working contract and they have to deliver their duty,' he said. Blatter said that, had he been fit enough, he would have gone to Israel to see a World Cup qualifier. 'I have to travel and I would have been to watch Austria play in Israel if I had not had a problem with my leg,' he said. 'And now I understand Chelsea have been eliminated [from the UEFA Cup], so the god of football was definitely looking down.'

FIFA sought to keep the footballing calendar on track following the events of 11 September. 'Football cannot ensure peace, but we have a duty to offer a message and a better understanding of the world,' said Blatter. 'I was at the Munich Olympics in 1972 and they stopped the Games for just one day. It was not cancelled, because life must continue. The youth of the world have a right to play their sport. We played football three days after 11

September in Iran and other Arab countries and people stood for sixty seconds to honour those who had died [in the United States].

'I'm concerned about security, but I pray to Allah, the god of football or whoever, that the world's most popular game is not disturbed.'

Marcel Desailly insisted that an Achilles injury – and not concerns over the unrest in the Middle East – had caused him to pull out of the tie. 'When we heard the name of our rivals in the draw, we all hoped that the club would react by saying we should play on a neutral ground,' he said on his official website. 'The club's managers explained to me that they asked the British Embassy in Israel whether there were any risks to play that game considering the current context. They obtained certain guarantees, knowing you can never have absolute security, but Chelsea decided to show the example: if we were not going then some other teams might not have wanted to go either. As for me I will not go to Tel Aviv, but it has nothing to do with all that stuff. I'm suffering from my left Achilles and it is linked to a problem with my teeth.'

UEFA reassured Chelsea that they would not be penalised for playing Hapoel with an understrength line-up. A spokesman for European football's governing body insisted that, with six players refusing to join the party flying out from Heathrow, manager Claudio Ranieri would have just nineteen players from which to select his starting XI. Asked if UEFA would be taking action over the Blues fielding a depleted team, the spokesman said, 'I'm sure we won't. It's the same as when you have players injured. There's a list of twenty-five eligible players named at the start of the season and they have to select the players from these twenty-five.' Quizzed as to why UEFA did not switch the match to a neutral venue, he added, 'We've been in contact with Chelsea and they're willing to travel to Tel Aviv. The match will go ahead there.'

Celestine Babayaro travelled to the Middle East and his agents, Wembley-based First Artist Corporation, revealed that he was concerned about the trip.

First Artist chief executive Jon Smith said, 'He's a little bit apprehensive, but he's there to play for his team and he's fully committed to that. Everyone's apprehensive about flying at the moment.'

The Chelsea 'volunteers' who did travel looked delighted by first impressions as they found relaxed surroundings. 'I think we'll have a bigger problem at Elland Road on Sunday than anything we face here,' said the chairman Ken Bates. 'More intimidation probably.'

Far from being whisked from the plane to their bus by armed guards before the game, the visiting party queued through passport control and milled about in the semi-chaos of Ben Gurion Airport for more than fifteen minutes as all and sundry passed by. If there was special security unit on hand, it was hard to spot. While Claudio Ranieri, John Terry and others wandered to the baggage carousel, most of the squad gathered by the offices of Smile Tourist Services before ambling into the sunshine. Celestine Babayaro read *OK!*, Mark Bosnich posed for a picture. 'My family kept ringing me up and asking if I was going,' Terry said. 'Of course they were worried, but there was never a problem as far as I was concerned.'

Hours earlier, the Israeli politician Rehavam Zeevi had been assassinated by a Palestinian gunman in a Jerusalem hotel. There was a day of mourning and a minute's silence was planned before kick-off, but Ranieri said that his focus remained unchanged.

The closest thing to danger came at the airport when a cameraman tripped beside Frank Lampard as the midfielder walked through a throng of Israeli press. Next to the door of the team bus stood two security men with guns, but the atmosphere was hardly threatening.

'Everyone had to make their decision and live with it,' said Bates.

The managing director Colin Hutchison was less bullish. 'We respect the decision they've made,' he said. 'We've tried to explain to them that the West Bank and Gaza Strip are a different world, but, if they are under pressure from their family and are uneasy about the situation, it would be wrong to force the players.'

Hapoel's chairman Moshe Theumim did not argue. 'We understand some of their hesitations,' he said, 'but there was no need because this is a totally safe place. There is a kind of disappointment, but Chelsea are a great club and we feel honoured we are going to see them.'

Ranieri scarcely seemed worried about returning to Israel, where he had spent part of his honeymoon twenty-five years earlier. At Heathrow the coach had sat studying his English textbook. 'I lived for four years in Sicily and three years in Spain,' Ranieri said. 'In Spain there is Eta, in Sicily there is the mafia. There were lots of attacks on important people. I'm sure in Tel Aviv it's like London.'

It is clear that Bates felt strongly about fulfilling the fixture. 'We've been fighting for the whole of European football,' said the chairman. 'Otherwise teams will start saying, we're not going here and we're not going there.'

The thought of a possible two-year ban from European competition also influenced Chelsea's thinking. About 125 of their fans also travelled from England.

Chelsea, who played without the Fly Emirates logo on their shirts, planned to exploit what Ranieri described as a slow Hapoel Tel Aviv back line. 'In my opinion, my players are very focused on the game and not on another situation,' said the manager. Chelsea lost the away leg 2–0 as those who did turn up didn't expect such problems on the pitch. Chelsea, reduced to ten men early in the second half following the ill-discipline of Mario Melchiot, capped a miserable performance by conceding two goals in the final five minutes to suffer their first defeat of the season. They were teetering on the brink of a humiliating, financially harmful UEFA Cup exit.

'It will be very hard to stay in the UEFA Cup,' said Ranieri. 'It's not so bad if it's one goal, but two makes it very difficult. It was incredible.'

Shortly after the finish, Hapoel re-emerged to salute their fans and enjoy the biggest victory in the club's history. Chelsea, who mustered not a single testing effort on target, could merely hang their heads. Even before Melchiot's dismissal they had been dominated by a skilful side. Only Terry, who conceded the eighty-ninth-minute penalty with which Hapoel took the lead, and the debutant goalkeeper Mark Bosnich, emerged with any credit.

At the start of Ranieri's reign he saw his team go down 2–0 at St Gallen and bow out of the UEFA Cup. This was worse, though, coming at a time when the Italian was settled in his job and trying to turn Chelsea into title contenders.

Melchiot let the side down by kicking Shimon Gershon off the ball, retaliating to being pushed. The home team played with plenty of heart and talent, whereas too many Chelsea players lacked verve. 'I didn't see the sending-off,' Ranieri said, 'but things like that are not good. We shouldn't be doing these things and I have already spoken to him.'

That such key players as Petit, Gallas and Desailly were missing failed to excuse this result. Only the seventeen-year-old Joel Kitamirike, making his debut at centre-back, was not an experienced first-team player. 'The side gets used to playing with more or less the same players,' Ranieri insisted. 'Tonight that wasn't possible. I don't want to talk too much about the players who stayed at home.'

Hapoel were scarcely bothered by who they faced. 'This is one of the greatest moments in Israeli football,' said their coach Dror Kashtan.

Hapoel had caused nervous moments in the first half with their attacking approach. But for three saves by Bosnich after Melchiot's dismissal, they might have lost more heavily. Despite his performance the goalkeeper was less than happy. 'I was told I would be playing twice this season, but it did not work out like that,' he said. 'I did not even look on the board [when the team was pinned up], but it was fortunate I was selected and I did my best for Chelsea.'

The only threatening spell they managed came after Melchiot's red card, when Lampard hit the side netting and Zola briefly sparkled.

Security fears proved unfounded, but in these troubled times it turned into a night to remember for the home side. 'With the things we are going through, it shows how sport can bring a lot of joy to this community,' said Kashtan.

Chelsea had looked likely to survive until Terry handled on the floor when Ilan Bachar burst into the area and Gershon scored from the spot. To make matters worse, Sergei Kleschenko beat Bosnich with a header in the final minute of injury-time. Gershon had said beforehand that 'after hearing that London and Liverpool were under threat of anthrax, we may be frightened to travel to the away leg'.

Ranieri's team were then held 1–1 at home as Hapoel secured the best-ever result by any Israeli team in European club football. The 'Six' and the entire team left the field looking as if they wished they had not turned up. For the second consecutive season, Ranieri had suffered another embarrassing early exit from the UEFA Cup.

The previous year it was Switzerland's St Gallen; this time it was the minnows of Hapoel Tel Aviv who became the first Israeli side to reach the third round of this competition. The visitors enjoyed luck at Stamford Bridge and were helped by fine goalkeeping, but Chelsea only had themselves to blame. Ranieri's side wasted several chances before and after Milan Osterc made it 3–0 on aggregate before half-time. And, although Gianfranco Zola salvaged a draw on the night, Ken Bates expected more for his £31 million summer investment.

Despite the painful defeat, the players who went to Israel had refused to castigate their non-travelling team-mates. 'No one's held anything against the lads who didn't go,' said John Terry.

Some supporters, however, were less impressed with the Six's attitude. Five of those who stayed behind were given a chance to turn things round by starting. Petit, one of the absentees a fortnight ago, came close to setting up a goal inside four minutes, his free-kick being headed wide by Mario Stanic, as Chelsea set about trying to rescue matters in a controlled, rather than a frenzied, fashion.

It was still one-way traffic as Chelsea poured forward against a Hapoel side who pulled eight bodies behind the ball but, in playing two strikers, had come with more than simply defending in mind. Urged on by an estimated 3,000 noisy fans, they knew an away goal would make life all the more difficult for Ranieri's players.

That did not look likely to begin with, and Chelsea could have turned the tie inside twenty minutes as chances came thick and fast. Three fell to the usually lethal striker Jimmy-Floyd Hasselbaink, who saw two efforts saved by the goalkeeper Shavit Elimelech. He also put a header wide.

So little had been seen of Hapoel as an attacking force that Mark Bosnich might have been on the bench, where he had spent more of the previous eighteen months than he might have cared to remember. There was the occasional nervous moment for Chelsea fans, but Hapoel's breaks initially came to nothing.

More worrying for Chelsea was that their early stream of opportunities began to dry up as the half wore on and Hapoel settled. Having survived the early onslaught, the Israeli side steadily came forward with more menace.

'Keep your heart pills handy,' Ken Bates had written in the programme, and there was real call for them when Hapoel scored in the thirty-sixth minute from their first chance. A poor pass by William Gallas was intercepted by Istavan Pishont, who enabled Osterc to beat the onrushing Bosnich and leave Chelsea needing to score four times.

Elimelech was forced into three saves before half-time and Stanic again headed wide, but Chelsea were pumping balls into the area rather than building with any great skill and it was no surprise that Ranieri made a triple change at the interval to play with four forwards.

One of the new arrivals, Mikael Forssell, hit the post not long after Hasselbaink headed wide as Chelsea streamed forward. Yet it needed a good stop by Bosnich to deny Osterc just before the hour and retain at least some hope for Chelsea. Zola, responded with a twenty-yard goal from Hasselbaink's pass, but the damage had already been done.

Ranieri hailed his team's 'brilliant performance' and their 'good spirit' after they were dumped out by the Israeli minnows. Despite the embarrassing aggregate defeat, Ranieri spoke positively about his players. 'The result went against us, but the performance was brilliant for Chelsea. I think my players deserved to win tonight, but in the end it is Tel Aviv who go through because they were calm, they kept possession and they countered well. I am disappointed with the result, but happy with the spirit of my players. This is a big blow because it was important for us to go forward in the UEFA Cup. We are building something here and this match was important.'

Ranieri conceded that the mood in the Chelsea dressing room after the game was naturally down. Not surprisingly, feelings were different among the visitors, where Hapoel Tel Aviv manager Dror Kashtan hailed his team's achievement as a huge moment for Israeli football and for the country as a whole. He said, 'There is a great feeling about what we have achieved. The players did a terrific job and showed great courage. The people back in Israel are already celebrating a glorious moment for the nation.' Kashtan singled out his goalkeeper Shavit Elimelech, who produced a series of heroic saves to deny Chelsea. 'I give him ten out of ten – and I have never before given anyone ten!' he said.

Five months later, UEFA stopped all international fixtures from being played in the troubled country.

V

Gianluca Vialli to Terry Venables

Gianluca Vialli is the most successful manager in Chelsea's history, even though he was only in charge for a short spell before being controversially sacked by the then chairman Ken Bates only a handful of games into a new season.

Ray Wilkins worked as a coach with Vialli on a temporary basis while Graham Rix was detained at Her Majesty's pleasure and he has no doubts about the Italian's place in Chelsea's history. Wilkins told me, 'Luca was a fantastic manager and yet now he is working for Sky Italian. In my view, it is a great loss to the game.

'Luca is Chelsea's most successful manager in terms of winning trophies and he will be for a while to come.

'He is the type of manager who reflects his days as a player. He was totally dedicated, 100 per cent behind the cause and knows the game inside out.

'It was terribly unfair that he was sacked in the circumstances in which he lost his job, and it is not my place to go into the reason but, in fact, I have no idea why someone as successful as Luca should have been sacked.'

As a player, the Italian legend had his problems in his very first season after joining the club coached by Ruud Gullit. He began well enough: the clever flicks and goalscoring prowess were still alive in the veteran, whose last appearance for Juve came when he lifted the European Cup. But injury curtailed his run of form, and he never quite regained his place. He ended the season sitting out the FA Cup final and in open conflict with Gullit.

Gullit only sent Vialli on to the Wembley pitch for the last few minutes: after eighty-eight minutes and thirty-three seconds the Italian finally made his Cup final appearance – he got the biggest cheer of the day.

Vialli commented afterwards, 'This is my first winners' medal in England, but I hope it won't be my last. I will put this medal alongside the one I won with Juventus in the Champions League last year. It means just as much to me, even though I only had a couple of minutes. The reception I was given was fantastic. My relationship with the supporters and my life in London will be the two biggest factors when I come to decide what I will do next season. Now is not the time to talk about my future. Now is the time to enjoy our Cup success. You know, I have been here before: at the end of my last match with Sampadoria I was crying because we had lost the Champions League (against Barcelona) and I wanted to leave having won something. Today, the atmosphere is completely different. I am very happy to have been a part of the final; it was great.'

Vialli was back at the Bridge in 2004 for a Chelsea Pitch Owners' Tribute Dinner in his honour, where he was flanked by Wilkins and Dennis Wise. Vialli was afforded a hero's welcome in the West Stand's Hilaire Beloc Suite attended by 350 fans. More than £12,000 was raised during the evening for Vialli's designated charity, the Vialli and Mauro Foundation for Research and Sport.

That night Vialli said, 'The only comparison I can see is that the club is still trying to move forwards and become a better club and win things. The chairman is not here any more and we have a new chairman, a lot of new players and, since I left, a new stand. Things are looking very good and Chelsea seems to be a very solid and strong side this year. I think that the manager is very determined, very ambitious and a winner, so I don't think anyone would be wrong to predict Chelsea winning some silverware this season.'

He regrets not being able to see as much of Chelsea these days as he would like. He explains, 'I can only see them on television at the moment because I am working for Sky as an analyst so I commute every Saturday and Sunday. I've not had a chance to come to Stamford Bridge yet, but I see Chelsea on television a lot.'

He has been linked with a potential takeover bid for Millwall, one that he has denied, but he would like to return to management: naturally, his ambition is to return to Chelsea one day. Vialli is now a dad and he and his

en Jose Mourinho signed Didier Drogba for £24million from Marseille, he told the yer that he would be catapulted into the same elite group of players as Thierry nry. With Drogba being a great fan of the French footballer, Mourinho's words pired the player.

John Terry has progressed through the ranks from the Chelsea Youth Academy to becoming captain of his side. He was voted PFA Footballer of the Year by his fellow professionals.

ank Lampard enjoyed a sensational season in Chelsea's centenary year. He has gone om strength to strength under the guidance of Mourinho and was voted Sports Writers' ayer of the Year.

Above: A modern-day Stamford Bridge.

Below: The famous Shed End was erected in 1930 and has become the focal point for Chelsea's most dedicated fans.

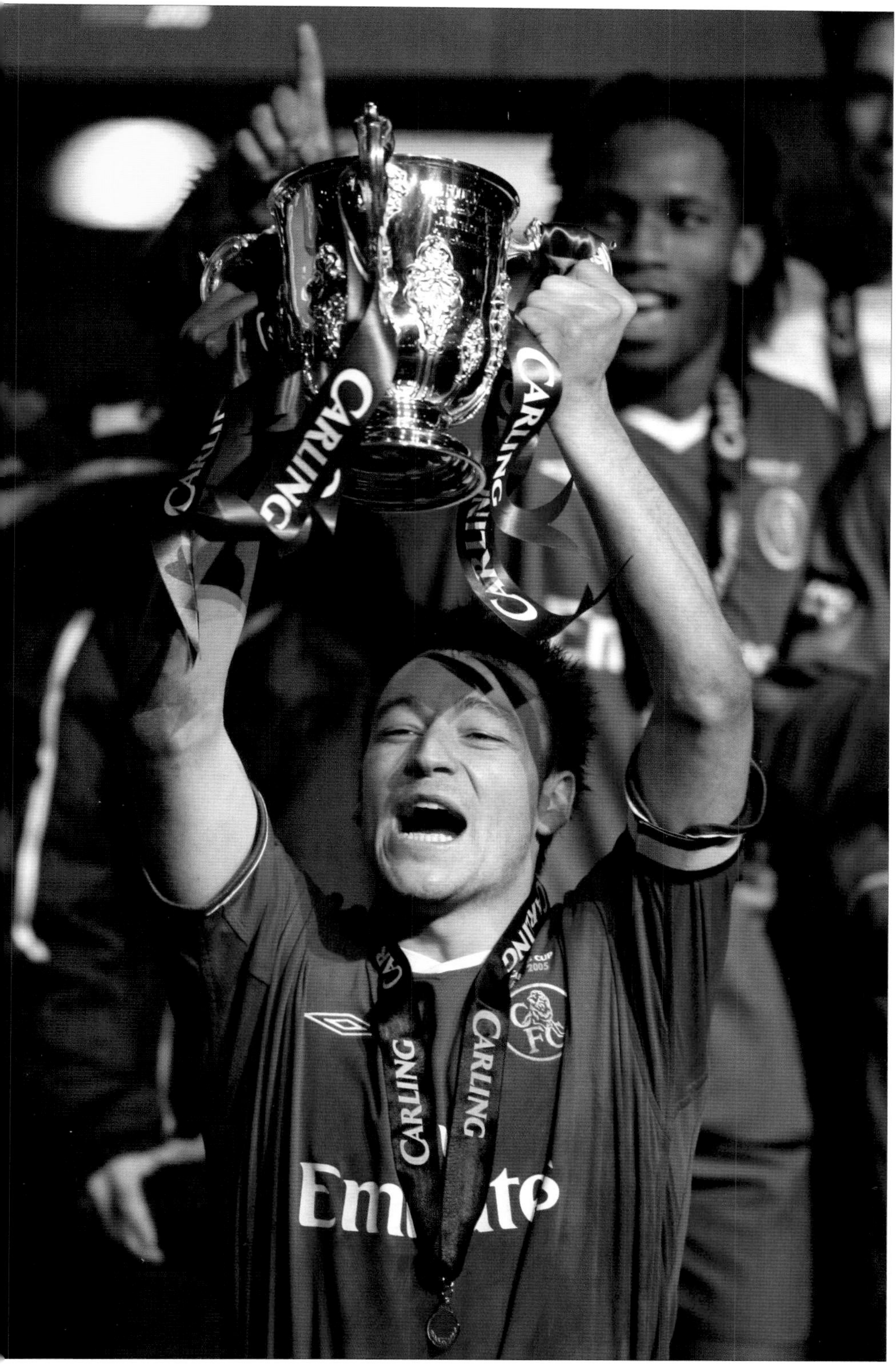

lsea won their first silverware of the season when they beat Liverpool in the Carling
Final. John Terry proudly lifts the cup.

Frank Lampard, Eidur Gudjohnsen and John Terry celebrate their triumph in the Carling Cup.

›roud manager congratulates his players.

Celebrations all round as the players celebrate their first league championship in fifty years during their centenary season.

wife Catherine have moved back to London. 'I would rather go back to managing in the Premiership straight away, but I have a feeling that it would be easier and better to go back to Italy, stay a couple of years there, do well, get stomach ache and get upset just like you always do when you are managing an Italian side, and then come back to London.'

Graham Rix was often credited for doing much of the coaching under Vialli, and indeed even Gullit. Rix won two FA Cups, one League Cup and the Cup-Winners' Cup while at Chelsea as assistant to Gullit and Vialli.

He collapsed with encephalitis, something kept secret by Chelsea because it came so soon after he had been released from prison after 184 days and nights in a cell in Wandsworth. Rix, now the director of football at Oxford United, was, in 1996, entrusted by the FA with England's brightest young talents – including a youthful David Beckham – at an international Under-20 tournament. Glenn Hoddle had asked Rix to join the senior camp on a match-by-match basis, but Gullit, the Chelsea manager at the time, refused to release the man in demand.

Rix contributed to a haul of five trophies at Chelsea and, under Vialli, was doing far more than simply overseeing training sessions. 'I remember in the Cup-Winners' Cup final against Stuttgart [in 1998] when we were drawing at half-time,' he said, 'Luca said, "If you want to make a change, you make one. Just don't take me off." We had Zola and Hughes on the bench and, although Franco had been injured, I brought him on for Flo. He scored seventeen seconds later to win the Cup. That was obviously luck, but I liked the fact that Luca trusted me to make those big decisions. I still think I've got a lot to offer. Whether it is Zola and Desailly or Stevie Basham at Oxford, I would like to think there isn't one footballer I have worked with who would have a bad word to say about me. I've had opportunities at Portsmouth and Oxford since Chelsea, but I don't think I was given enough time in both cases. I spent two years out of work before and, without wanting to sound big-headed, I think it is a waste if I am not working with footballers.'

Rix wants to be a manager, but enjoyed his greatest success in the assistant's role at Chelsea. He was revelling in his work when he was arrested, charged and then sentenced to one year in prison after admitting to having had unlawful sex with a fifteen-year-old girl. The conviction did not prevent him from working – indeed, Chelsea kept his job open – but Rix knows that there was bound to be a stigma once he was placed on the sex offenders' register. Rix believes that the six months he served was a heavy punishment. 'I had never been in a police station before and suddenly I was on my way to prison without saying goodbye to anyone. Wandsworth was a tough, tough regime and for the first few days in my diary I was writing, "What on earth am I doing in here?" But I never wrote that I didn't deserve it. I couldn't afford to get bitter. It was a very, very strong test because you don't know who you can trust – warders, prisoners – and obviously everybody knew me. It has made me tougher, because nothing anyone can do will be worse than being locked up for six months. It has also made me a better man, because it gave me time to think about what was important in life.'

Rix's fame might have invited trouble but, to the contrary, prison was full of Chelsea supporters happy to keep an eye out for him. 'It only takes a second to smash a sauce bottle and there were some tough cases in there, but I never had problems. I got to paint the cells, which was one of the better jobs. I got paid £8 a week which, funnily enough, was the same money I was on as an Arsenal apprentice.'

Released in September 1999, Rix crept out at dawn to avoid the media. A few hundred yards away, sitting in a car on Wandsworth Bridge, Vialli was waiting. 'He took me to Chelsea Hotel and I had a big breakfast and a glass of Guinness. It tasted great at seven in the morning.'

He was soon back at work, but another traumatic year was to follow. Six months after regaining his freedom, Rix left the training ground one day feeling fit and healthy. 'I drove half a mile and suddenly started feeling dreadful. I pulled into a garage and rang Gwyn Williams (the assistant manager). By the time a couple of the lads came out to get me, I was sprawled all across the front seat. There was vomit everywhere and I was unconscious. They didn't know if it was a stroke or a brain haemorrhage, and they thought at first that it might have been some kind of stress reaction to being in prison. It took weeks to diagnose that it was encephalitis [an inflammation of the brain brought on by a viral infection]. I couldn't walk to the shops or remember anything, and at the 2000 FA Cup final I was totally spaced out. Somehow, Chelsea kept it quiet. Some people are left permanently damaged, but I recovered after about six months – just in time for Luca to get the elbow. Then Ranieri came in and for four months Ray (Wilkins) and I just used to come in and sit on a football. It was a little bit disrespectful, to be honest. I know the players were embarrassed by it.'

Rix was squeezed out twice more, at Portsmouth after Harry Redknapp's arrival and at Oxford, where he spent only six months in the dugout before making way for a new regime led by Ramon Diaz.

At the age of forty-seven, Rix believes that he is too young to abandon the training ground.

He represented Arsenal 464 times in midfield. It was Rix's cross that allowed Alan Sunderland to score the dramatic FA Cup final winner against Manchester United in 1979. A year later, Rix missed the decisive penalty in the Cup-Winners' Cup final against Valencia. He spent fourteen seasons at Arsenal up to 1988 before playing for Caen, Le Havre and Dundee. He was capped seventeen times for England, filling in for the injured Trevor Brooking in the 1982 World Cup finals in Spain. He joined Chelsea as youth coach in 1993, but came out of retirement to play at the age of thirty-seven.

Chelsea made history at Southampton when Vialli fielded a team without a single British player but at least he had a bench that contained five English players – two of whom came on. During the 2004–05 season, Arsenal reignited the debate about foreign imports when they fielded an entire squad of foreigners for their Premiership game with Crystal Palace at Highbury.

Vialli still harbours a dream that he will return as Chelsea manager one day. He was livid when he heard that his former chairman, the man who sacked him, was looking to take over another club. Vialli fired a broadside at Bates when he was looking to buy Sheffield Wednesday before he eventually settled on Leeds United. 'He has a go at the new owner and Peter Kenyon, saying you have to support your manager, but the first thing Bates said he would do at Sheffield Wednesday is to sack the manager. That really made me laugh.'

Terry Venables will forever be associated with Chelsea: he was one of the highest-profile products of the Chelsea youth system that won the FA Youth Cup in both 1960 and 1961. He was also an ever-present in the promotion-winning team of 1962–63, even though he didn't turn twenty until January 1963.

Right from the start Venables was different; he would write match reports on the coach journeys home from away games.

In his first season back in the First Division, he was made captain. Tactically astute from the word go, he was the team's midfield general. He can be credited with the progression of wing-halves and inside-forwards to the modern-day playmaker. He wanted to discuss tactics with the manager, took the free-kicks and penalties and generally orchestrated the way the team played.

Chelsea put together their first three consecutive top-five places with the highlight being a third in 1965 – a position that fell in the middle of that sequence.

But he went too far, as, perhaps, he was always destined to do in his life. Even at an early age, he tried to usurp manager Tommy Docherty's authority, and lost.

Chelsea journeyed to Rome during a European campaign of enormous promise and Venables took it upon himself to change the tactics, moving Marvin Hinton back to sweeper when Docherty had ordered a back four. Venables lost the captaincy soon afterwards.

In 1965, Venables won two England caps, and so became the first player to be capped at every level: schoolboys, youth, Under-23 and senior.

But Docherty had had enough of his interference on the training ground and even in matches. Venables's departure from the Bridge, however, was one of the most contentious issues in the club's history.

Docherty's relationships with some players were strained – none more so than with Venables. Many years later, Docherty reflected, 'He was always the ringleader, the King of the Kids, a good player among the youngsters, in charge of them so to speak. They followed him and looked up to him and he knew it.'

Docherty put Venables up for sale, explaining, 'It was a move I had been considering for nearly a year. And, though it was a controversial decision, with possible disastrous results to the team and their important programme, I felt a lot better when I had done it. There is only room for one boss – the manager. And for months Venables had been trying to run the playing side of the club or, at least, had made it difficult for me to do so. Time and again at training sessions he would openly disagree with what I was trying to put over or, by dumb insolence on his very expressive face, try to make me look small in front of the other players.'

Semi-final defeats in the FA Cup and Inter-Cities Fairs' Cup against Barcelona followed. The Doc also kicked out George Graham, Barry Bridges and Bert Murray. While Venables moved on to Spurs, Graham forged a formidable career at north-London neighbours Arsenal.

Adored at the Bridge, Venables never found the same rapport with the fans at White Hart Lane, even though he was part of the Tottenham team that beat Chelsea in the 1967 FA Cup final.

When he went into management, which he was always destined to do, he took his close friend from his Chelsea days Allan Harris with him as his assistant.

After being hailed as the manager of the team of the 1980s at Crystal Palace, he moved to QPR and then on to Barcelona, where he won the Spanish league title. He returned to England as manager of Spurs and ended up as chief executive and co-owner with Alan Sugar, but that ended in an acrimonious departure following tales of financial irregularities, for which he was banned as a company director for seven years after a Department of Trade and Industry High Court case.

Venables's association with Barcelona is remarkable. He first went to the Nou Camp as a twenty-three-year-old in Docherty's flamboyant young side in 1966. He played 237 first-team games for Chelsea, making his last appearance in a Fairs' Cup tie against Barcelona in the Nou Camp just before Docherty sold him to Tottenham. He returned to Barcelona as a coach for three years and steered them to the European Cup final in 1986.

'It's a stadium with a special atmosphere,' said Venables, who was manager when the visit of Juventus in the European Cup quarter-final in March 1986 set a Nou Camp attendance record of 120,000.

More than 100,000 watched when Barcelona beat Chelsea 5–1 in the quarter-final in April 2000, but such is the turnover of players these days that none of those who played over two legs in the 6–4 aggregate defeat five years ago still remains at Stamford Bridge.

'It was very different in my day,' recalled Venables. 'A lot of the players when I was there spent most of their careers with Chelsea ... Ronnie Harris, Peter Bonetti, John Hollins, Eddie McCreadie, Peter Osgood, Marvin Hinton, Charlie Cooke.'

It was the arrival of Cooke from Dundee in April 1966 that ended Venables's seven-year stay at Stamford Bridge. His last game was that 2–0 Fairs' Cup semi-final defeat in Barcelona. Cooke's first game was in the return leg at Stamford Bridge, which Chelsea won 2–0 thanks to two own goals.

In those days, a third match was required when the aggregate scores were level. This time Barcelona won 5–0 at the Nou Camp – a match beamed back to Stamford Bridge, where 10,000 fans watched the game on six giant screens. It was the first European tie transmitted in this way.

At the time, Venables was one of six Chelsea players called into Alf Ramsey's forty-strong squad for the 1966 World Cup. The others were Bonetti, Hinton, Hollins, Osgood and Barry Bridges, although only Bonetti survived the cut and made the final twenty-two.

'We had a good young side with a growing reputation,' Venables recalled. 'The average age was about twenty-two and we got to the FA Cup semi-finals in successive seasons. Then Tommy Docherty got a bit impatient and decided he needed a couple of new faces. That was the end of me.'

Chelsea remain his first love in football. He has two season tickets and watches most home games, often with his grandson. 'They're brilliant at the moment. They break hearts! They don't let you score. The teams with the best players will win the trophies, and the best players cost the most money. It's always been that way. Until recently, Manchester United and Arsenal bought the best players. Now Chelsea can buy them, too, but, in their case, you've also got to give a lot of credit to the coach. Jose Mourinho knows what he's doing. You need more than luck and a fat chequebook to enjoy the success he's had.'

Now sixty-two, the entrepreneurial spirit still burns but, from a footballing viewpoint, he's happy enough now sharing his opinions with the nation – and watching Chelsea.

'Defensively they're brilliant and because of that they're particularly effective away from home. If Chelsea score, you can almost see the energy and confidence levels of the opposition drain by 20 per cent because they know they're not going to score against them. They've got to get past Claude Makelele and the back four and then still beat the best goalkeeper in the Premiership. Petr Cech has had a fantastic season. So have Frank Lampard and John Terry. They've been sensational. But the one who's made the difference this season is Arjen Robben. He's a great player and he's taken some of the pressure off Damien Duff. Last season, opposing defences could concentrate on Duff. Now they have to split their forces and look after two of them.'

He still fitted in being manager of England and took the nation to the semi-finals of Euro '96 at Wembley – the high point of his career – before resigning for a variety of reasons, one of them that he had to fight a court battle with Sugar, the other that the then FA chief executive Graham Kelly had only offered a one-year extension to his contract ahead of the tournament.

He moved on to become manager of Australia and then back to England with Portsmouth before more financial problems led to another hasty exit.

Venables tried his luck at just about everything, from co-writing a novel that was turned into a television series, *Hazell*, to becoming a television pundit, a wine-bar owner at Scribes West in Knightsbridge and developing a leisure complex in Spain.

W

Ray Wilkins and Dennis Wise

Few players epitomise Chelsea more than Ray Wilkins and Dennis Wise. Two former club captains – although vastly different in their styles of play – and from different generations, they came together as manager and coach at Millwall. Both also dovetailed at Chelsea and played a leading role in the Vialli period.

Wilkins first discusses his playing career at the Bridge. 'It was a sheer delight, that's how best I can describe it, happy memories of a wonderful time. We were all homegrown players who had come through the youth system and it was more like a boys' club, going to play with your mates ... it was a lovely time.'

Four months before his nineteenth birthday, Wilkins was named captain of Chelsea. He had already played nearly thirty games for the club, but his emergence coincided with traumatic times: as new manager Eddie McCreadie brought in the youth brigade, the club hurtled towards relegation.

Wilkins, who is now a star Sky TV pundit and recently confirmed his decision to follow Dennis Wise from his joint coaching role at Millwall, continues with his recollections of his playing days. 'It was just a shame that the club was experiencing financial difficulties and we had become somewhat of a yo-yo club: great times when we were promoted, great sadness when we were relegated.'

Wilkins won his first England cap when he was twenty. Over the next three years, he won twenty-four caps to become Chelsea's most capped player – taking over that record from McCreadie. He played an attacking midfield role, full of flamboyance, and was top scorer in 1975–76 with twelve goals. 'Yes,' says Wilkins. 'I did get a fair amount of goals in those days, believe it not.' He captained the side to promotion the following year and was required to change his role when Ken Shellito became manager: with it, his attacking prowess became muted.

Wilkins had inevitably outgrown a struggling club and moved on to Manchester United for a new club record sale of £850,000. The year Chelsea went to the brink of relegation to the Third Division, he scored an outstanding goal at Wembley as Manchester United won the FA Cup. He went on to captain England and win eighty-four caps. He also moved on to play for AC Milan, Paris St Germain and Glasgow Rangers. He returned to England in his thirties to star for QPR and played on until he was forty. He recalls, 'I used to enjoy my attacking midfield role but, when I moved to Manchester United, the manager Dave Sexton had a completely different role for me and, as we all know in this game, what the manager wants he invariably gets.'

Wilkins linked up in coaching with Ray Lewington at Crystal Palace, whom he had known from his Chelsea youth and first-team days.

Dennis Wise became only the third Chelsea captain to lift a major trophy when the club won the FA Cup. He was a member of the original Dons 'Crazy Gang', when they surprisingly beat the formidable Liverpool team of that era and won the FA Cup in 1988: he was voted Wimbledon's Player of the Year that season.

He signed for Chelsea for a record £1.6 million in 1991. First game ... Man of the Match as he scored the winner. Second game ... sent off. He was caught drink-driving and banned. He even played for England and was a favourite of chairman Ken Bates. He scored Chelsea's first winner at Liverpool in twenty-six years and celebrated by jumping into the crowd. He won a goal-kick in the dying seconds of a League Cup tie with Newcastle, picked up the ball, kissed it and got booked for that.

Ian Porterfield switched him from the wing to a more influential midfield role. Glenn Hoddle made him captain.

He starred against Leicester, playing head tennis with a fan while an opposing player was injured. Hoddle stripped him of the honour of leading the team. Wise looks back: 'He knew I cared about being captain and the only way he felt he could see me coming to my senses was to take it off me.'

He regained the captaincy when Ruud Gullit took over as boss. Under Hoddle's management, he had captained the team to the FA Cup final in 1994: he did so again in 1997, with Gullit in charge, when they finally won at Wembley to end a twenty-six-year wait for silverware. He had played in the final with painkilling injections to quell an injury. When Gullit strolled into an ecstatic Wembley-winners' dressing room carrying the FA Cup minus its top and plinth, his skipper had just finished a television interview. 'Look at the Yet!' Wise shouted across the room. A broad smile creamed Gullit's features. Typical irreverance form Wise, and an even more typical good-natured response from the manager. His 'lovely boys' as he called them had won the FA Cup and ended such a long wait for silverware. That night Wise led the singing and the drinking at the banquet.

But, under Vialli, the honours just kept rolling in.

⚽ ⚽ ⚽

Graham Rix was the coach under Vialli, and a vital ingredient to both the boot room and the manager's development in the dugout. Rix was going to be a hard act to follow when he went to prison, found guilty of under-age sex. Wilkins recalls, 'Luca asked me to come and help out on a temporary basis because of what had happened to Graham Rix. It was a wonderful time and I thoroughly enjoyed it working with such world-class footballers.'

Could Wilkins, who had played during such financially crippling times, ever have believed that an Abramovich would have come along? 'Probably not!' he said, but Wilkins is thrilled that the present, and indeed the future, looks 'bright' – another one of his typically understated assessments.

Wilkins tells me, 'The money that Mr Abramovich has stumped up is well documented, but money alone isn't enough to put together the kind of feeling you now have about Chelsea. Don't get me wrong, it certainly helps, but there are other ingredients vital to the mix.

'I went across to Cobham to see the guys the other day and I must say I was impressed. In life, at football clubs, at varying periods, there has been big money available to spend on players, but in reality it is how you spend it that counts, and the way Chelsea have spent the money is absolutely first class. The training ground facilities are wonderful. Yes, it has been an immense amount of money, but they have a fabulous squad of players as a result of that spending. And, from what I can gather, the club have had a "result" in putting all that money into hands of Jose.

'I contacted the club to ask for permission to go to the new training camp, because I was intrigued by it all, and although it is a closed shop I was invited down. You know I used to be captain at the club, but half of the current team probably don't even recognise me! Of course, I knew players such as John Terry and Eidur Gudjohnsen from my time coaching with Luca, and had the opportunity to chat to quite a few of the players. I also had a chat with Jose, and I found him an extremely positive type of guy. It was interesting to see how he works with the players: in fact, it was quite an eye-opener. The work ethic was most certainly evident, so too was the enjoyment and laughter to go with the very serious side of the new manager's regime.

'Jose is just first class, just like the training facilities. He is fantastic, a breath of fresh air into our game. He is a winner. He says it as he sees it and that is rare in this day and age.

'I sensed a wonderful atmosphere at their training complex. The atmosphere was that this is the right place, an atmosphere of winners, an environment for winners, with absolutely nothing left to chance.

'Off the field, Peter Kenyon talks about the club being self-sufficient by the year 2010 and one can only hope that he is right. But, to achieve that, he must make Chelsea a world brand close to Manchester United. With the kind of ambition at that place, though, I see no reason why they cannot do that.'

Until recently, Wise was manager at Millwall – Wilkins was his coach – and Wise's links with Bates remain strong. After the former chairman took over at Leeds United, Wise was immediately linked to the job of manager at Chelsea's traditional foes.

Wilkins still harbours ambitions to return to management himself. 'I had a couple of goes at it, and both times it ended up unfulfilled, not disastrously, but unfulfilled. I would like to have another bash; it's just finding the right place to do it. I know it's more of a comfort zone working in television and I enjoy working in the media – and you can probably tell how much I enjoy commentating on Chelsea – but there isn't quite the same buzz and banter.'

As for Wise and his place in Chelsea's history, he says, 'He was an influential captain, and I have coached him. He deserves the utmost respect for his achievements as a player at the club. He did a very good job, particularly as Luca's captain, but it also has to be said that he played in an awfully good side, one that could and should have won the championship. Perhaps it might have done had Luca not been sacked.

'But just look at the foreign imports that came in ... I would say that they have been the best crop of foreign players any club have imported in this country – Gullit, Zola, Vialli, Poyet, Petrescu, Desailly, Leboeuf, Di Matteo. I should imagine Arsenal run them close with Henry, Bergkamp, Pires, Ljundberg, Petit and Overmars, but even at Manchester United, once you go past Cantona and Schmeichel, there haven't been a lot of truly world-class performers who have made a major impact in English football the way that the foreigners have at Chelsea.'

X

Xenophobia

Chelsea have imported some of the biggest-name overseas stars from all over the globe, some earning as much as £100,000 a week and costing up to £24 million in transfer fees.

When Luca Vialli became the club's second foreign coach, succeeding Ruud Gullit, he fielded the first complete team of foreign players ever to play in English football. As a result, Chelsea have become a focal point of attention and, on occasions, the centre of the debate about xenophobia in English football.

Jose Mourinho pledged that he will never follow Arsène Wenger by having an entire squad full of foreigners. Wenger did not name a single Englishman in his sixteen-man outfit for a 5–1 win over Crystal Palace in the 2004–05 season. Mourinho, who has seven Englishmen in his twenty-three-man squad, plans to bring in more home-based players. Mourinho said, 'We have three or four home players involved in every domestic match. I really believe in home players. I think Peter Kenyon and Mr Abramovich feel exactly the same. The club is investing in youth football and, in a couple of years, we will be ready to answer the demands of UEFA in relation to that. It's important, although you can do it without them. The best proof of that is the success Arsenal have had over the last few years with a lot of foreign players. But that's not the point.

'As a foreign manager, I feel responsible for the English clubs and the

English national team. I would never forget that or the future of youth football at the club. The supporters fall in love with players they feel are the club. If kids can see John Terry, Frank Lampard and Joe Cole, these kind of English boys in the club, it's easier for them to say, "Yes, we'll go to Chelsea, because we believe in their philosophy." I think it's easier.

'But I don't think you need to be made in the club to be a part of it. But it helps having English players. I want to have the best young players in England. You have to show young kids and their parents that they have a chance to succeed at this club.'

Terry is Chelsea's only homegrown player. Arsenal's only first-choice star to progress through the ranks is Ashley Cole, and he is wanted by Chelsea!

Wenger dismissed the idea that his foreign policy was damaging to England's future, insisting that quality overseas players help raise the standards of homegrown youngsters. 'If you look at the England team, you have Ferdinand, Ashley Cole, Rooney, Owen and Gerrard. You have never had so many stars. I feel it is getting stronger. The top players have benefited from the influx of foreigners. If every club has, say, only three foreign players, you would have more English players, but the quality of the team would definitely drop. That is the choice I must make. There are other teams with many foreign players, not just Arsenal. There is Liverpool, Chelsea and also Bolton.'

Mourinho is against FIFA proposals to ensure that each squad includes a certain number of players from their youth system. He added, 'It is a good idea, but you cannot implement this in a few months. We are spending a lot of money on youth systems, but we will not have lots of young English players in a few months.'

Some of Chelsea's foreign imports have been wonderful ambassadors for the club, from Ruud Gullit to Franco Zola to Marcel Desailly. The very first foreign player to wear the blue of Chelsea was anything but a mercenary. He was called Nils Middelboe.

Arriving in 1913, the outstanding left-half had already appeared in the Olympic final for Denmark against Great Britain, winning a silver medal, and had won thirteen caps for his country, but he played for Chelsea in the true amateur tradition – he didn't even take a penny in expenses.

'Expenses,' he said. 'What expenses? I came here by bus and shall go home on one. Lunch? I should have had to take lunch if I hadn't been playing football. Expenses? I ought to pay the club for a fine afternoon's sport.'

Such an attitude would put some who have ripped off the club in recent years on their expenses alone to shame.

His work came first, though, which did not give him many free Saturdays. His most regular performances came during the First World War. When war ended, he became captain whenever he was available, yet when he left, in 1921, he had played a mere forty-six peacetime official games.

His team-mates clubbed together to give him a parting gift, a silver cigarette box inscribed: 'To our captain and comrade – one of the best.' That was the only gift he ever accepted. He died in Copenhagen in 1976.

Since Ossie Ardiles and Ricky Villa emerged as exotic imports in 1978, English football has been awash with players from all over the world, but the top foreign stars have only been a recent phenomenon at the Bridge.

Now Chelsea can boast some of the best and worst examples of the way the Premiership has been dominated by foreign players.

From Ruud Gullit's 'sexy football' to sex and drugs for Mutu, who was tempted into taking drugs in the belief that it would improve his sex life. The twenty-five-year-old striker, who admitted to using a banned drug but denied it was cocaine, had been linked to a string of stunning models. Mutu, who began daily one-hour counselling sessions, claims he did not take cocaine but a substance aimed at improving his sexual performance. 'I am not hooked on drugs. I categorically deny this. The only reason I took what I took was because I wanted to improve my sexual performance. It may sound funny, but it is true. I did not take cocaine. I took something to make me feel good.'

The Romanian, who joined Chelsea from Parma in August 2003, made a whirlwind start to his English career with Chelsea and was branded as the new Zola, but he then had little impact on the team after falling out of favour with Claudio Ranieri in the second half of the Italian's final season in charge. Mutu managed only two brief substitute appearances under Jose Mourinho.

When Mutu arrived he brought with him bags of confidence. 'I will succeed where other Romanians have failed because I am Adrian Mutu. If you doubt that, then wait until you see me on the pitch. The rules of football are the same wherever you play. I have confidence in myself to play well. I'm told that it is maybe more physical in England, but I know I'm quick enough to get away from my opponents and do things for the rest of the team. Since the very moment when I found out that Mr Abramovich was interested in the club and wanted to pursue a number of well-known names in European football, I realised he was a president who wanted to put a very competitive team together. Chelsea want to make a name for themselves and I want to be part of that. This is the most important thing I've done in my career. I decided the day I heard about Chelsea wanting me that I would come. I look at the squad and see a powerful team with a lot of championship material. If we can make a team out of all this talent, we will certainly do well.'

Ranieri said, 'If a striker can score eighteen goals in Italy, then he can score anywhere in the world and that is why Adrian will be very important for us. He is a different player to Gianfranco, but I hope the fans will take him to their hearts in the same way.

'We have to be consistent and show that we are linking together more and more. I understand that people want to put me under pressure. Last season, when I could only bring in Quique De Lucas, you all wanted to kill me. Now I have the money to bring in the players I want for us to win. I know it might be a problem with so many players now. It is important that everybody understands our philosophy has changed. We must be like Real Madrid, Juventus, Inter and AC Milan. Whether the players play or don't, they must realise that they are all important for the team.'

Mutu added, 'I hope that I won't disappoint the fans and I want to help the team win. If Crespo comes, it will be a problem for the manager to play us together. Now I just have to do my job against Leicester.'

When, on the stroke of half-time, Mutu's free-kick flew straight into the wall and rebounded to him on his debut against Leicester, he let fly with a follow-up effort that rocketed into the far corner of the net. A montage of the magical Zola was played on the giant screens, but there was a new master of tricks and skills in Mutu. Leicester manager Micky Adams observed, 'That's what you pay £15.8 million for ... not that I would know!'

Mutu was pleased to get through the game after a hectic week when he had to catch five planes to reach Donetsk for Romania's 2–0 win over Ukraine, a game in which he scored both of the goals. He also had a nasty gash on his right hand for which he required nine stitches. 'My goal was a great start, but that's not the most important thing. The style is not important and I'm just pleased it went in. My father is a mathematician, so I obviously inherited his sense of angles! The style and beauty of the goal is not as important as the weight of the three points. If it hits the back of the net, it's good enough. I hope it's a good omen and I want to carry on in this way. I was delighted that the crowd took to me straight away. I was running on empty, but they gave me wings!

'I love my tricks and flicks and like to entertain the crowd. Fans in England appreciate these fine touches as there are not many players around who can play like that. My arm was quite badly gashed, but the Premiership's not bad if you can take the knocks. I was pleasantly surprised at the amount of space I found. In the future, I may be marked more closely, but I should still be able to create gaps for others and allow them to play.

'Zola was a great player for Chelsea and cannot really be replaced. He was a unique personality and I can only try and raise my game to his level. I don't see myself purely as a forward. I like to operate as a second striker, linking play from the midfield. I bring something different. Many English strikers are all about power, but my game is based on speed and fantasy. I am a Latin player and love to have the ball at my feet so I can go past defenders.

'For a player who wants to make a name for himself in the international arena, this is the only club.'

When Mutu first arrived, Ranieri said, 'Mutu will be the second striker. He is young and scored many goals in Italy, which shows he is dangerous and he is clever and strong. I have said Jimmy is a shark and Carlton Cole a lion. Mutu is another predator – I have a zoo!'

Mark Bosnich was in such a state when he was drug tested positive for cocaine that he entered a specialist institution.

Then Bosnich demanded an investigation into who had 'fingered' him. The release of the unauthorised information almost pushed Bosnich over the edge. He attempted to obliterate the nightmare he had endured as his career crashed at Chelsea. He had been ordered to train with the kids by Claudio Ranieri, and had once even been overlooked for a place on the bench – the young reserve 'keeper was called up instead. Bosnich's lavish wages and celebrity lifestyle couldn't compensate for a once-glittering career that was rapidly going downhill.

While Paul Merson had been backed by Arsenal at the time of his drug confession, Chelsea, at the time under the chairmanship of Ken Bates, did not follow the same path and sacked the 'keeper.

Bosnich was on a basic salary of just under £30,000 a week topped up with loyalty payments that were built into his contract and which were payable at the start of each season after he had signed on a Bosman free transfer from Manchester United. He had a contract that ran to June 2004: the total value of that deal was in excess of £3 million and possibly as much as £3.5 million.

Bosnich was concerned about why the FA-Sport UK drug-testing unit came to test him in the first place. The suspicion is that, for the first time, the FA doping unit were possibly tipped off about Bosnich and came down at the invitation of the club. Chelsea told him to find another club.

With his professional career in ruins and his relationship with model Sophie Anderton failing, the Aussie descended into a personal abyss. The disgraced star is still battling his addiction, which followed his sacking by Chelsea in 2002.

Bosnich said, 'I never touched drugs until I was thirty-one, but once it got hold it became a massive struggle to break free. I was slowly killing myself, but I didn't care. Now I have a new agent, Angie, who has convinced me there are things in life worth giving up cocaine for.'

Chelsea's Foreign Legion has been a cocktail of the Good, The Bad and The Ugly. Bad boys are easy to find in Mutu and Bosnich, but the good guys range from Gullit to Weah, both former World Footballers of the Year.

Weah played one season for Chelsea, and has more recently been seeking a new career as a candidate to run for the presidency of Liberia.

Weah, thirty-eight, who lives in the United States, but who enjoys almost godlike status in his native country, says, 'I will be a candidate in the presidential election. I have no choice but to accept the people's request.' Youth, business and political groups petitioned for Weah to stand in the West African country's first free and fair elections in more than two decades. Liberia emerged from fourteen years of civil war in August 2003, when Charles Taylor was forced into exile. At the time of writing, the country was being ruled by an interim government led by Gyude Bryant. A friend of Weah said that a recent meeting with Nelson Mandela had persuaded 'King George', as he is known in Liberia, to stand in the election. Weah will join more than twenty other candidates who have announced that they will run in the election. Although he has only a basic education and little political experience, many commentators believe that Weah's popularity in the football-obsessed nation and the paucity of other strong candidates make him a realistic contender. 'Oppong [Weah] is capable of winning because he is the most popular man in the country,' said Sam

Dean, publisher of the *Independent* newspaper in Liberia. 'But the question is: can he rule the country?'

The peace accord in Liberia remained shaky and hundreds of thousands of refugees who fled the civil war still remained outside the country. Corruption still dogs all levels of society and thousands of former combatants are unemployed, with little prospect of finding jobs.

Many of the country's three million inhabitants see Weah – who serves as a goodwill ambassador for the United Nations Children's Fund and has received worldwide acclaim for his humanitarian work – as the only man who can bring the country together. 'After several years of bloody and fratricidal war that destroyed unity in the country, Liberians need a true patriot, a humanitarian, and George Weah has the potential to redeem the nation by reuniting Liberians,' read a petition published in the local press in September 2004.

Weah's humble beginnings resonate with a desperately poor population. One of fourteen siblings born in a shanty town in Monrovia, he established himself in local leagues before moving to Europe. Fast and strong, with a knack for scoring spectacular goals, he enjoyed huge success with Monaco, Paris St Germain and AC Milan. In 1995, he became the only player in history to win the European, African and World Player of the Year titles in a single year. He won the FA Cup with Chelsea in 2000, and later had a brief spell with Manchester City. As player-coach of the Liberian national team between 2000 and 2002, he made Liberia one of Africa's most competitive teams before quitting because of political interference. But it was his generosity off the pitch that consolidated Weah's regal status in Liberia. In 1995, when the national team faced suspension by FIFA over outstanding fees, he paid the US$5,000 shortfall. At the African Cup of Nations the following year, he purchased equipment, clothing and aircraft tickets for members of the squad and its management staff.

He was not immune to the violence that gripped the country. After criticising Taylor in 2002, his home was burned down and members of his family were attacked.

There haven't been many clubs signing a Russian, but with a new Russian owner that was almost a natural progression. The arrival of Alexei Smertin raised a few eyebrows, however, because, after costing Roman Abramovich's club a reasonably big fee, he was loaned straight away to another club! A player signed for £4.2 million from Bordeaux, more than most Premiership clubs can afford, and immediately loaned out to Portsmouth, took some explaining. The twenty-eight-year-old midfielder was looking to return home to Torpedo Moscow until Abramovich's personal involvement. Big Italian clubs often sign players and then farm them out to gain experience and Chelsea were the first English club to follow suit.

'In principle, we have agreed everything and Alexei will sign a four-year deal with Chelsea,' Paulo Barbosa, the player's agent, said at the time of the move.

Smertin had to accept the arrangement as he said, 'It's probably the best possible solution for me right now. I need to get accustomed to life in England and to the Premiership, and I need to learn English. Playing for Portsmouth will mean that I have a smoother transition.'

Smertin was amused by the suspicions that had been aroused by his loan deal. 'People have been watching too many old movies about spies and stuff! There is nothing dodgy about my move to England. I am here because I, and Chelsea, want me to be here. It is good for Chelsea because they have so many new players trying to find their feet, and it is good for me because it allows me the time to adapt to the country and the style of football. I think that, after a year with Portsmouth, I will be ready for the challenges at Chelsea. Very few Russians have ever played, let alone succeeded, in England, so it is sensible not to rush.

'Part of the confusion has come from the fact that I was supposed to be going back to Russia, but then suddenly came to England. There is no question that Roman helped me, but he did not just buy me to get me out of France at all costs. Claudio Ranieri also liked me as a player and played a part in the negotiations that brought me here.'

The Russian connection played its part. 'Of course,' Smertin admits, 'because Roman had watched me play and wanted me to join his club. But that is not strange. Many chairmen suggest players to their managers.'

Smertin saw Abramovich in those early days with Pompey. 'Yes, several times. Whenever I go up to London, we try to meet for lunch or just to catch up. I did not know him at all before my transfer to Chelsea, but now that we are two Russians in England we have lots more in common. We always have loads to talk about.'

But Smertin was called up by new coach Jose Mourinho and formed a part of his plans.

Which is more than can be said about Juan Sebastian Veron; Claudio Ranieri tried to achieve what Sir Alex had failed to do with the Argentine. 'I've always had good links with South American players. Only Ariel Ortega was a little difficult at Valencia, but all the rest, Careca at Napoli, Enzo Francescoli at Cagliari, Daniel Fonseca at Cagliari and Napoli, Gabriel Batistuta at Fiorentina and Claudio Lopez at Valencia, I had a good relationship with. Veron is very intelligent; he doesn't always need to be always saying, "I'm the best." He's a fantastic man.'

He thought his 'Little Witch' – the nickname fans had given him in Italy – would flourish. 'Do I believe I will get more out of Veron? Yes. It's difficult to say why he didn't do it at Manchester United, but I think I have a very good link with Argentinean players and if I link well with Veron he will be a different player. I think I can get more out of him, it's a feeling.'

And Veron's best position? 'In the middle.' So why play him on the right in Slovakia? 'It was the first match. I cannot change too much. I may be the Tinkerman but I'm not stupid.'

David Mellor had savaged the decision to sign Veron, questioning its validity because of links to Zahavi. He now admits that he was wrong. 'As for Veron, I am a sinner come to repentance. I worried that he was spoiled, but an early encounter with another sceptic changed his mind, and should have changed mine. Well, before Sunday's Premiership encounter, my friend reported how fit and determined Veron was. Which was exactly how he looked, with end-to-end running and accurate passing, not to mention that goal. Already, Chelsea are building themselves around Veron and this could be a season to rival the one with Lazio three years ago where some of the most unforgiving fans in the world hailed him as a hero among heroes.'

Veron's one season at the Bridge was fraught with problems, including a burglar who threatened to kill his two young children with a machete and who was subsequently jailed for life. Junkie Wayne Harley – who had a string of burglary and ABH convictions – was told he was a danger to the public. At the trial, Judge Charles Tilling said, 'You terrorised an entire household by threatening them with a machete. The people you terrorised included two very young children.'

The judge, who said Harley may have been high at the time, added, 'I regard you as representing a continued risk of causing serious harm to the public. Therefore, the sentence I pass is one of life imprisonment.'

The thief, who took £70,000 in gems in the raid on the Chelsea star's £2.5

million home, burst into tears and a woman in the gallery yelled, 'No!' As he was led away he shouted, 'Tell her I love her.' Harley, who has spent almost half his life behind bars, will be eligible for parole in just over four years. The masked robber had made the Verons and their children – a son, three, and a daughter, two – wear pillowcases over their heads in the raid in Barnes, south-west London. He broke in through a window in January and confronted Veron's mum and aunt in a bedroom, Kingston Crown Court, Surrey, heard. Prosecutor Philip Bennetts said, 'He demanded money and jewellery, banging his machete on the bed as he made his demands.' He then went to the room where Argentina skipper Veron, twenty-nine, and wife Maria were sleeping. Their children were in a nearby bedroom.

Mr Bennetts said, 'Veron and his wife awoke when the lights went on and they saw the defendant had a machete in his hand. He told them not to do anything strange or he would kill the children.'

Harley demanded keys to a safe, money and jewellery and made Maria give him the rings she was wearing. When their daughter wandered into the room he let her climb into bed and made Veron fetch his son as well. After asking about the value of their house and cars, the burglar ordered them to put pillowcases on their heads.

Mr Bennetts added, 'Having completed his search of the room, he told them to go into the bathroom. He told them not to go near the window as somebody was watching outside.'

The burglar fled in a van at about 8am, but soon fell asleep. He set off again but crashed and was arrested shortly afterwards. Harley, of Wimbledon, south London, admitted aggravated burglary – his fourth conviction for the crime. His lawyer Simon Draycott QC said, 'He acknowledges what he did was a terrible thing and he's remorseful.'

The Verons are now in Italy, where the star is on loan to Inter Milan, but have been kept informed of the case. Outside court, Detective Constable Brian Hizzett said, 'It's a just sentence. He's a predatory burglar.'

Chelsea had thought they had paired two of the best Argentineans, Veron and Crespo, but it never had much of a chance. Crespo had played in front of Veron since they were teenagers in Argentina. Crespo said at the time of his move to English football, 'I always talk to Seba and he spoke very highly of Chelsea. That is why I am here. It is always easier for me when Seba is in the team. I have played most of my best football with him in Italy and for Argentina. Manchester United and Arsenal have dominated the Premiership for many years, but we intend to break that up and make sure we challenge for the Premiership. The world of football has been shocked by what has been happening at Chelsea. We might not have the prestige of Real Madrid and others yet, but that will come. Here we can write our own history. I met Mr Abramovich only briefly, but I have seen from the way he watches games that he is passionate about football, and with a businessman like him behind us anything is possible. Playing in the Champions League is always stimulating. Inter Milan reached the semi-finals last year and to get that far you need both a lot of quality and a little bit of luck.'

English football had not had a high profile in Argentina since the days of Ardiles and Villa. Crespo added, 'English football has not been so popular in Argentina since Ardiles and Villa were at Tottenham, but I hope we can revive that interest. At the moment, there is only Spanish and Italian football on the television at home, but I hope that Seba and I at Chelsea will put a stop to that.' How long had it taken him to decide? 'Not too long because the two clubs had made an agreement,' said Crespo.

Inter Milan's Christian Vieiri raged at allowing his strike partner to leave. But Crespo explained that the 'economic crisis' in Italian football had meant that his move was 'simple'. The financial problems in Italy offered an opportunity to British teams who, he claimed, were 'not so far behind Italian football'. He added, 'Real Madrid, Juventus and Inter have been building their history for a long time. Now we'll try and write our history for the future. To get to that stage, you need a lot of quality and a little bit of luck. Hopefully, we'll have a bit of luck, because I'm convinced that we have the quality. It's all about the growth of the team – and, if we achieve union in the team, we'll go far. I'm a very positive and optimistic person and I'm convinced things will go in the best possible way. I'll do everything I can to make sure they do. I know in my country anything which smells English is not very well looked upon, but between Juan Veron and myself we're going to try and turn Chelsea into a club which has supporters out there. Of course, it's an interesting prospect to link up with Juan, we are great friends. We first got to know each other in 1996 at the Atlanta Olympics. Before that, we'd always been opponents. I was with River Plate and he was with Estudiantes, and then Boca Juniors. When we both found ourselves in Italy, he was on his own at Sampdoria and I was in the same situation at Parma. We used to encourage each other if we were feeling low. It was the first time we had left our home country, and we had left behind the way of life that we knew so well. So that's how our friendship started and it has remained strong ever since. He says that, with a bit of luck, we can turn English football upside down. Argentina wear light blue, Chelsea royal blue and next to me there will be Veron. If I shut my eyes, I'm going to think that I'm in Buenos Aires.'

Ardiles believed that the striker is as good as Raul and Ruud van Nistelrooy. Ardiles said, 'I rate Crespo very, very highly. He is one of the best strikers, right up there with van Nistelrooy, Henry, Raul and Ronaldo. Chelsea will be quite a force with him this season and have such a strong squad now. Can they win the Premiership? Certainly. They will be fighting Manchester United and Arsenal all the way.'

Ardiles added, 'By the time he left Argentina for Italy, he was already a big, big star. He is a big, strong guy and he is a winner. He is aggressive, quick, good in the air and has a very nice touch. He scored a lot of goals in Italy in a difficult league. In England the game is more open, so I think he will score even more goals. I think he will be a great success. He is the number-one striker for Argentina right now. The others, like Saviola and Aimar, play around him – that's how good he is.'

Crespo would not have to face the same problems that Ardiles had to contend with. 'The biggest problem was the language and other stuff that will no longer be a worry for him because of globalisation and developments in communication systems,' he explained. 'Crespo will be able to bring as many friends and family over from Argentina and Italy as he wants. He'll settle well.'

Crespo declared, 'The advantage of having an Italian coach who speaks Spanish is sensational. I won't suffer any handicap because of the language. Ranieri has a very good reputation in Italy. I know he's been following me and that he asked Abramovich to buy me.'

Ranieri admitted, 'This is my biggest test as a manager. People want to put me under pressure, but I will work in the same way. I want to see a team with the new players linked together. My philosophy is to get them all helping each other. It's a challenge whenever new players arrive, as the manager is under pressure to get them all playing together.'

Crespo signed a four-year deal. Ranieri said, 'You can play the greatest football in the world, but it's no good if you don't put the ball in the net. And it's my neck that is on the block! Crespo is a fantastic striker who scores a lot of goals. That is what can decide tight games. He was the second top scorer in the Champions League for Inter Milan last season. That is very important. He's very fast, good in the air and I am delighted to have him. He attacks space superbly and is strong and clever.

'It is more difficult to score in Italy because they have a defensive culture. England is different, but he'll adapt. Crespo's characteristics are good for English football. I now have five strikers and can pick two every week. In September and October, we will have games every three days, so it's important to give the players a rest. He is another champion who wants to fight and never gives up. He is my new little lion ... and I like lions!'

Crespo told Chelsea TV how much he had enjoyed the 'wonderful welcome'. 'It was very satisfying; it was great to be in front of our home fans. This move is very important to me because it's a great sporting chance and a great social chance with a great group of players. Mario Stanic, he was at Parma with me, and I played against Desailly. I also know all the other players, but I've never played against them. I've come here to win things, not just to participate. We will do everything we can to win things. I see myself as the first striker, but I have no problem if the manager wants me to be the second striker.'

'Here there is everything to win. The prestige will come. The history can be written. This is the challenge that I put upon myself.'

Crespo said the spending spree had 'surprised the world', never mind Serie A. Veron's reaction was ultra-positive. He felt that the club was now in a position to challenge Manchester United's supremacy. Veron said, 'The two teams are obviously very different; however, Chelsea's activities in pre-season show they can also make it to the level United are at. There are very few clubs in the world like Manchester United, but I think Chelsea can also become as big, if not bigger, than they are.'

Veron insisted that the duo would be even more successful than Ardiles and Villa, the last two Argentineans to link up at an English club, both of whom starred when Spurs won the FA Cup in 1981. Veron said, 'I think Hernan and I are going to surpass their achievements.'

Veron's early displays suggested that he would finally do himself justice. Veron said, 'Italian and English football are very different, and perhaps that is what caused the change in my form over the last few seasons. But I feel I can make it in the English game, too. What I aspire to do is to leave the same image of myself in England as I did in Italy. I want to be seen as a champion – as both a professional and a person. I didn't have my flow for United. One of the problems could be that I played out of position, but what I lacked was the continuity more than the actual position. Last season, I felt I was in some of my best form before I got injured against Leeds – so maybe Mark Viduka was to blame for injuring me. It was unfortunate I could not show my all at Old Trafford, but I don't regret anything. What I have to show now is only to the people of Chelsea – the manager, the players and the fans. I will play in whatever position I'm asked and that comes down to the manager, but my favourite is in central midfield where I can attack.'

Ranieri was banking on Veron to bring the best out of Crespo. 'Veron and Crespo have known each other since they played together for Argentina's Under-21 team. They have a good link together and Veron will be able to explain to him all about English football. Crespo is a good leader on the pitch. He's a new champion for us. He is a fantastic striker and could be very important to the team. I will try and speak to the Italian FA about whether he can play on Saturday.'

But the arrival of Jose Mourinho saw the departure of the expensive Argentine imports, with Crespo shipped off on loan to AC Milan, and Veron to city rivals Inter. After shaky starts both were thriving again.

In their place came some wonderfully gifted stars, none more so than Petr Cech, who set about setting new records for shut-outs.

Overall, players such as Zola, Gullit and Roberto Di Matteo reflect the highly professional attitude of the majority of overseas players to have arrived at the Bridge. 'The Rock', Marcel Desailly graced the club, making 222 appearances after singing from AC Milan shortly after winning the World Cup. He captained Chelsea on ninety-four occasions and won the European Super Cup, FA Cup and Charity Shield with the club. His equaliser against Liverpool on the final day of the 2002–03 season put Chelsea on the way to a victory that secured Champions League football, which in turn was crucial to the decision of Roman Abramovich to buy the club. He retired as a Chelsea player after a hip injury.

The emergence of Terry and Gallas as one of the strongest defensive partnerships in the Premiership limited his appearances in his final season, before he headed off to play in Qatar. 'It was a diffcult decision because I love the club. I've been here for six years and I will support them for the rest of my life. I'm still feeling the pain that we didn't win the Premiership, but there's a future coming and I'm sure Chelsea will win it.' He was wanted by

Crystal Palace, Portsmouth and Celtic, but joined Al Lttihad for a season, also rejecting the chance to become coach to the country where he was born, Ghana. But he plans to take the Ghana job in the future. Frank Leboeuf is also playing now in Qatar.

Emmanuel Petit helped Arsène Wenger to lift his first-ever title in England and quit Highbury five years ago for Barcelona. He almost ended up playing for Manchester United on his return to England, but chose Chelsea instead. He received a telephone call from Sir Alex Ferguson, but opted instead for a return to London and joined Chelsea. Yet he still maintains that the best manager he ever played for was Wenger. He says, 'Maybe I should have joined Manchester United when they came in for me before I joined Chelsea after Barcelona, as I would have liked to have played for Ferguson, too.'

Petit, thirty-four, was released when Jose Mourinho arrived and was forced to quit the game after failing to recover from a knee injury. Despite training with Arsenal for a few weeks, the former Gunner and Chelsea midfielder, failed to regain full fitness. Petit won the World Cup with France in 1998 and his partnership with Patrick Vieira was central to Arsenal's 1997–98 Double success.

He said, 'Just before Christmas [2004] I became certain I would never get back to my physical level. I knew it was over. Twenty years of my life have ended. It's like a little death. All the images of my career came through my head. You must suddenly get into real life. Football players live in a bubble.'

He added, 'Arsenal lost the plot after losing their unbeaten record to Manchester United. They lost their focus completely on the Premiership. Their new target is undoubtedly the Champions League. Over the last ten years it has been Arsenal and Manchester United for the Premiership, but Chelsea are growing a lot. The big difference in Chelsea is their confidence and team spirit. They have very good players. Arsenal may not have retained the title but, along with Manchester United, they have been the most successful club in the past ten years. They are now content for United and Chelsea to fight for the title between themselves as they have a new target. Their success in the Champions League depends on injury and suspensions and if they can avoid these they have a very good chance.'

After eight years, Celestine Babayaro thought he had seen it all. At twenty-six, the left-back had played for, and outlasted, three managers – Ruud

Gullit, Gianluca Vialli and Claudio Ranieri. He saw young players arrive and old favourites leave, part of the natural evolution of a dressing room. But nothing prepared him for the impact of Abramovich's millions.

'What has happened at Chelsea under Abramovich is like nothing else that has happened before,' said the Nigerian international who, after almost a decade in west London, delivers his words with an accent more King's Road than Kaduna, his family home in Nigeria. 'He came out of nowhere. Nobody expected someone like him to take over Chelsea. The amount of money he has invested is unbelievable. So many players came and went, the dressing room always had different faces in it, everything changed so quickly.' Babayaro made 197 appearances for Chelsea following a £2.25 million move from Anderlecht in 1997. Significantly, though, only five of those were made during the historic 2004–05 campaign.

Having left Nigeria aged just fifteen, Babayaro was still only nineteen when he moved to Chelsea. He grew up at the club and became a familiar face in a river of new arrivals. But, having survived the cull under Ranieri, the first manager given unlimited access to Abramovich's chequebook, he was not so fortunate under Mourinho. With little hope of regular football, and having lost his place in the Nigerian national side, Newcastle were the first to offer him an escape. 'There was no hesitation when I found out Newcastle were interested in me. I'd been at Chelsea for eight years, but I had five months left on my contract. I could have stayed, the manager told me that. I'd thought about signing a new contract, but I wasn't playing regularly. I was the longest-serving player at the club. I'd seen players and managers come and go. I'd played under four different managers and that is not an easy thing to do. Every footballer worries when a new manager takes over, because he comes in with his own players. He has new ideas and you worry that you will not be part of those plans. But I was always OK, I always stayed.

'When Jose came I didn't start to think, 'I don't have a future at the club.' I thought it would be the same as it had been – difficult, but if I got my head down and worked hard, I'd stay. When I spoke to Jose, he told me I'd get a fair chance. He said everyone would get a fair chance, but I got a couple of injuries. I missed my chance.

'Until Roman Abramovich took over, there was nothing to choose between Chelsea and Newcastle. We were at the same standard. Both looked like they might be able to win the title, but never managed it. Then it all changed because of Abramovich. It is not the same Chelsea I joined, but they are doing so well and I'm pleased for them. I'm happy here, though [at Newcastle]. It was the right decision. Things have not gone as well as we'd like on the pitch, but we can change that. It's about a new beginning for me. I could have been a part of what is happening there. I could be playing in the Champions League and challenging for the Premiership title. But why would I want to do that? After eight years it was time to move on. I would have gone in and trained hard every day, but I didn't know if I'd ever get in the team. Now I have a spring in my step. If I win a trophy at Newcastle, I will retire a happy man. That would be a massive thing to do, because they haven't won anything in so long.'

He won an FA Cup-winner's medal and a European Super Cup trophy, but he believes the transformation from also-rans to runaway leaders is largely down to one man. 'Mourinho's great strengths are confidence and organisation. He knows exactly what he is doing. He came into Chelsea and changed everything. Some people say he's arrogant, but I just think he has confidence in everything he does. He's instilled that into the boys and they really believe in themselves, which is a big change for Chelsea. Last season we went into games thinking it was going to be hard and we might get a draw, but this year they expect to get three points from every game. No one even thinks about the possibility of losing. Mourinho's approach to the game is so professional; he's the most thorough manager I've worked with. We used to watch videos before every game, but Mourinho made us watch the same video three times. A couple of days before the game, he puts down notes on each player's peg of who you're playing against so that everyone knows their job.

'There's this incredible feeling of togetherness and belief that they're going to succeed.'

Y

Youth Team to £20 Million Academy

Jose Mourinho stressed his desire to build the club's future around homegrown players. Claudio Ranieri spent more than half of his final season's transfer money on foreign imports, but Mourinho started the clear-out with Seba Veron, a £15 million signing, by sending him out on loan to Inter Milan.

When Mourinho first arrived at the Bridge, he observed, 'Last night I was spending my night analysing a document about the academy, because I have to be ready for my feedback in relation to this document. I try to be very organised and I try to explain to the Board what I like, and because of that I'm making a few documents for the Board to explain what I want and what I like. I think it is [youth development] crucial. The biggest quality of the team is to play as a team. I don't know a successful team [which does not] play as a team. We must have a nucleus of strong personalities, and if possible with people with the culture of the club. With the Bosman law the door is open completely to go a different way, but we should recover a little of that spirit. So if you ask me would I like to have many English players in your team – yes, I would like – and when I finish my contract would I love to have a heart of Chelsea boys made in the club – I would love it and will work for it.'

Anyone who thinks Mourinho cares only for big-money signings should have seen him on the morning before the prestigious, high-profile supercharged Champions League draw in Monaco. He might have been the man who had led Porto to triumph in Europe's elite tournament, but he had more crucial club affairs to see to, including the youth structure. He was watching Chelsea Under-13s from behind one goal.

'That's the second time he's been down here in two weeks,' said Chelsea's academy director Neil Bath. Mourinho had to leave before the end of the youngsters' game against Ajax. 'Jose's produced a document for the [academy] coaching staff and scouting staff which sets out the philosophy he'd like to see,' said Bath. 'He's very clear about the type of player he'd like coming through and what he wants to see with the young boys, particularly at the older end when they're starting to progress to the reserves and first team. He fully understands that the needs and requirements of seven- to thirteen-year-olds will be different and he likes the practice we're doing with the younger ages. He wants players who are physically, technically and tactically capable of playing in the first team and have experienced the systems of play and the typical training methods that he implements for the first team. So we have spent time watching his training sessions and reading up on his philosophy. Our role is to ensure that, when a young player does get an opportunity, they're aware of what's coming because they will have experienced it.'

The plans for the £20 million development of a 3,338-square-metre site at Cobham in Surrey will see Chelsea enjoying superb facilities. It will also give Mourinho a proper base after having to share with their landlords, London University's Imperial College. Abramvoich said when he took over, 'I don't believe the model of Real Madrid would fit in the English structure. I see Chelsea being in between Manchester United and Real Madrid. At Manchester United, there is an academy that is preparing future players. But, when you have to make a purchase, you do.'

Mourinho's attention to detail has dovetailed with Abramovich's vision over the new headquarters. The new training ground will have fifteen pitches, six of them laid to the highest Premiership standards, three with undersoil heating, one indoor artificial grass pitch for winter use, and a state-of-the-art treatment and rehabilitation centre. Planning conditions imposed by Elmbridge Borough Council before they granted permission means that the main building will be built down, with an underground 'bunker' surrounded by a moat, and with a grass roof to blend with the environment.

Chelsea's need for a new base was identified by Abramovich when he bought the club from Ken Bates after being bemused by the quality of facilities at the club's rented home at Harlington near Heathrow Airport. The Surrey site, close to the homes of a number of Mourinho's squad, and which will also play host to the club's youth and academy teams, fits the bill perfectly.

Mourinho said, 'This is fantastic news for Chelsea. One of the reasons I joined was the commitment that Mr Abramovich and the Board showed about investing in youth.

'With the academy, youth, reserves and first team all on the same site, this will act as an inspiration for the young players at Chelsea. A modern training ground is important for first-team players. The club needs its own home for training and top players want to know about the facilities and their environment for work before they join a club. If we can tell them we have the best training ground, this is a big advantage.'

Kenyon added, 'The Cobham development is central to the future of the club and we are delighted we now have the final go-ahead. Developing homegrown players is a vitally important goal for Chelsea.'

Part of Mourinho's brief when he came to Chelsea was to oversee an improvement in the academy. The fact that Chelsea hosted the Premier League academy Under-13 event, which also featured Ajax, Celta Vigo, Bayer Leverkusen, Fulham and Liverpool, showed a different side to the club from the moneybags version. 'They've given me a brief that their long-term plan is to have homegrown talent rather than to invest year after year,' said Bath, whose coaches include the former Chelsea players Damian Matthew, Eddie Newton and Jason Cundy. 'With the work that's going on at such younger ages, who knows, in eight, nine, ten years' time we might find ourselves with seven or eight players in the first team, which is both my target and the club's.'

The academy system, which began six years ago, allows Premier and Football League clubs to work with players from the age of seven rather than twelve. 'Ajax, who are renowned for their production of players, said their stats have shown that when they took the boys early – at seven, eight and nine – they have produced a better quality of player,' said Dave Richardson, the Premier League's director of youth. 'We think we have a system ... which will produce a level of player that means our leading clubs don't have to seek so many from further afield.'

Chelsea hope Michael Mancienne, an England Under-17 international, will fulfil his potential. Mourinho's eye was also drawn to a twelve-year-old goalkeeper. 'My goalkeeping coach is ready to work with him now and again to teach him a few things,' he said. 'And this kid needs a lot of support, because he comes from Bosnia and he lost his father and mother in the war.'

The manager feels his trips to the academy can help the club's search for talent. 'Every kid and parent needs motivation to be in Chelsea,' he said. 'And it's a big boost for them to try to join us if they feel I'm there, involved.'

Chelsea chief executive Peter Kenyon explained that the club had gone for Mourinho because they felt he would change Chelsea for the better. 'The next generation is about becoming a dominant force in the Premier League and building Chelsea into a truly big European club. That's about successive years of winning trophies. In order to do that we have to take a completely different approach to perhaps the Chelsea of old. Youth development is an important factor in that. It's not just about continuing to buy the big-name players.

'This is about building a cohesive team from youth right the way through to the first team, so it's completely revamping the way that we go about our football programme and, at that point, we felt it was necessary to look for a new manager. We wanted the next generation. We wanted somebody to work with for the next five, ten years, so age was an important factor. So was track record, someone who will take this academy through to [the] first team. If you look at a lot of Europe, their structure is to have a football director and a first-team coach and what we wanted to do is to combine that, and get somebody who would take the holistic view of identifying the nine-year-olds, signing them as YTS at sixteen, as pro at seventeen, and hopefully bringing them through to the first team, because that is the heart and culture that Chelsea wants to do. At the same time, Chelsea is always going to have big-name players, so the ability of that man to manage the big stars as well as the stars of tomorrow was a key component.'

Abramovich personally made a surprise visit to Arsenal's London Colney training ground to examine their state-of-the-art training facilities with a view to making improvements at his own club. The club spent £15 million purchasing land to develop a training complex in Cobham, Surrey, but had yet to receive planning permission when the inspections of other big club's training facilities took place.

Clubs like Chelsea and Arsenal were at the forefront of major changes planned by UEFA regarding quotas of homegrown players. UEFA's policy was to crack down on the number of foreign stars allowed in some of the leading clubs to prevent them 'hoarding' the best players. Instead of stockpiling Europe's finest, Mourinho and Wenger, plus all of the English clubs in European action, will have to include up to eight 'homegrown' stars in their twenty-five-strong Champions League or UEFA Cup squads. UEFA also want the rules extended to the Premiership and domestic competitions, but have come up against strong opposition from clubs in England and Italy.

The new quotas are being phased in for European competitions and will be introduced for the 2006–07 season with clubs needing to include a minimum of four homegrown players in a squad. That number will be increased to six the following season and then to eight in 2008–09.

Arsenal, Chelsea, Celtic and Rangers, along with Ajax, were the five clubs out of thirty-two in the previous season's Champions League who would not have had enough homegrown talent in their squads. Of the eight homegrown stars needed by 2008, four will have had to be trained by the club's own academy, and four trained as youngsters by other clubs in that country. UEFA define a club-trained player as one who has been registered for a minimum of three seasons with the club between the ages of fifteen and twenty-one.

Last season, Chelsea had John Terry, Robert Huth and Lenny Pidgeley as academy-produced stars with Glen Johnson, Joe Cole, Frank Lampard (all West Ham), Wayne Bridge (Southampton) and Scott Parker (Charlton) trained elsewhere in England.

Arsenal fell short with Ashley Cole, Justin Hoyte, Stuart Taylor, Ryan Garry and Jeremie Aliadiere as homegrown, and only Sol Campbell trained elsewhere in England. Manchester United had no problems meeting the eight homegrown criteria. Liverpool had Jamie Carragher, Steven Gerrard, Neil Mellor, Stephen Warnock, Richie Partridge as homegrown, but only Chris Kirkland trained elsewhere.

The Premier League was confident that the UEFA measures will not be implemented for the domestic competitions. A spokesman said, 'As all Premier League clubs have the potential to play in European competitions, they do have an interest in this issue. UEFA clearly believe that they have a robust enough legal position to introduce the changes within their competitions. However, it is extremely unlikely that such a rule change will be introduced in our domestic competition.'

Sepp Blatter, president of FIFA, has accused major clubs of creating a 'high-stakes trade in humans' by snapping up players from less-developed areas of the world in a desperate search for talent. He fears increasing 'globalisation' is weakening the bond between clubs and their local fan base. Many countries, including 2006 World Cup hosts Germany, believe the lack of opportunity for local players is harming the national team.

Lars-Christer Olsson, chief executive of UEFA, said, 'The squad must be limited to twenty-five to stop some of the bigger clubs hoarding players and not playing them. This is unacceptable.' He says that in the last ten years there are 30 per cent less domestic stars playing in their own top-flight European leagues.

David Davies, executive director of the English FA, said, 'There is significant opposition from our own Premier League clubs and from some Italian clubs. We understand the motives, we know why this has to happen, but there will be more talking before any decision is made.'

Clubs like Arsenal and Chelsea were busy recruiting young players from all over the world for their acadamies. Sporting Lisbon threatened to make a formal complaint to FIFA after accusing Chelsea of making illegal approaches for three of their players. The Portuguese club issued a statement on their website which claimed that they were going to take up the issue with football's world governing body. The players are Adrien Silva, Fabio Ferreira and Ricardo Fernandes – all members of Sporting's youth side. Sporting claim that the trio trained with Chelsea without permission and that the London club's reply to a fax indicated their desire to 'recruit some of Sporting's players at all costs and with little regard for FIFA's fundamental rules on such matters'. A Chelsea spokesman later confirmed that the club had contacted Sporting Lisbon over 'three of the club's amateur youth players', but that the only Portuguese youngsters who were now on trial at Stamford Bridge came from Felgueiras and Pedras Rubras.

Chelsea's players decamped to Cobham, departing their outdated training ground at Harlington, under the flight path of Heathrow Airport, for the tree-lined streets and private roads of stockbroker-belt Surrey.

Their assortment of Bentleys and black 4x4s cruised into King's College sports ground in the nearby village of Stoke D'Abernon. Wealth is everywhere in Cobham, in which a three-bedroomed end-of-terrace house sells for about £300,000 and a multi-roomed mansion can cost up to £6 million.

Roman Abramovich, the billionaire Chelsea owner, will feel at home in Cobham and many of the players live in the town, anyway. The club's new

£20 million complex, with a large dome covering its indoor pitch, had not been completed, but the transition was smooth.

Gone are the days of the valuables' bag, hiding cherished possessions. Chelsea's new training Cobham training ground will be fitted with padded jewellery boxes. The club even installed £10,000-worth of sunbeds after players asked for somewhere to top up their tans! They reckoned that sunbeds were the only item missing from their luxury complex.

The club kitted out their new training complex in the ultimate footballer brand – Louis Vuitton, with £200,000 of the French firm's wallpaper and furnishings for the reception and changing rooms. Lockers for the players will be lined with Louis Vuitton leather.

Pampered Manchester United players had heated boot pegs installed at their Carrington training ground. Arsenal stars are having a beauty parlour built in their new Ashburton Grove ground in north London.

Cobham FC, the Combined Counties League club, are positively beaming at their new neighbours. Their part-time players are not paid – they have to find £60 a season each for kit and the privilege of playing at the Leg of Mutton Field, their ground. 'We get by,' Chris Woolston, the chairman, said. 'I'm a big Fulham fan, but I don't mind Chelsea being here at all. Once they've settled in, we might contact them to see if we can help them or they can help us. We could perhaps stage their women's matches or whatever. It would be great if they could put something into the local community.'

John Terry and Wayne Bridge dropped in to watch Cobham Under-17s training. 'It made our kids feel like a million dollars,' Woolston said – and Arjen Robben helped to turn on Cobham's Christmas lights.

As a teenager, Terry had the choice between Manchester United and Chelsea. Despite being a southern Red, he preferred to stay in London. His time as a trainee has shaped his captaincy, proving the value of promoting talent from within. 'As a YTS lad, you can travel a long way to the club and it was difficult for me. I struggled at the time because my mum and dad didn't have any money. I had to borrow where I could for things like driving lessons.

'So now some of the money from the senior players goes to helping out the younger kids. It is from the players' pool, the fines for being late and so on. Some will go to something like the tsunami appeal and some to helping out young players.'

Ted Drake brought the first championship to the Bridge in 1955, but he also had a sense of purpose about the development of young talent. In the championship year, Chelsea also won the Football Combination, the South-East Counties and Metropolitan Leagues.

Promising youngsters such as Peter Brabrook, Bobby Smith and Ron Tindall were bursting to break through at this time, but there was a conveyor belt of talent coming through the youth system, nurtured by Dick Foss and Albert Tennant.

Jimmy Thompson, a player for the club in the late 1920s, often donned a disguise to scour the playing fields of east London to pick up some of the finest young talent in the country, including Jimmy Greaves and Terry Venables.

Thompson provided the raw material, while Foss and Tennant developed the youth system. Yet, the then manager Tommy Docherty dispensed with Thompson: it came as a major surprise at the time.

Fast forward to the current era under Jose Mourinho. John Terry epitomises the homegrown player at the Bridge. He mixes with the club's young professionals, pays for some of them to take driving lessons and subsidised a party for them at Christmas.

Claudio Ranieri was criticised for not overly involving himself in anything other than the senior team. Mourinho is different. 'He has been outstanding with me from day one,' said youth-team coach Rodgers. 'He is very open and has plenty of words of encouragement. He has a methodology for the way the game should be played and the way the club should go, tactically, technically, physically and socially. There is this feeling about Chelsea that we haven't produced our own players. I know I had that preconception, but since I've come here I've discovered that, since the Premier League was formed, a total of twenty-two players have come through to make their first-team debuts for the club, players like John Terry, Jody Morris, Jon Harley, Michael Duberry, Muzzy Izzet and others.

'The ideal is to produce young players like John Terry who will progress through to the senior team and stay there, but otherwise players will sometimes move on for a fee which can help finance the academy. We're already seeing some young players coming through. Steven Watt was excellent against Scunthorpe, and Nuno Morais did well in an unfamiliar position at left-back. Ultimately the supporters love their own. They can especially identify with a young player who they've seen develop at the club over a period of time. John Terry is the prime example, but we are working hard to ensure that there will be others in the future.'

Z

Gianfranco Zola and Pini Zahavi

Franco Zola received the ultimate accolade when he was voted by Chelsea fans as the club's greatest-ever player.

Zola played 312 games for the club after joining for £ 4.5 million from Parma in November 1996. He scored the only goal against Stuttgart in the European Cup-Winners' Cup final in 1998, and won two FA Cups (in 1997 and 2000) and the Coca-Cola Cup (1998). He was also voted Footballer of the Year in 1997.

Zola was delighted at the chance to thank his adoring Chelsea fans after the club arranged a tribute match at the Bridge. Zola left Stamford Bridge just before Roman Abramovich's takeover.

At the time of his sudden move to Italian side Cagliari, the thirty-eight-year-old midfielder spoke of his regret at not being able to show his appreciation to Chelsea's fans after seven seasons with the club. But he was given an emotional farewell on Sunday, 8 August 2004, a week before the Premiership season kicked off.

When the match was officially announced, Zola said, 'This is a perfect occasion to say farewell to the Chelsea supporters. When I left, it happened quite suddenly. I wasn't expecting it, and I've had so many fans coming over to watch the games in Cagliari it has been astonishing. I'm really looking forward to this game. It's something I was hoping for. I can't wait. What Chelsea are doing for me is fantastic because they have a very busy schedule and to find the time to organise a game like this is fantastic. I won't be able to say thank you enough. And I just can't wait to be with the fans again.'

Chelsea chief executive Peter Kenyon said, 'We are absolutely delighted to be able to stage this match in tribute to Chelsea's greatest player. We look forward to him gracing the Stamford Bridge pitch one last time and we are certain it will be a memorable day for our fans.'

Zola urged Jose Mourinho not to abandon Chelsea's English players in pursuit of the Premiership title. The club's Portuguese head coach signed five foreigners in the summer, but Zola believes homegrown stars, such as captain John Terry, could prove just as important. He said, 'In this country you have to have a core of English players. English players are vital and when I first came here Dennis Wise and Steve Clarke were the spine of the team. English players are very important, have a great spirit and will be pushing the others in the right direction. Chelsea don't have Wise, but John, Frank Lampard and Joe Cole are really good guys. They have good character and will help achieve a winning mentality.'

Zola played the last twenty-seven minutes in a 3–0 win over Spanish side Real Zaragoza. Didier Drogba scored his third goal in three games for his new club, with a Gabriel Milito own goal and a late Scott Parker strike completing the scoring, as Chelsea finished their preparations for their opening game of the 2004–05 season, against Manchester United.

Zola was impressed with the changes that had taken place at his old club and believed that Chelsea had what it takes to win the Premiership.

He said, 'My one regret was that we didn't win the Premiership, but this team has all the ingredients to be a winning side. The team is really good and strong in every part of the pitch. I trained with them the other day and was really impressed with their commitment. Winning the Premiership is not the easiest task, but they will be very up for it. They have the strength and the desire to do it. If I was to bet, I would bet on Chelsea this year.'

Zola signed a one-year contract extension at Cagliari that will enable him to finish his playing career in Serie A, but is considering the possibility of returning to Chelsea as a coach afterwards. Assistant manager Steve Clarke said, 'I would love to see him back at this club in whatever capacity. He'll always be a fantastic ambassador for Chelsea and will always get a fantastic reception. He's got a young family, but if it's possible for him to come back he'd be more than welcome. He gets instant respect and that's very important in management. Not only is he a fantasic footballer, he is a fantastic person.'

Ken Bates took the brunt of the criticism for losing Zola, but the chairman of the time made it clear he had not personally been dealing with players' salaries for some time, first handing over to former chief executive Colin Hutchinson and then Trevor Birch. Bates says, 'When Gianfranco signed a two-year extension in 2001, we increased his salary by £1 million a year. We felt our new offer was all we could afford, given the financial constraints we had until the takeover. Now he's gone to Cagliari for less than he'd earn here. He could also have gone to Qatar and earned £4 million tax free in a year. But Sardinia is his home and he wanted to go and play there. We'd love him to come back with Cagliari for a charity match at the end of the season. I'd like him to wear a Chelsea shirt for forty-five minutes and a Cagliari shirt for forty-five minutes.'

Chelsea considered buying Cagliari and enquired how much it would cost to turn it into a nursery club, but the approach failed. Zola's agent Fulvio Marrucco said, 'Chelsea were desperate to keep him and would have done almost anything to get a deal.'

Ranieri had one lingering regret – Zola. 'We were talking about his new deal and told him the "old" Chelsea couldn't afford the extra money he wanted. I had no idea the new owner was coming because it was a secret until the very last moment. Franco had agreed terms and, even though Chelsea made such a good offer under Mr Abramovich, Franco came back and said, "People like us are born to sell dreams and, in Cagliari, they really need me in order to start dreaming great dreams once more."'

Ranieri was upset. 'I really wanted Franco to stay, but he and the club could not agree over wages. I'm not surprised about what has happened because I talked to him two or three days ago and things were going in that direction. Chelsea should have made a bit more effort to keep him, but maybe they were involved in other matters. From a technical point of view, we have lost a great player and a great ambassador. When the Queen decided she should arrange a dinner for Italians in the UK, Zola was on the list. It's going to be impossible to replace him in the hearts of the supporters. His loyalty, generosity and technical skills were all put at the disposal of our club and he was a vital leader in the dressing room.'

Zola said it was 'painful' to leave. Asked if he would have stayed had he received an improved offer before 1 July, he said, 'Yes. I wasn't thinking of leaving and had put all my offers on standby. But the renewal of my contract went on and on until 1 July, when my contract expired. Then I had to do something. I couldn't keep the other people waiting as that would have been disrespectful to them. So I decided to go. Chelsea made me a better offer on 2 July, when the transaction between the old owners and the new owners happened. They came to me with a better offer and that gave me a really bad couple of hours. But, unfortunately, it was too late. It wouldn't have been correct to take it, because Cagliari had followed me for such a long time. The renewal of my contract happened at a bad, bad moment. Chelsea were in a bad situation and we couldn't make an agreement. But I'm not putting any blame on Chelsea as they had so many more important things going on than renewing my contract.'

Zola joked that Henry would be the perfect replacement for him – if only the Frenchman could match him for speed!

So who could replace Zola? 'I can't give advice, I'm just a miserable football player! I think there are players around, more than one, who could replace me. It's finding them and getting the team that owns them to release them. But with the financial potential that the club has got now, they can force many things.'

Zola urged Abramovich not to make a rash decision on Ranieri. 'I can understand that these people, as they've put money in, will be very demanding with the manager and everyone. But, hopefully, they will also understand that things don't come straight away in football. I've seen teams in Italy spend huge amounts of money, not have success and then sack the manager. In football, you need time, patience and the club to support the team. The new man has a big responsibility on his shoulders. Hopefully, Chelsea are in good hands ... I hope he does the right things for the fans. I have not met him, but what has happened at Chelsea in the last few days is an incredible story and I pray he loves this club and gives the supporters the satisfaction they deserve.'

Zola sensed a degree of apprehension about some players when he said his goodbyes. 'There is a lot of uncertainty and I can understand that some players will be feeling anxious. Everything has happened so quickly and the players need someone to reassure them. I don't think the team needs too many changes, maybe a couple of new players, but I'm sure the manager is aware of what is needed.'

Zola urged caution in the transfer market. 'Money can give you many things – a new car, a new team – but it can't buy everything. To win things in football is not just about buying big players, but creating the right environment for the team to work. The financial potential the club has now means it can do many things, but I don't think this team needs too many players to improve, just ones in certain positions. Chelsea came fourth last season and were in contention for the title until Christmas. A couple of players in the right place will make them very competitive.

Zola's only regret was leaving without the title. 'I don't think Mr Abramovich is interested in coming second to anyone, be they Arsenal or Manchester United or whoever. He is not spending this money to help the taxman in England. He is spending it to win, and every Chelsea fan should welcome it with open arms. Claudio Ranieri has done a good job since joining Chelsea, but I don't think he will get too long to win the league. Maybe two or three years but not any more, because football owners have very little patience. Chelsea have certainly bought well, but it is no use buying the best players in the world if they do not want to play as a team. If Chelsea can do that and perform as a unit, they can win the league. It is true we did well and were always in the top four or five, but I left Chelsea with one major regret, that we failed to win the league. I just hope the fans at Chelsea now get the success they deserve and that they win the league. Everyone kept telling me about how they had only won the title once, in 1955, and that has to end. I will be dancing for joy if they do it this season and the credit must go to the manager, the players and, of course, Mr Abramovich, if they do. The championship has been a two-horse race in recent years and now it is definitely three. I would love it if Chelsea were at the front at the final post.'

Pini Zahavi has played a pivital role in the Roman Abramovich regime, masterminding numerous acquisitions.

And not only players, the Israeli agent was also behind the poaching of Peter Kenyon from Manchester United. Zahavi was also a leading figure in bringing Abramovich to the Bridge in one of the most spectacular takeover deals in English football history.

He then clashed big time with Ken Bates, who refused to acknowledge his intermediary role in the takeover. Zahavi had originally met with Bates and the chief executive at the time, Trevor Birch, to discover their availability and the price of players that Chelsea needed to sell to ease their acute cashflow crisis: the conversaton then switched to a potential takeover. The fall-out of Zahavi's row with Bates has been ongoing.

But Zahavi was well compensated as he brought several key players to the club. The moment Abramovich took control, Zahavi embarked on a whirlwind tour of Europe's most glamorous footballing cities ... Tuesday it was Paris; Wednesday, Turin; Thursday, Milan; and Friday, Monaco, and his travels across the globe have hardly stopped in pursuit of players for the new Chelsea regime, in addition to his other clients, of course.

Invariably, it is not simply a matter of one agent pulling off a deal. The player has an agent, and sometimes another agent has the authorisation for the transfer from a club. Transfers might involve numerous agents.

Abramovich had a 'hands-on' approach in all transfer dealings. He enjoyed the chase. Within a few days of owning Chelsea, Abramovich said, 'This is what the pleasure is all about: to participate in the game and the selection process. The coach will determine which areas are in need of new players. I will participate in that discussion and analysis. I like Thierry Henry and I also like Sol Campbell. But I'm not going to name any other players because their price will just go up.'

The system started off with Zahavi and Birch haggling over fees and personal terms until they were agreed in principle. At that point, Birch would call one of Abramovich's chief aides and confidants, Richard Creitzman. When Abramovich was happy with each of the deals, Creitzman talked to Eugene Tenenbaum, who controls the access to Abramovich's funds, and who acts as Abramovich's interpreter, as well as being a key adviser. Tenenbaum releases the funds from one of Abramovich's numerous bank accounts straight into Chelsea's current account.

Birch observed at that time, 'The business works at the speed of light now. We tell Roman what it costs, and he sorts it out. Simple as that. There's such a buzz around the place.

'This is the job that I came into football to do. I never imagined it at the level it's escalated to here, but being able to run a football club with big sums available is wonderful. It's completely different from what I was doing two months ago. Last pre-season we only brought in de Lucas on a free transfer and, all of a sudden, we have a menu of the world's best players. It's a dream job. To have all these funds available is great. Any club in the world would want to be in that position. Before Roman Abramovich took over, we had made preparations for restructuring and rescheduling our finances. That's what we had been working towards for sixteen months.'

'There are a lot of discussions with Claudio,' Creitzman insisted. 'Roman knows the players who have come in. He does not know them inside out or tell you how many goals they scored last year, but he watches videos and goes through cassettes on a lot of players. Agents all over have been sending him cassettes, and if Claudio says "yes" then they go ahead. Videos get sent to Roman and he talks to Claudio and he talks to other people.'

Creitzman is a Barnet supporter who was born and raised in London, educated at Surrey University, and then left England to work in Moscow and become part of the new Chelsea owner's business empire. Creitzman has been Head of Corporate Finance at Sibneft since 2001. He prepared the initial report on how the Russian might buy into a football club. Creitzman says that Abramovich 'takes a strategic look at management and is not so hands-on'.

Abramovich discusses transactions from his offices in Chukotka, Moscow, his Knightsbridge home or on his private yacht. He says, 'I have videos sent to me of the players we want to buy before I agree to go ahead with it. Of course, there is no point having money if you can't spend it, but I don't throw my money away either.'

Abramovich spelled out his philosophy. 'This is not a business venture. I am focused on the game, the beauty of the game. This is simply for my love of football. Buying Chelsea is a way to realise my ambitions myself. Through a great team you can realise your ambitions through a great game. Chelsea should be an international team. The best players need to play. What they have now is nearly a top European team. I am prepared to invest in the club and see the club be successful and, of course, I will be looking to buy players.'

Abramovich made it plain that money was no object in securing the players of his choice, although Zahavi told me, 'I won't allow him to be ripped off.'

Chelsea Facts and Figures

Founded in 1905 by Mr H.A. Mears
Biggest Win: 13–0 v. Jeunesse Hautcharage, 29 September 1971
Heaviest defeat: 1–8 v. Wolves, 26 September 1953

Top five attendances over 70,000 at Stamford Bridge:

82,905 v. Arsenal, 12 October 1935, Football League (ground record and second ever highest for a league game)
77,952 v. Swindon Town, 13 April 1911, FA Cup Round 4
77,696 v. Blackpool, 16 October 1948, Football League
76,000 (est) v. Tottenham Hotspur, 16 October 1920, Football League
75,952 v. Arsenal, 9 October 1937, Football League

Top five largest attendances at Chelsea matches at other grounds

100,000 v. Tottenham Hotspur, 20 May 1967, FA Cup final, Wembley Stadium
100,000 v. Leeds United, 11 April 1970, FA Cup final, Wembley Stadium

100,000 v. Stoke City, 4 March 1972, Football League Cup final, Wembley Stadium
90,000 v. Millwall, 7 April 1945, Football League Cup final South, Wembley Stadium
80,000 v. Charlton Athletic, 5 April 1944, Football League Cup final South, Wembley Stadium

Honours

Premier League Winners 2005
League Division One Winners 1955
FA Cup Winners 1970, 1997, 2000
FA Cup Runners-Up 1915, 1967, 1994, 2002
FA Cup Semi-Finalists 1911, 1920, 1932, 1950, 1952, 1965, 1966, 1996
European Cup-Winners' Cup Winners 1971, 1998
European Cup-Winners' Cup Semi-Finalists 1995, 1999
European Super Cup Winners 1998
League Cup Winners 1965, 1998, 2005
League Cup Runners-Up 1972
Charity Shield Winners 1956, 2000
Charity Shield Runners-Up 1971, 1997
League Division Two (Old) Winners 1984, 1989
League Division Two (Old) Runners-Up 1907, 1912, 1930, 1963, 1977
Full Members/ZDS Cup Winners 1986, 1990
FA Youth Cup Winners 1960, 1961
FA Youth Cup Runners-Up 1958

Managers

John Robertson 1905–06, David Calderhead 1907–33, T. Leslie Knighton 1933–39, William Birrell 1939–52, Ted Drake 1952–61, Tommy Docherty 1962–67, Dave Sexton 1967–74, Ron Suart 1974–75, Eddie McCreadie 1975–77, Ken Shellito 1977–78, Danny Blanchflower 1978–79, Geoff Hurst 1979–81, John Neal 1981–85, John Hollins 1985–88, Bobby Campbell 1988–92, Ian Porterfield 1992–93, David Webb 1993, Glenn Hoddle 1993–96, Ruud Gullit 1996–98, Gianluca Vialli 1998–2000, Claudio Ranieri 2000–04, Jose Mourinho 2004–

Player of the Year 1967–2004

Peter Bonetti, Charlie Cooke, David Webb, John Hollins, John Hollins, David Webb, Peter Osgood, Gary Locke, Charlie Cooke, Ray Wilkins, Ray Wilkins, Mickey Droy, Tommy Langley, Clive Walker, Peter Borota, Mike Fillery, Joey Jones, Pat Nevin, David Speedie, Eddie Niedzwiecki, Pat Nevin, Tony Dorigo, Graham Roberts, Ken Monkou, Andy Townsend, Paul Elliott, Frank Sinclair, Steve Clarke, Erland Johnsen, Ruud Gullit, Mark Hughes, Dennis Wise, Gianfranco Zola, Dennis Wise, John Terry, Carlo Cudicini, Gianfranco Zola, Frank Lampard

A–Z of Every Chelsea Player

Laurence ABRAMS (1914–20)
Rati ALEKSIDZE (2000–02)
David ALEXANDER (1939–45)
Les ALLEN (1954–59)
Clive ALLEN (1991–92)
Jack ALLISTER (1949–52)
Joe ALLON (1991–92)
Leonard ALLUM (1932–39)
Gabriele AMBROSETTI (1999–2003)
George ANDERSON (1927–29)
Sylvan ANDERTON (1959–62)
Jimmy ARGUE (1933–47)
James ARMSTRONG (1922–28)
Ken ARMSTRONG (1946–57)
James ASHFORD (1920–25)
Trevor AYLOTT (1975–79)
Jimmy BAIN (1945–47)
Tommy BALDWIN (1966–74)
Joe BAMBRICK (1934–38)
Eamonn BANNON (1979)
George BARBER (1930–41)
Ned BARKAS (1937–39)
Darren BARNARD (1990–95)
Anthony BARNESS (1992–96)
William BARRACLOUGH (1934–37)
Fred BARRETT (1920–27)
Jim BARRON (1965–66)
Brian BASON (1972–77)
Sid BATHGATE (1946–53)
Thomas BAXTER (1919–20)
Dave BEASANT (1989–93)
John BELL (1920–23)
Walter BELLETT (1954–58)
Walter BENNETT (1922–24)
Roy BENTLEY (1948–56)
Paul BERRY (1953–60)
Walter BETTRIDGE (1909–22)
Sidney BIDEWELL (1937–46)

Hugh BILLINGTON (1948–51)
Alan BIRCHENALL (1967–70)
Ted BIRNIE (1906–10)
Sid BISHOP (1928–33)
George BISWELL (1928–29)
Michael BLOCK (1957–62)
Frank BLUNSTONE (1953–64)
Mickey BODLEY (1985–89)
Gordon BOLLAND (1960–62)
Winston BOGARDE (2003-04)
Peter BONETTI (1959–79)
Petar BOROTA (1979–82)
Mark BOSNICH (2001–03)
A.G. 'Baishe' BOWER (1923–25)
Jimmy BOWIE (1944–51)
Andy BOWMAN (1951–55)
Tom BOYD (1991–92)
John BOYLE (1964–73)
Peter BRABROOK (1955–62)
Terry BRADBURY (1957–62)
James BRADSHAW (1909–10)
Billy BRAWN (1907–11)
Ronald BREBNER (1906–07 and 1912–13)
Billy BRIDGEMAN (1906–19)
Barry BRIDGES (1958–66)
Harold BRITTAN (1913–20)
Ian BRITTON (1971–82)
Mike BROLLY (1971–74)
Johnny BROOKS (1959–61)
William BROWN (1911–13)
John BROWN (1912–15)
William BROWN (1924–29)
Dennis BROWN (1962–64)
John BROWNING (1919–20)
Robert BUCHANAN (1911–13)
Peter BUCHANAN (1936–46)
John BUMSTEAD (1976–91)
Harry BURGESS (1935–45)
Craig BURLEY (1989–97)
Robert BUSH (1906–07)
Dennis BUTLER (1960–63)
Geoff BUTLER (1967–68)
Michael BYRNE (1905–06)
David CALDERHEAD (1907–14)
Jock CAMERON (1907–13)
David CAMERON (1920–26)
Bobby CAMPBELL (1947–54)
Paul CANOVILLE (1981–86)
John CARR (1928–31)
Robert CARTER (1929–33)
William CARTWRIGHT (1908–13)
Tony CASCARINO (1992–94)
Len CASEY (1954–58)
Pierluigi CASIRAGHI (1998–99)
Sidney CASTLE (1923–26)
Petr CECH (2004–Present)
Laurent CHARVET (1998)
Alec CHEYNE (1930–32 and 1934–36)
Wilf CHITTY (1931–38)
Gary CHIVERS (1978–83)
Jimmy CLARE (1977–81)
Steve CLARKE (1987–98)
Neil CLEMENT (1996–2000)
David CLISS (1956–62)
John COADY (1986–88)

Jack COCK (1919–23)
Carlton COLE (2001–Present. On loan 2003–Present)
Joe COLE (2003–Present)
Nick COLGAN (1992–98)
Michael COLLINS (1951–57)
John COMPTON (1955–60)
Charlie COOKE (1966–72 and 1974–78)
David COPELAND (1905–07)
James COPELAND (1932–37)
Peter CORTHINE (1957–60)
Colin COURT (1954–59)
Allan CRAIG (1933–39)
James CRAIGIE (1905–07)
Jackie CRAWFORD (1923–34)
Hernan CRESPO (2003–Present. On loan 2004–Present)
Nick CRITTENDEN (1997–99)
Jimmy CROAL (1914–22)
Stan CROWTHER (1958–61)
Carlo CUDICINI (1999 – Present)
Jason CUNDY (1988–92)
George DALE (1919–22)
Sam DALLA BONA (1998–2002)
Jimmy D'ARCY (1951–52)
Alex DAVIDSON (1946–48)
Gordon DAVIES (1984–85)
Ed DE GOEY (1997–2003)
Quique DE LUCAS (2002–03)
John DEMPSEY (1969–78)
Marcel DESAILLY (1998–2004)
Didier DESCHAMPS (1999–2000)
Roberto DI MATTEO (1996–2002)
Alan DICKENS (1989–93)
William DICKIE (1919–21)
Murdoch DICKIE (1945–46)
Alan DICKS (1951–58)
Bill DICKSON (1947–53)
Perry DIGWEED (1988)
Kerry DIXON (1983–92)
Jim DOCHERTY (1979)
Tommy DOCHERTY (1961–62)
George DODD (1911–13)
Billy DODDS (1986–89)
Hugh DOLBY (1909–12)
Len DOLDING (1945–48)
Charles DONAGHY (1905–07)
Mal DONAGHY (1992–94)
Alexander DONALD (1930–32)
Tony DORIGO (1987–91)
Angus DOUGLAS (1908–13)
Andy DOW (1993–96)
Sam DOWNING (1909–14)
Phil DRIVER (1980–83)
Didier DROGBA (2004–Present)
Micky DROY (1970–85)
Michael DUBERRY (1993–99)
Keith DUBLIN (1983–87)
Sam DUDLEY (1932–34)
Damien DUFF (2003–Present)
Bernard DUFFY (1923–27)
John DUNN (1962–66)
Gordon DURIE (1986–91)
Charles DYKE (1947–51)
Robert EDWARDS (1951–55)

Sidney ELLIOT (1928–30)
Paul ELLIOTT (1991–94)
Timmy ELMES (1980–82)
Bobby EVANS (1960–61)
Norman FAIRGRAY (1907–14)
Mark FALCO (1982)
Joe FASCIONE (1962–69)
Peter FEELY (1970–73)
Edward FERGUSON (1920–23)
Willie FERGUSON (1921–33)
Chris FERGUSON (1927–30)
Albert FERRER (1998–2003)
James FERRIS (1920–22)
Michael FILLERY (1978–83)
William FINLAYSON (1920–23)
Steve FINNIESTON (1971–78)
Robert FLECK (1992–95)
James FLETCHER (1905–06)
Tore-Andre FLO (1997–2000)
Harry FORD (1912–24)
Craig FORREST (1997)
Mikael FORSSELL (1998–99 and 2003–2005)
Dick FOSS (1936–52)
Willie FOULKE (1905–06)
Steve FRANCIS (1981–87)
Charlie FREEMAN (1907–20)
Roger FREESTONE (1987–91)
James FREW (1922–27)
Les FRIDGE (1985–87)
James FROST (1906–07)
Lee FROST (1976–80)
Paul FURLONG (1994–96)
Hughie GAILACHER (1930–34)
James GALLON (1919–21)
John GALLOWAY (1946–49)
Chris GARLAND (1971–75)
Bill GARNER (1972–78)
GEREMI (2003–Present)
Derek GIBBS (1955–60)
George GIBSON (1933–39)
Michael GILKES (1992)
Ray GODDARD (1946–48)
Tony GODDEN (1986–87)
Bjarne GOLDBAEK (1998–2000)
Joe GOODWIN (1905–06)
Len GOULDEN (1945–50)
George GRAHAM (1964–66)
Danny GRANVILLE (1997–98)
Billy GRAY (1949–53)
Jimmy GREAVES (1957–61)
Ron GREENWOOD (1952–55)
Bob GREGG (1933–38)
Robert GRIFFITHS (1931–41)
Frode GRODAS (1996–98)
Jesper GRONKJAER (2000–04)
Eidur GUDJOHNSEN (2000–Present)
Ruud GULLIT (1995–98)
Kevin HALES (1979–83)
Gareth HALL (1986–96)
Harold HALSE (1913–21)
Ian HAMILTON (1967–68)
Steven HAMPSHIRE (1997–2000)
Colin HAMPTON (1914–25)
Alfred HANSON (1938–46)
Augustus HARDING (1906–13)